Nidderdale: Or, an Historical, Topographical, and Descriptive Sketch of the Valley of the Nidd, Including Pateley Bridge, Bishopside Dacre Banks, Harwith, Brimham Rocks, Stonebeck Down, Ramsgill, Stonebeck Up, Middlesmoor, Fountains Earth, Greenhow Hill,

William Grainge

Nabu Public Domain Reprints:

You are holding a reproduction of an original work published before 1923 that is in the public domain in the United States of America, and possibly other countries. You may freely copy and distribute this work as no entity (individual or corporate) has a copyright on the body of the work. This book may contain prior copyright references, and library stamps (as most of these works were scanned from library copies). These have been scanned and retained as part of the historical artifact.

This book may have occasional imperfections such as missing or blurred pages, poor pictures, errant marks, etc. that were either part of the original artifact, or were introduced by the scanning process. We believe this work is culturally important, and despite the imperfections, have elected to bring it back into print as part of our continuing commitment to the preservation of printed works worldwide. We appreciate your understanding of the imperfections in the preservation process, and hope you enjoy this valuable book.

NIDDERDALE;

OR,

An Historical, Topographical,

AND

Descriptive Sketch

OF THE

VALLEY OF THE NIDD,

INCLUDING

PATELEY BRIDGE, BISHOPSIDE,
DACRE BANKS, HARTWITH, BRIMHAM ROCKS, STONEBECK DOWN,
RAMSGILL, STONEBECK UP, MIDDLESMOOR, FOUNTAINS EARTH, GREENHOW
HILL, AND THE STUMP CROSS CAVERNS.

BY WILLIAM GRAINGE,

*Author of "The Battles and Battle Fields of Yorkshire," "Castles
and Abbeys of Yorkshire," &c., &c.*

PATELEY BRIDGE:

PUBLISHED BY THOMAS THORPE;

LONDON:

T. T. LEMARE, PATERNOSTER ROW.

1863.

THE NEW YORK
PUBLIC LIBRARY

521832

ASTOR, LENOX AND
TILDEN FOUNDATIONS
R   1911   L

PREFACE.

LITTLE preface is required to introduce this small book to the notice of the public, the title alone sufficiently explains its aim and objects ; that something of the kind was needed is obvious, from the fact that there is no other work in existence descriptive of the district of which this volume treats ; nor, ever has been, with the exception of a small tract by the late William Weatherhead, published in 1839 ; and which for many years has been entirely out of print. The notices of Nidderdale also in general topographical works are of the most meagre and unsatisfactory kind.

> "It lay like some unkenn'd-of-isle
> Beside New Holland."

The beautiful scenery and general importance of "the valley of the Nidd," are certainly deserving of a more minute and extended description than has ever yet been given of them, alike for the satisfaction of the inhabitants, as a guide to the pleasure-seeking tourist, and also as a means of making its beauties and capabilities more known to the world. This want, the publisher has undertaken to supply, at a considerable cost and risk to himself, trusting that a generous public will so far appreciate his endeavours as not to allow

vi PREFACE.

him to be a loser by the undertaking. It is also with feelings of satisfaction and something of pride, that he would point to this History and Description of his native valley, as the *first book* ever printed in Nidderdale. To the friends who have assisted his labours, and aided his subscription for the illustrated edition, his best thanks are due. Errors and imperfections of necessity the book will contain, as those are inseparable from all human productions.

> " Of old, those met rewards who could excel,
> And those were praised who but endeavoured well."

Whether he may deserve the first of these the public must decide, but he certainly does feel that he has some claim to the latter.

To the tourist and occasional visitor, it is only necessary to say that the matter of this book is arranged in such a manner as to suppose the whole valley to be seen in four days, making excursions from Pateley Bridge as a centre ;— the first, to be devoted to Pateley Bridge, Bishopside, Bewerley, Bewerley Hall, and the beauties of Ravensgill and Guy's-cliffe ; the second, to Dacre, Hartwith, and Brimham Rocks ; the third, to the upper part of the valley, including Ramsgill, Middlesmoor, Stean-beck, Goyden Pot, and the scenery in their respective neighbourhoods : the fourth, would be fully occupied in visiting and exploring the mining ground around Greenhow-hill, and the yet untarnished beauties of the Stump Cross Caverns.

The mineral productions and manufacturing industry of the valley have long been known, but that, the more ready access given to the " great world" by the recently opened railway,

PREFACE.

vii

will give an impetus to the latter; and encourage the more ample developement of the former cannot be doubted.

The Geology and Botany of the valley are but slightly touched upon, and in these departments an ample field remains for further research and enquiry, which it is to be hoped this book will be the means of stimulating and directing.

With these few remarks, this (the first book issued from the Nidderdale press) is consigned into the hands of the public.

CONTENTS.

—o—

NIDDERDALE.

	PAGE.
Situation, Extent, Etymology	1
Geological formation	2
First Inhabitants. British Celt	4
Roman occupation	5
Division into Townships	6
Nidderdale from Domesday Book	7
held by the Barons De Mowbray	9
given to the Abbeys of Fountains and Byland	9
Ancient Roads, Bridges, &c.	11
Survey for a Railroad in 1818	12
Railroad constructed in 1862	13
Description of route from Harrogate, Ripley, Hampsthwaite, Birstwith, Wreaks	14
Darley, Dacre Banks, Castlestead, Bewerley Hall, Pateley Bridge	15

PATELEY BRIDGE.

	PAGE.
Situation, Etymology	17
Description	19
Old Church—situation	19
Description of	20
Inscriptions in Church-yard, &c.	21
New Church—situation, when built	23
Description of	23
Inscriptions, Living, &c.	24
Registers, Extracts from	25

CONTENTS.

ix

Chapels—Wesleyan Methodist	28
Primitive Methodist	28
Poor Law Union	28
Mechanics' Institute, Banks, &c.	29
Market, Fairs, Feast	30

BISHOPSIDE.

Situation, given to the Archbishops of York	31
Inclosure of Common Lands	32
Wilsill	33
Raikes School, Foundation, Endowment, &c.	34
Glasshouse Mill, Smelthouse Mill, Fellbeck	35
Bollershaw Grange, North Pasture House, Fellbeck House	36
Mineral productions, Agricultural Statistics, Population, &c.	37

BEWERLEY.

Situation, Early Owners	38
Mowbray Charters	39
Pedigree of the family of Yorke	41
Bewerley Hall	53
Old Monastic Chapel	53
The Grounds—Ravensgill	55
The Crocodile Rock	58
The Trough, Baal Hills	59
Guy's-cliffe	60
Castlestead	63
Grassfield House	65
Eagle Hall	65
Family of Taylor—of White	66
Bridgehouse-gate, Chapel	68
Bewerley Village	69
Mineral productions of Bewerley	69
Agricultural Statistics, Population, &c.	70

DACRE.

Situation, Boundaries	71
Early Owners	72

CONTENTS.

Dacre Village, Chapel, &c.	73
Friends' Burial Ground	74
Braithwaite School, Dacre Pasture, Enclosure, &c.	74
Hayshaw	75
Harewell Hall	76
Family of Lupton	77
Low Hall	78
Dacre Banks, Village, Mills, &c.	78
Charles Gill—Account of	79
Church, &c.	79
School	80
Population, Statistics, &c.	81

HARTWITH.

Situation, Boundaries, &c.	82
Early Owners	83
Brimham Rocks	84
Hartwith Chapel	95
Foundation, Endowment, &c.	96
Charities, Inscriptions	98
Hartwith School	99
Brimham Hall	100
Lodge	101
Winsley Hall	102
Spring House, Family of Danson, &c.	102
New Bridge	104
Hardcastle Garth	105
Dougill Hall and Family of Dougill	106
Summer Bridge	108
New York	108
Low Laith	109
Braisty Woods, Pedigree of the family of Skaife	110
Enclosures, &c.	113
Population, Statistics, &c.	114

CONTENTS.

xi

STONEBECK DOWN.

Situation, Boundaries, &c.	115
Early Owners, Family of De Mowbray	116
Heathfield	118
Gowthwaite Hall	119
Dr. William Craven	121
Riddings Gill	123
Colthouse	124
Ramsgill	124
Church	125
Ancient Chapel	126
Eugene Aram—Account of	127
Blayshaw, Pit Dwellings, &c.	133
Stean, Tenure of Lands, &c.	135
Mineral Productions, &c.	137
Population, Statistics, &c.	138

STONEBECK UP.

Situation, Boundaries, &c.	139
The River Nidd, Source, &c.	140
The Lodge	141
Woodale	142
Deadman's Hill	144
Goydon Pot	145
Limley—Family of Bayne	147
How Stean Beck	150
Park Foss	151
Stean-gill-foot	154
Eglin's Hole, or Cavern	155
Middlesmoor	156
School	157
Chapel; when built, Consecration, &c.	157
Inscriptions	160
Charities	161
Registers	162
Terrier	165

xii   CONTENTS.

Land Owners, &c. 168
Mineral Productions 170
Geological Section 172
Statistics, Population, &c. 173

FOUNTAINS EARTH.

Situation, Early Owners, &c. 175
Thwaite House 177
Lofthouse 177
Sikes Grange, Longside, Helks 181
Bouthwaite 183
Calval Houses, Holme Houses 184
Sigsworth Grange 185
Statistics, Population, &c. 186

GREENHOW HILL.

Smelting Mill 188
Sunside Mining Company's Works 192
Geological Section 194
Village of Greenhow Hill 195
          Church 195
          Parochial District 196
Craven Keld, Craven Cross 199
Earthquake 200
Thomas Blackah, the Poet 201

STÜMP CROSS CAVERNS.

Situation, Discovery 204
Description of 205
Season for Visiting the Valley 211
Dwellings in the Dale 213
Roads, &c. 214
Inhabitants, Language, Manners, Customs, &c. 216
                 Appendix at the end.

Nidderdale.

NIDDERDALE, or Netherdale,* is an extensive and beautiful valley in the West Riding of Yorkshire, extending in a south-easterly direction from the mountain of Great Whernside to Dacre Banks on one side, and the rocky wonders of Brimham, in the township of Hartwith, on the other, at which points it may properly be said to terminate, though the river Nidd, which gives name, fertility, and beauty to the valley, continues its course between slopes of varied extent, until it has passed the castle-crowned rocks of Knaresbrough; afterwards its waters traverse a plain country, through a rich alluvial soil, until finally they mingle with those of the Ouse at Nun-Monckton, after a remarkably crooked course of more than fifty miles.

Great diversity of scenery exists in this valley : in some places wild and grand, in others mild and beautiful ; yet, generally, blended into pictures of endless number and variety,

*A great deal of learning has been displayed on the etymology of this name ; it has been derived from the Hebrew *Nacash*, a serpent—from the Celtic *Nathair*, also a serpent—from the Danish *Nidur*, a murmuring stream—from the British *Nedd*, turning and whirling, and *dour*, water ; and from *Nidd*, under, below, or covered—which last derivation is probably the true one ; unless *Netherdale* be only the *Nether*, or lower valley, in contradistinction to the vales of the Wharfe and Aire, which have the same direction, and with reference to Netherdale, might be called the upper vallies ; as the *Netherlands* are, strictly speaking, the *low-lands*, so *Netherdale*, after all, may only be the *lower dale*.

A

combining with the softer beauties of the green and fertile vale, with the river winding down its centre,—extensive patches of woodland on the upper slopes, a back ground of dark-brown or purple moors above, girdled at times by precipices and vast masses of rock. Occasionally the sides of the hills are cut into by wild and shaggy glens, or gills, clothed with hanging woods, presenting to the tourist who has the courage to explore their lonely recesses exquisite pictures of mountain scenery. The towering Whernside, the wild rocks of Brimham, the volcanic mount of Greenhow, with other kindred heights, ranging from 800 to 2,300 feet above the sea level, form its natural boundaries.

"Where the rainbow comes—the cloud,
And mists that spread the flying shroud,
And sunbeams, and the sounding blast."

The formation of this valley is due to a grand convulsion of nature, which at some remote period of the earth's history upheaved the mass of limestone in Greenhow-hill, and Stean-beck, forming the lofty heights of Whernside, and casting upward to the north-east the heavy masses of millstone grit which appear on Fountain's Earth Moor, the crags above Yeadon, Brimham Rocks, Plumpton, and Spofforth; leaving a deep, crooked, and rugged cavity in the naked rock, which afterwards abraided, partly filled up, and smoothed, by the rushing currents of a tumultuous sea, formed the picturesque valley of the Nidd. This rending of the earth's crust has evidently taken place after the deposition of the magnesian limestone, and before the commencement of that of the new red sandstone; as the former rock has been thrown upward, and rent into fragments all along its south-western edge, as is observable in the formations beneath Knaresbrough Castle, and northward by way of Farnham and Burton-Leonard;—while the new red sandstone to the eastward does not appear to have been subjected to any such violent displacement.*

This formation of the valley, so conducive to natural beauty, grandeur, and sublimity, was also the origin of its mineral and vegetable wealth, by disclosing the veins and beds of metals and minerals with which its hills are stored; and forming a receptacle in the hollow below for the rich sediment washed from the sloping hills above. · The lead, coal, slate, ironstone, limestone, and gritstone mines and quarries are all due to this violent breakage of the strata; as well as the romantic scenery, wooded glens, rich meadows and pastures which ornament its sides and bottom.

After this event, many ages, such as are measured by the life and death of man, must have elapsed before the soil was fitted for the habitation of the ruminant animal, or the rational being. The eye of the profound philosopher can alone read the pages which contain the annals of this great pre-historic period; they are written in, and on rocks, in vast diluvial mounds, and in terraces which have formed the shores of inland lakes or sea estuaries. At length the fullness of time was complete, and man became an inhabitant of the earth, but

*Professor Phillips estimates the thickness of rocky matter removed by this displacement at 700 feet. His words are, "The lowest pebbly grit group known in the whole region south of the Tyne, is found everywhere almost in contact with the top of the limestone in the districts of Nidderdale, Greenhow-hill, and Kettlewell. At Greenhow-hill and Grassington its inferiority of position to the bold crag grits of Brimham and Symon's Seat is most certain, and the measures which I have taken in the upper and lower parts of Nidderdale, (above Lofthouse, at Brimham, Guy's-cliffe, Darley, &c.) and about Greenhow, justify the assertion that at least 700 feet of shales, flagstones, and grit rocks, with one or more seams of coal and cherty beds intervene."—*Geology of Yorkshire,* vol. ii., p. 59.

NIDDERDALE.

his first settlement and actions are alike lost in the dark mist of antiquity.

The first human inhabitants known to have occupied this valley were the British Brigantes; a race at once warlike and pastoral, shepherds, hunters, and warriors from necessity. At that time we can safely say the country was an uncultivated wilderness; the limestone hills, then as now, covered with short sweet herbage, the moors to the eastward thickly set with a wood of fir, oak, willow, birch, alder, hazel, and all trees indigenous to similar soil and climate; the valley itself partly pasturage, partly wood, the haunt of the wild boar, the roebuck, and the deer. A few burial mounds, the names of a few hills and streams are nearly all that remain to remind us of the existence of the British tribes in this valley.*

About 70 years after the advent of Christ, the armies of Rome began the conquest of the territory of the Brigantes, and though resisted by the undisciplined bravery of the natives with pertinacious obstinacy, the complete conquest was achieved by Agricola about the year 80. The conquerors penetrated into this valley, destroyed the forests on the hills to the east-ward, worked the mines on the west, and established a small station or camp on one of the warmest spots in the valley,

*On the enclosure of the common in 1862, a stone axe or celt, in a fine state of preservation, was found at a place called the *Brae*, about a mile from Pateley Bridge; it is six inches in length, three across in the widest part, and about one-and-a-half inches thick, of an oval shape, finely rounded, and tapering to an edge, at which part it is the widest. The stone of which it is composed is a very compact grit, exceedingly hard, and capable of being polished. Though not well adapted as an offensive weapon in war, it would form an invaluable instrument to a hunter, both for the skinning of animals and the dividing of their flesh. It probably formed part of the equipments of a British hunter on the moors twenty centuries ago. It is at present in the possession of Mr. G. H. Strafford, commissioner for the inclosure.

close to the river, a short distance below Pateley Bridge. The reason why they destroyed the woods was, that the thickets sheltered the Britons; and also from their fastnesses they could issue upon the convoys of their masters, cut them off, and again retreat to the woods for safety. From the remains dug out of the peat, it is evident that many of the trees were of great age and bulk, and from marks yet remaining, that they were partially cut by the axe, and partially destroyed by fire. This destruction of wood appears to have been the cause of the formation of peat, by the interrupting the drainage of the waters by the mass of fallen trunks and branches; previous to that period there is every reason to believe that, what are now extensive patches of peat was dry ground, as, when the peaty soil is cut through, as is frequently the case in digging it to dry for fuel, the roots of the ancient forest trees are found standing upright, rooted on the spots where they originally grew. That the Romans worked the mines of Greenhow we have the most satisfactory proof in the existence of pigs of lead bearing the Roman stamp. Two of these were found at Hayshaw Bank, near Dacre Pasture, in 1785; one of them, preserved at Ripley Castle, bears—

IMP. CÆS: DOMITIANO. AVG. COS: VII.—BRIG.

thus proving that these pigs were cast as early as the year 81, of the Christian era; the syllable BRIG. indicating the territory in which they were raised. The camp was of a rectangular form, the shape generally used by that people, and yet bears the significant name of Castlestead. It retained its original form until the year 1862, when Mr. George Metcalfe built a house in the area, and sloped the agger for his gardens and grounds.

Of the two next grand historical periods of early English history, the invasions and conquests of the Saxons and Danes, we have no records, literary or monumental, pertaining to this valley; yet the names of places, as well as the language and personal appearance of the inhabitants, are sufficient proof that both these people formed settlements here.

When the Kingdom was divided into parishes, for the more efficient teaching of the gospel, which took place during the seventh century, Nidderdale, notwithstanding its extent and distance, was apportioned to Ripon and Kirkby Malzeard, the former twelve, the latter eight miles distant; a proof that the country at that time was ill cultivated and thinly inhabited. Bishopside, Dacre, and Bewerley were given to Ripon; Hartwith-with-Winsley, in the lower part, and what was afterwards known as the townships of Stonebeck Up, Stonebeck Down, and Fountain's Earth, in the upper part of the valley, were given to Kirkby Malzeard. These districts were formed into chapelries, known as those of Pateley Bridge, Hartwith, and Middlesmoor, but this took place long afterwards, when the population had considerably increased.

After the Norman conquest, we begin to find written records of this valley and its owners; the first of these is the invaluable Domesday survey, made by order of William the Norman, and completed about the year 1086; it also shews the wild, uncultivated state of the country at that time, from the imperfection of the survey, and the small value of the land. Bishopside, the township in which Pateley Bridge is situate, had been given by the Saxon king Athelstane to the Archbishops of York, more than two centuries before the conquest, and their possession was not disturbed by that event. Amongst the lands of Thomas, Archbishop of York, enumerated in that survey, within the *Leuga*, or Liberty of St. Wilfrid, at Ripon, we find *Wifleshall* (Wilsill) and *Kenaresforde :* this latter place has hitherto been unappropriated, but we think it might be applied to Pateley, and the district immediately around it, on the same side of the river; the termination *ford*, certainly indicates a crossing place over a river, or considerable stream; and the ford here may have received the name of *Knares*, or *nere*, either from *knares*, hills, or from *nere*, the *near* ford, in contradistinction to some more distant one, as that at *Wath* (a name of the same signification), a short distance above, near the boundary of the manor. The names of the places are only given in the first entry, but in *Clamores de Eurewicscere* (Claims in Yorkshire) is a summary of the Archbishop's lands in *Borgscire* (now Claro Wapentake), in which the same names, and also quantities are given :—

" In *Wiveshall* two carucates. In *Chenaresford* one carucate and a half."[†] No value, separate from the other lands with which they are entered, is given.

Amongst the lands of Gospatric occurs the following entry, evidently applicable to the same place :—

" In Neresford, Gospatric, half a carucate of land to be taxed. He has the same, and it is waste."[‡]

The whole of the lands mentioned in what we suppose to be now known as the township of Bishopside is only four carucates, or about 480 acres, a quantity so small, that we can only suppose it to apply to the lands enclosed at that time.

The name of Hartwith does not appear in the survey, but

*Bawdwen's Domesday Book, p. 54. †Ibid, p. 256. ‡Ibid, p. 219.

8 NIDDERDALE.

Brimham is evidently the substitute, and was then held by three owners. Erneis de Buren held—

"Manor. In Birnebeham, Gospatric had three carucates and six ox-gangs to be taxed. There is land to two ploughs. Ernegis has it, and it is waste. Value in King Edward's time twenty-three shillings."*

Giselbert Tison held—"In Birnebeham, Gamelbar had two ox-gangs to be taxed."† And lastly, Gospatric had—

"Manor. In Birnebeham three carucates of land and two ox-gangs to be taxed. Land to two ploughs."‡

The above quantities are slightly altered in the *claims*, where they stand thus—

"In Birnebeham, Gospatric, three carucates and two ox-gangs. In the same place G. Tison, two ox-gangs. In the same place Erneis, half a carucate."§

Bewerley and Dacre are mentioned together as belonging to Erneis de Buren.

"II Manors. In Burelei and Dacre, Gospatric had six carucates of land to be taxed. There is land to four ploughs. Ernegis has it, and it is waste. Value in King Edward's time fifty shillings. Wood pasture two miles long, and two broad. The whole four miles long, and three broad."||

The quantities afterwards given are three carucates in each place. The only other place in the valley mentioned is *Higrefeld*, now Heathfield, in the township of Stonebeck Down.

"Lands of Berenger de Todeni. Manor. In Higrefelt, Gamel had two carucates to be taxed. Land to two ploughs. Berenger now has it, and it is waste. Wood pasture one mile

---

*Bawdwen's Domesday Book, p. 207.   †Ibid, p. 194.   ‡Ibid, p. 217.
§Ibid, p. 256. ||Ibid, p. 207.

long, and half broad. The whole manor one mile long, and one broad. Value in King Edward's time twenty shillings."*

Neither Stonebeck Up nor Fountain's Earth are mentioned in any form in the survey; and with the exception of the Archbishop's lands, of the value of which we cannot speak with certainty, the others are all returned as waste; a melancholy proof, that even the remote situation of this valley had not saved it from the rapacity of the Norman soldiery.

In less than a century after the Domesday survey was made, all the lands in Nidderdale, with the exception of Bishopside, were in the hands of the potent family of Mowbray; and were by Roger, the first baron of that name given away, with slight reservations, to religious houses; to that of St. Mary, of Fountains, he gave Brimham, including Hartwith and Winsley, Dacre-with-Bewerley, and Fountain's Earth, which last place probably acquired its name from this donation:—To the monastery of his own foundation at Byland, he gave the forest of Nidderdale, an extensive district, now constituting the townships of Stonebeck Up and Stonebeck Down; so that the whole of the valley was held by three proprietors—the Archbishop of York, and the Monasteries of Fountains and Byland. These ecclesiastics devoted it to pastoral purposes, to the grazing of sheep, cattle, horses, and pigs; establishing Lodges, Granges, and Dairies in suitable places; occasionally enjoying a little recreation in hunting the game in the valley and on the uplands, not forgetting to make use of the lead mines which were within the limits of their respective grants; the lead of Greenhow covered the roofs, and marble, hewn from

*Ibid, p. 128.

the bed of the Nidd, decorated the clustered columns of the stately monastery of Fountains, in the day of its highest greatness. The abbots' smelting house was situate in a corner of Hartwith, at the place which yet bears the name of Smelthouse; the ore being carried thither on account of the abundance of fuel in that neighbourhood. Between Winsley and the head of the Nidd, there were eighteen different stations occupied by servants of the convent of Fountains; those of Byland were fewer in number, as their possessions were of a wilder and less valuable kind. The monks were the best farmers of their times, and enclosed the land of the valley as far up the slopes of the hills as they deemed it of sufficient value, while the commons above were occupied as sheep walks by their numberless flocks, for they were great wool merchants as well as farmers. Chapels were built by the brethren of Byland at Ramsgill, and by those of Fountains at Bewerley, for the accommodation of their shepherds and servants. The monks held possession of their respective lands until the dissolution of the monastic orders in England, when they came into the hands of the crown, and were shortly afterwards granted out to different owners; and, after being held for short periods by different parties, the royalties of the manors of Bewerley, and the Forest of Nidderdale, with a great part of the soil, became the property of the family of Yorke, now of Bewerley Hall, in which they yet continue. The lords of Studley Royal obtained the manorial rights over Fountain's Earth; the Ingilbies, of Ripley Castle, over Dacre; and the Norton's, lords Grantley, over Brimham and Hartwith. Notwithstanding the formation of the See of Ripon, the Archbishops of York, or more properly at present, the Ecclesiastical Commissioners, are yet the superior lords of Bishopside.

Owing to the steepness of the hills, and the spongy and desolate nature of the surrounding moors, the approaches to the Dale were always difficult, and at some seasons of the year dangerous. The Romans doubtless obtained access to their camp at Castlestead by a vicinal branch up the valley from Hampsthwaite, where their main road from Isurium (Aldbrough) to Olicana (Ilkley) crossed the Nidd ; though we are not aware that any traces of it have been discovered. This was probably used as long as it continued in repair, and afterwards the valley was entered by nothing but trackways, impracticable to wheel carriages. The two high, narrow arches over the Nidd, one at the bottom of the township of Fountain's Earth, the other in Hartwith, both bearing the name of *Newbridge* (though old structures), are types, or representatives of this age. They are only adapted for pack-horses and foot passengers, and inconvenient as we deem them now, were vastly superior to the more ancient ford or wath. In Leland's time, about 1536, the lower Newbridge, and one at Pateley, were of timber. The road from Kirkby Malzeard to Fountain's Earth and Pateley, even to the commencement of the present century, was nothing but a trackway across the moors, indicated to travellers in misty weather and in winter by tall, upright pillars of stone, some of which yet remain. It was only in the year 1756 that an act of Parliament was obtained for repairing and widening the road from the borough of Ripon to the town of Pateley Bridge, which, until a very recent period, was one of the most frequented roads into the valley. The *old* road from Knaresbrough and Ripley wound its toilsome way over the craggy moor of Brimham ; and it was only a few years ago that the more level road, called the *new line*, was formed from Burnt Yeates to Summer Bridge. Skipton could only be reached then, as now, by the steep ascent of Greenhow; and to reach Otley, the traveller had to encounter the rugged heights of Guy's-cliffe, and the desolation of the middle of Knaresbrough Forest.

The rapid descent of the waters of the Nidd, and its lateral branches, affording much motive power, and many fine situations for mills and manufactories, the bleaching and spinning of linen yarn was introduced into the valley, principally into the townships of Dacre, Hartwith, and Bishopside, where it has continued to flourish ever since. The difficulty of bringing the raw material to the mills, and afterwards conveying the manufactured goods to market, was felt to be a serious drawback by those engaged in the business; and means of remedying this defect were sought as early as the year 1818, when the country between Knaresbrough and Pateley Bridge was surveyed by Messrs. Telford and Palmer, for the purpose of forming a railroad; the distance being 14¼ miles, the cost of a single line of railway, with passing places, was estimated at £88,890. This scheme, however, proved abortive, and nothing further was done until the year 1849, when the Leeds and Thirsk Railway Company surveyed a route, and obtained powers for the construction of a branch railway from their main line at Starbeck to Pateley Bridge; the times proving unpropitious, the powers of that act were permitted to expire in 1851, from which time unremitting exertions were made to obtain for Nidderdale railway communication. The success with which these efforts were at last crowned is mainly due to G. Metcalfe, jun., Esq., aided by the following principal

NIDDERDALE. 13

landed proprietors in the valley—viz: The Rev. H. J. Ingilby, John Greenwood, Esq., M.P., John Yorke, Esq., G. Metcalfe, Esq., Hanley Hutchinson, Esq., T. F. A. Burnaby, Esq., and Messrs. Thorpe and Co. In 1859 power was obtained by the North Eastern Railway Company to construct a single line of railway from near the village of Nidd to Pateley Bridge. The first sod was cut near Killinghall Bridge, in September, 1860, by the Rev. H. J. Ingilby, of Ripley Castle, and the finished road was opened to the public May 1st, 1862; thus placing the inhabitants of the lower part of the valley in direct railway communication with all parts of the kingdom. The contractors for the line were Messrs. Cail and Towns, of Newcastle-on-Tyne; the length 11¼ miles, and the cost £8,000 per mile.

As the formation of the railway will be the means of inducing many to visit this district, who would not otherwise have done so, we will briefly describe the route, noting the objects on each side most worthy of attention, before proceeding to give a more detailed history and description of the Valley of the Nidd.

Harrogate is the starting point, from which the distance to Pateley Bridge is 14 miles. For rather more than two miles the track is along the main line of the North Eastern Company's Railway, until after passing the river Nidd by a lofty viaduct of seven arches, we suddenly turn to the westward, leaving on the right hand the ancient church, village, Hall, and station of Nidd, and proceeding with the river almost close on the left. Before reaching the Ripley station, the line passes along a cutting through an unconformable patch of magnesian limestone; the station is close to the river, with the village of Killinghall at some distance, on the opposite side, to the south, and the small town of Ripley about a mile to the north. The last is one of the best built in the county; it can also boast an elegant Town Hall, or Hotel de Ville, erected in 1854, to the memory of the late Sir William Amcotts Ingilby, Bart., by his widow; an ancient church, with many interesting monuments; a Castle, surrounded by a park and pleasure grounds, the residence of the family of Ingilby for more than 500 years. The station stands, and the railway passes for a short distance on a piece of low ground, which has at no very remote period formed the bed of the river. The wooded hill on the right is called *Kirk Sink,* from the parish church of Ripley having stood there previous to the year 1400 when by a slip of the bank, the river at that time running immediately below it, the sacred edifice sunk or slided into the water. Passing onwards, on the left may be seen the mansion of Hampsthwaite Hollings, built by the late John Williamson, Esq., and a little further the village of Hampsthwaite, with its church almost close to the water. On the right, but not visible from the railway, is the small, antique hamlet of Clint; close to which, on an eminence, are the slender remains of Clint Hall, a manor house of the family of Beckwith for many generations. The next station is Birstwith, close to the bridge, and immediately adjoining the neat and well-built village of Wreaks, with its elegant, decorated church, standing gracefully with its tall spire on the slope of the hill, the crest of which is crowned by Swarcliffe Hall, the residence of John Greenwood, Esq., M.P. Wreaks is situate in what was formerly the Forest of Knaresbrough, and is one of the sweetest spots in the neighbourhood; the white stone-built cottages, located among the trees and gardens, the church, and church-yard, with its sepulchral monuments, are models of neatness and refined taste. Soon after leaving this station, a partly wooded, partly craggy hill, comes almost down to the river on the left, and adds to the variety of the scenery; a short distance further and the railway crosses to the southern side of the river by means of an iron girder bridge, and leaves Darley, a straggling village, with a small new church, on the left, and soon afterwards reaches the third station—Dacre Banks, a small manufacturing village. Now we are fairly within the district properly called Nidderdale, and to which our subsequent inquiries will be principally confined. The woody slopes of Hartwith and Braisty Woods, and the rock-crowned and romantic heights of Brimham rise grandly as a back ground to the picture presented by the busy hive of manufacturing industry on the right; the same scenery again frequently comes into view from different points, until the railway re-crosses the river by another iron girder bridge, and then passes Glasshouse Mill, the manufacturing establishment of the Messrs. Metcalfe; on the left, rising rapidly and shutting in the valley on that side, appear the woods and lofty rocks of Guy's-cliffe. In the centre of the valley stands Castlestead, the elegant castellated seat of Mr. George Metcalfe, erected in 1862, on the site of an ancient Roman camp, and approached by an iron bridge across the river. This mansion may be styled the architectural gem of the valley, and its situation within the area of the old encampment gives it an interest it would not otherwise possess. The mansion and grounds of Bewerley Hall, seat of John Yorke, Esq., are next observed on the same side; and while contemplating the beautiful park-like fore-ground rising from the river, on which the Hall stands, backed by the lofty woods of Ravensgill, the engine slackens speed, and finally comes to a stand at the station of Pateley Bridge, which forms the terminus of the Nidd Valley Railway. Before reaching this point much beautiful scenery is passed on both sides of the railway, to which the river contributes considerably by adding to the variety, sometimes as a lively impetuous current, rushing along a stony course, sometimes as a bright and brimming flood, when dammed for utilitarian purposes; it is seldom hid from the view, except for very short distances when passing through a cutting, and near the Dacre Banks station. Passing along the bottom of the valley by the easiest way, the line presents no triumph of engineering skill over natural obstacles; a cutting through a bed of hard rock near the Dacre Banks station being the heaviest work along the route. The stations are small substantial buildings of stone, and all nearly alike. Though but a single line, it will be of great utility to the country through which it passes, affording facilities for the increase of the trade, and the developement of the mineral riches of the valley; at the same time, though of minor importance, it will open out a new district to the tourist and health seeker, where they may roam at leisure amid the wildest mountain glens, and imbibe health and strength from the purest mountain breezes, receiving a welcome from a people at once hospitable and independent.

From this preliminary sketch we turn to the more immediate object of our inquiry, NIDDERDALE, commencing with Pateley Bridge, which may properly be denominated its capital.

PATELEY BRIDGE

Is a market town and chapelry in the parish, liberty, and diocese of Ripon, Wapentake of Claro, and West Riding of Yorkshire; situate at a distance of twelve miles from Ripon and Masham, nine from Ripley, fourteen from Harrogate (by railway), seventeen from Knaresbrough, fifteen from Skipton and Otley, thirty-two from York, and 224 from London. In the centre of Nidderdale, which abounds with beautiful and romantic scenery, immediately adjoining Brimham Rocks, within easy distance of Studley, Fountains Abbey, and Hackfall, with the rocks and caves of Craven, Barden Tower, Bolton Priory, and the beauties of Wharfdale only a few miles to the westward, it is favourably situate for the accommodation of the tourist about to explore this most interesting portion of Yorkshire.

At what time the town was built we have no direct information; it did not exist under its present name when the Domesday survey was made; though, probably, at that time it was a cluster of shepherd's huts near the place where the river was crossed, and known as *Nereford*, while the land around it was the *ley* or field of the *Pate*, or Badger, (an animal formerly numerous in the dale). When the bridge was built and the ford disused, the old name was discontinued, and that of the field and bridge substituted, when the place henceforward became known as Pateley Bridge.

Forming part of the Liberty of the sainted Wilfrid of Ripon,

18 NIDDERDALE.

it was possessed by the Archbishops of York from a period long anterior to the Norman Conquest; who exercised within it all the rights of royalty, with an almost unlimited control over the lives and property of the inhabitants; appointing their own magistrates, coroner, and other officers, and holding courts for the trial of all offences, with the power of life and death. About the middle of the thirteenth century a small chapel was erected here, and this and the adjoining townships of Bewerley and Dacre attached to it as a cure for souls, under the patronage of the Dean and Chapter of Ripon. The profits derived from the working of the lead mines on the adjoining hills, and the favourable situation of the town as a place for bringing the produce of the dale to market, were not unobserved by its owners, and in the year 1319 Archbishop William de Melton obtained from King Edward II a charter for a weekly market, and several fairs to be held here; from which we may infer that it had at that time acquired something of wealth and importance.

Lying remote from the great routes of traffic and war, the site of no castle or religious house, nor the residence of any distinguished family, Pateley presents but few incidents to the local historian. Leland slightly mentions it in his *Itinerary**
as " Patley Bridg and Village, a membar of Ripon Paroche."
He does not appear to have visited it, but had his information merely on hearsay; he says the bridge was of " tymbre."

The town consists of one main street, extending from the steep slope of the hill eastward to the river westward, and two small branches—one along the road to Ripon, called Souter

*Vol. 8.

or Souther, and another towards the New Church and Union Workhouse. At the bottom is the bridge crossing the river Nidd, a substantial fabric of three arches, and built at two different periods.*   The main street is narrow, and the houses placed close together, so that a considerable population is found dwelling on a very limited space of ground. The houses are built of stone of excellent quality, but none of them present any remarkable features. The Nidderdale Brewery, built in 1855, at the point where the road from Ripon enters the main street, is a conspicuous object, with its tall chimney and castellated style of architecture.   The Odd Fellows' Hall, built in 1855, at a cost of £700, is an elegant and commodious building, but from its confined situation, does not show to advantage.

The Old Church, or Chapel of Ease, dedicated to St. Cuthbert, is now a ruin, with the exception of a small portion recently fitted up, where service is read over those who are interred in the old burial ground.   It is situate on the slope of the hill, nearly half a mile east of the town, approached by a road at once steep, rugged, and narrow.   From the appearance of the remains, it was probably built about the year 1250. The masonry is very rude, and in irregular courses; the original windows are small lancet lights, in pairs.   The ground plan is of a square form, about seventeen yards in length by fifteen in breadth, divided into nave and chancel, the last only distinguished by an elevation of three steps above the floor of

---

*On cutting a drain across the road, near the Bridge, in 1862, three different causeways were cut through at different depths; one of them was about three yards below the present surface, and had evidently led to a ford before a bridge was built, the others to a bridge at a lower level than the present one.

20   NIDDERDALE.

the first. The east window is of four lancet lights, divided by a transom. The walls are yet of the original height—very low on the sides—which, with the wide gables and disproportionate span of the roof, would always render it an unsightly building. In the interior the base of the pulpit yet remains, and four square blocks of stone standing above the level of the floor were the supports of the pillars that bore the galleries, of which there were three—on the north and south sides, and across the west end.* The walls of the chancel have been first covered with a slight coat of whitewash, then adorned with a series of inscriptions and ornaments in black paint, which have been obliterated by another coat of whitewash, or plaster, and again renewed in a different style ; this process appears to have been repeated three times, as is evident from the scaling of the plaster from the wall. On the southern side of the nave is a carved stone about eighteen inches high, bearing within a bordure something like a cross *patonce*. On the floor are divers sepulchral inscriptions, but none of interest. In what was the vestry, on an upright slab of gritstone, is inscribed in large letters, some of them joined to each other—

"Here lyeth the body of Henry Smyth of Age 88. Buried the thirteenth of Oct : Ano : Dom : 1632."

The tower, at the west end, is yet complete, and of a more recent date than the other portions of the building. It was erected only in 1691, when the Rev. Thomas Furniss was

*The following memorandum occurs in the Parish Register under the year 1683 :—" This year was erected one Loft in the north of the Chappel by the proper costs, and for the only use of the Worshipfull Richard Taylor of Walling Wells, Esq. together with his worshipfull uncle Richard Taylor of Newall Esq. and their assigns."

PATELEY BRIDGE.

curate, whose initials and those of the churchwardens yet remain over the entrance from the tower into the nave—

"T.F: H.W: T.W: W.E: W.G: 1691. M.G: T.Y:"

The burial ground surrounds the church, and is occasionally used for the remains of those who have expressed a desire to be buried near their relations. There are many tombstones, but few inscriptions that will arrest the stranger's eye. Near the south-west corner of the ground is the following, commemorating an extraordinary instance of longevity :—

"Mary Myers of Northwoods, departed this life on Tuesday the twentieth day of September, Anno Domini 1743, aged near 120 years."

At the west end of the church is a headstone recording the deaths of four children born at one birth—

"Here lie Ralph, William, John, and one still born, sons of Robert and Margaret Fryer of Pateley Bridge, born 15th and died before the 23rd of July 1755."

Another tomb bears—

"Justus ut ramus virescet retine quod habes, ut tuam coronam neme occipiat.

To the Memory of Anthony Buck of Kell House, who died the 17th of Nov. 1788, aged 53 years.

Also Mary his wife, who died July 24th 1820, aged 81 years.

'Mark the perfect man, and behold the upright, for the end of that man is peace.'

> The grave has eloquence, its lectures teach
> In silence louder than divines can preach,
> Hear what it says—Ye sons of folly hear !
> It speaks to you—lend an attentive ear !"

Though the church be in ruins, and divine service no longer performed within its walls, there is a solemnity attached to a church and burial ground which no other places possess. The most careless must reflect on his own destiny as he walks over the mounds beneath which repose the ashes of what were once sensitive beings like himself. Even this place, deserted though it be, will always be an interesting spot to the moralist and the antiquary. From the upper corner of the burial ground may be seen one of the finest pictures of natural scenery it is possible to imagine—a green and fruitful valley enclosed in a frame of mountains; on the left the shaggy rocks of Guy's-cliffe, crowned by a mock ruin, and the woods of Ravensgill close the prospect; in front rises the more distant, naked head of Coldstones; on the right, at the end of a long range of winding hills, is seen the dark and lofty form of Whernside at the head of the dale; within these bounds are seen the town of Pateley, Bewerley Hall, and the beautiful grounds around it, Eagle Hall, with the wooded knolls ascending the slope of Greenhow, the valley with its picturesque enclosures, studded at intervals with dwellings of almost every shape and kind, enlivened by the windings of the river, whose reaches gleam like silver as we view them from this eminence.

On the old road leading from the town to the church, a copious spring of pure water flows into a round stone basin, which is protected by a square dome of masonry, on the covering stone is the following inscription, which being some-what defaced through the lapse of time, was renewed in 1863—

"Ill Habits gather by unseen degrees,
As Brooks run Rivers—Rivers run to Seas.

The way to Church."

The Old Church having become ruinous, besides being inconveniently situated, it was determined to erect a new one on a larger scale, on a site nearer the town. The first stone of the new fabric was laid October 20th, 1826, and the finished building opened for divine service October 7th in the following year; the cost was upwards of £4,000, one half of which was granted by Parliament, the Dean and Chapter of Ripon contributed £50, and the remainder was raised by a rate on the inhabitants.

The present church, dedicated to St. Mary, adjoins the town on the north, standing pleasantly on an eminence, and consists of a nave with small chancel, and tower at the west end. The style partakes of the early English; the windows have acutely pointed arches with flowing tracery. The main entrance is from the west, through the basement story of the tower. The interior forms one large room, with a flat ceiling. The windows are of plain glass, with the exception of one at the north-east corner, which is a memorial to the late John Yorke, Esq., of Bewerley Hall, in stained glass, by Wailes, of Newcastle-upon-Tyne. The font is an elegant octagonal column of veined marble, with moulded base and cornice, placed near the entrance. There are no sepulchral inscriptions within the church. Against the south wall, a marble tablet bears—

"By the last will of Mrs. Margaret Lupton of the city of York, spinster; bearing date Aug. 12. 1766, was left to the Minister of this Church, and his successors for ever, the sum of Forty Shillings pr year, for preaching two sermons, one on the Twentieth of May; the other on the Seventh of November; giving on each of those days out of the above Forty Shillings, five shillings in bread to the Poor, as soon as the Sermons are over; a week's notice to be given that the Poor may come to receive it. The above to be paid out of her Estate call'd by the name of Glasshouse and Stock Plain &c. in Low Bishop side."

On the opposite wall, on a board, is an account of the endowment of Raikes School, by Mrs. Alice Shepherd.

Across the west end is a gallery, in which is placed the

24 NIDDERDALE.

organ. The whole church contains 800 sittings, of which 432 are free. In the tower is one bell, brought from the Old Church; around the neck of which is inscribed, in old English characters—

✠ Sancta Petre Ora Pro Nobis.

Between every word is a shield, bearing the sacred monogram IHS.

The living is a Perpetual Curacy, in the gift of the Dean and Chapter of Ripon, valued in 1707 at £26 3s. 4d., and in 1818 at £87 11s. 4d. per annum. In 1809 it was augmented with £200 from Queen Ann's Bounty Fund, to meet benefactions of £100 from the Dean of Ripon, and £100 from Mrs. Pyncomb's trustees; in 1811 with £300 from the Parliamentary Grant, to meet a benefaction of £200 from the Dean of Ripon; and in the same year with £1,000 from the same Grant; in 1812 with £200, and in 1821 with £400, both from the same Grant, by lot; in 1827 with £200, to meet a benefaction of £200 from the Dean of Ripon; and in 1832 with £200 from the Parliamentary Grant, to meet a benefaction of £200 from the Archbishop of York. The nett annual value is about £152.

The Registers commence in 1552; the first book extends to 1661; the first part of it, to the year 1602, has been copied from some older book; the writing is all in one hand, and the different entries are numbered in the margin. During that fifty years the number of Baptisms was 1,382, Burials 811, Marriages 306. The second book extends from 1662 to 1687, and contains some memoranda indicative of the state of the Chapelry at that period. On the last page is inserted the following :—

PATELEY BRIDGE. 25

"A true Copy of Henry Squire yᵉ Advocates opinion relating to our Surplice fees &c. In answ. to yᵉ Queries I sent to him, wᶜʰ. wt. they were will appear by his Ansewˢ.

If Marriages, Xtenings, & burials have been constantly had at yᵉ Church or Chapel of Pateleybridge, ye have doubtless a good right to yᵉ Dues accustomed for such p'sons as had those offices p'formed with yᵘ.

But as to such p'sons as are married &c, at Ripon, if they can make it appear yᵗ. they have constantly married p'sons yᵗ. were of your Parish or Chapelry & alwaies rece'd yᵉ fees, I think they may continue so to do.

And yet if those p'sons who have been married at Ripon have alwaies paid yᵉ Minister of Pateleybridge his Marriage dues also, he may well maintain a Suit for yᵐ. in yᵉ Spiritual Court. If yᵉ p'sons married wᵗʰ yᵘ had only a Certificate from Ripon, I see no reason why they should insist upon the Marriage Dues.

Lands of the Cistercian Order, whilst they are in yᵉ Owners hands, are privileged from paymt. of Tithes, if they did not belong to some of yᵉ Least Abbeys wᶜʰ came to yᵉ crown by Stat. 26, Hen.

As to the burial dues they must be customary or Voluntary, but the best rule is to be guided by yᵉ neighbouring churches. And the same I think as to yᵉ Parish Clerk.

90
Jan. 20. 16—. H. SQUIRE."
91

In the year 1683 occurs the following entry :—

"Given this yeare, and Intended towards a Library in the Vestry, now to that purpose chiefly erected, Two Bookes or Little ffolioes, viz. The Life of the Apostles and the Primative ffathers, The Gift of the Worshipfull Tho : Johnson, Alderman of Hull, Autore Dʳ Cave. Also given by him The Whole Duty of Man, Dʳ Taylor's Holy Living & Dying, with some other small pieces in 12ᵒ."

The third book extends from 1688 to 1715 ; on the fly leaf at the end occurs the following receipt :—

"For the biting of a Mad dog. Take 6oz of Rue shred, 4 oz. of Garlick pill'd and stampt, 4oz Mithridate or Venice Treacle, 4 spoonfull of scraped Tin. Boil these in two quarts of stale ale in a pot well covered, for yᵉ space of one hour & strain it & give of this Decoction in the morning, three mornings together—8 or 9 spoonfull warm to a man, or cold to a beast, 3 to a sheep, 4 times a day, p'vided it be given within 9 days of yᵉ bite. Bind to yᵉ wound some of the drugs it was strained from. This receipt was given by Dr. Troutbeck, and by him caused to be inserted in all Church Registers where he came for the good of people, for a certain cure."

At this time the Rev. Thomas Furniss was curate, who

NIDDERDALE.

appears to have been active and diligent in his duties—the tower to the Old Church was built during his time ; the vestry re-built, and three galleries erected ; a school was established at Bewerley, and many other public improvements effected. He died in 1735, and his assistant thus records his decease—

"1735, Jan. 20. Mr Thos. Furniss Curate of ye Paroch 58 years was buried ye 20th day, after I had been 5 years his curate. He was almost 90 years of age.

This curate's name was Harrison, who appears to have thought himself something of a poet, as well as a divine. Two specimens of his talent occur in the Register—

"1736. Oct. 12. Will. Needham, Clark of the Church buried ye 12 day.

> Farewell poor Clark thou'l say no more Amen,
> Nor sing thy Fa sol Fa's on earth again ;
> What tho. thou's gone to thy first dust to turn,
> One day thou'l rise again—then let's not mourn."

"Thos. Simpson, Poet of Bewerley buried March ye 24th of March, 1738.

> Here lies ye body of one, as yet you do not know it,
> To tell ye very truth, it's honest Tom the poet ;
> This versifying, witty Songster,
> Has oft employed his pen—bout many a Youngster ;
> All that these serious lines rehearse
> Man is immortal made by making verse.
>
> JAMES HARRISON, Curate."

To all whom it may concern, we give the following "rental of the Premises belonging to the Church of Pateley Bridge," as entered in April, 1738 :—

	£.	s.	d.		s.	d.
"Jno. Cowlin	1	9	4	Robt. Furniss for his House		
Thos. Raggs	1	9	0	called Priests Chamber	2	6
Roger Thompson	1	8	4	Stephen Downs	9	0
Ninian Proctor	1	6	0	James Scott	3	0
Stephen Lupton	1	2	6	Leonard Richmond	2	0
Jno. Ingleby		15	4	Thos. Pawson	2	6
Jno. Lupton		15	6	Francis Gouthwaite	1	6
Robt. Furniss		10	0	Rhos. Raggs—2/- & 2/-	4	0

This is paid every half year at Martinmas and May-day."

"A true Terrier of the Glebe Lands, Tenements, Tithes, and portions

PATELEY BRIDGE.

of Tithes, and all other rights belonging to the Parocial Chapel of Pateley Bridge, in the County of York, and Diocese of York, taken the 10th day of June, 1782, and exhibited at the Archbishop's Visitation, held at Ripon the 12th day of the month and year above written. 1st—The Parocial Chapel of Pateley Bridge had not at any time, nor at present has any Buildings, Glebe Lands, Tithes, or modus in lieu of Tithes belonging to it, save the Chapel Yard, with one House and Garden, situate in Pateley Bridge aforesaid, which House and Garden were assigned over some years ago by the last surviving Trustee to Mr. Furniss, the then present Curate, and his Heirs for ever, paying out of the same half yearly, to the Minister, at May-day and Martinmas, £12 0s. 6d. either time. 2nd—A Rent Charge of £20 1s. 4d. per annum, payable at May-day and Martinmas, out of several Estates lying in High and Low Bishopside, given by Thos. Beckwith, gentleman, proprietor of the aforesaid Estates, as for ever due to the Curate of Pateley Bridge, half yearly, at May-day and Martinmas. 3rd—The present furniture, books, utensils, &c., belonging to Pateley Bridge Chapel are these, viz. : 2 bells, 1 pewter flagon, 2 pewter plates, silver chalice, 1 blue plain cloth, 1 linen cloth, 1 napkin for the Communion Table, 1 pulpit cushion, 2 surplices, 2 common Prayer Books, and 14 Register Books. 4th—The land owners and occupiers are chargeable with the repairs of the Chapel and Chapel-yard stone. 5th—The Clerk and Sexton's wages (both which offices have been united into one) are paid by the Chapel Wardens, out of money collected by Assessments for the purpose, &c.; and the Clerk and Sexton is chosen by the Minister alone. In testimony of the above-mentioned, we the Minister and Chapel Wardens of Pateley Bridge aforesaid, have set our hands the day and year above written.

W. NEESOME, Minister.

GEORGE METCALFE,
MATTHEW GILL,
JOHN MOSS,
EPHRAIM ELLIS,
} Chapel Wardens."

In one corner of the church-yard an obelisk marks the place where repose the remains of the late Mr. Joseph Warburton; near the base is the following inscription :—

"Erected in Memory of Joseph Warburton, surgeon, by his numerous friends to record their sense of the loss which they have sustained by his premature death, and their respect for the great skill, integrity, benevolence, industry, and energy, which distinguished his character. He practised his profession in this place for thirty-three years, and died June 30th, 1841, aged 55."

The Wesleyan and Primitive Methodists have both chapels in this town, that of the former situate in Souther, on the right of the road leading to Ripon, is a plain building of stone, opened in September, 1776, and used ever since. Wesleyanism was early introduced into Nidderdale, John Wesley himself visiting Pateley at least seven times, the first on July 24th, 1766, when he preached in the open air. On May 1st, 1780, his fifth visit, he preached in the Old Church; on his next visit, April 29th, 1782, he preached in the present Chapel. The Primitive Methodist Chapel is near the Odd Fellows' Hall, on the right of the road leading to the New Church, and was built in 1855.

The Pateley Bridge Poor Law Union was formed in 1837, and includes fourteen townships,* extending over an area of 165,052 acres, which contained in 1851 a population of 9,280, and in 1861 9,532; an increase having taken place in the manufacturing, and a considerable diminution in the purely agricultural townships. The number of Guardians elected is twenty-one, of which number Bishopside and Bewerley return three each, Dacre, Hartwith-with-Winsley, and Menwith-with-Darley two each; the other townships only elect one each. There are also four ex-officio Guardians.

The Union is divided into five medical districts—the Northern, Central, Eastern, Southern, and the Workhouse. There are three Registration districts—Dacre, Pateley Bridge, and Ramsgill.

The paupers were accommodated in an old building which

*Bishopside High and Low, Bewerley, Birstwith, Bishop-Thornton, Clint, Dacre, Fountain's Earth, Hartwith-cum-Winsley, Menwith-with-Darley, Stonebeck Down, Stonebeck Up, Thornthwaite-with-Padside, Thruscross, and Warsill.

PATELEY BRIDGE.

29

had been used as a Poor-house previous to the formation of the Union, until the year 1863, when the present Workhouse was built, at a cost of about £3,500. The number of poor receiving relief January 1st, 1863, was 438; in-door, 27; out-door, 411. The total expenditure for the whole Union for the year ending April 6th, 1862, was £4,327.

The Nidderdale Agricultural Society was established in 1846; an Exhibition of Animals, Implements, and Agricultural Produce is held annually at Pateley Bridge.

A Mechanics' Institute was established in 1839, which has been regularly supported, and of considerable benefit to the town and neighbourhood. The number of members is about sixty. The library contains 900 volumes, amongst which are many valuable standard works. The reading-room is supplied with the London and provincial papers, Magazines, Reviews, &c. The annual soirée is regarded as a social re-union by the inhabitants of the town.

There are three Banking establishments—branches of the Ripon Old Bank, Knaresbrough and Claro, and Yorkshire District Banks. The Savings' Bank was opened in 1837, and in the first year the deposits amounted to the sum of £1,200.

The Secret Benefit Societies established in the town are— the Odd Fellows, whose meetings are held fortnightly in their own Hall; the Ancient Order of Foresters, whose meetings are held fortnightly at an Inn; and the Golden Fleece, who hold their meetings monthly, also at an Inn.

Since the passing of the Reform Bill, in 1832, Pateley Bridge has been a polling place for the election of Knights of the Shire for the West Riding of Yorkshire.

The Market is on Saturday; the Fairs are held on Easter,

NIDDERDALE.

Whitsuntide, and Christmas Eves ; September 17th, if on a Saturday, if not, on the Saturday following ; on the first Tuesday after October 10th, and on the Saturday before Martinmas. A Fortnight Fair for Cattle is held every alternate Saturday throughout the year

The annual FEAST is on the first Sunday after the 17th of September, but commences on the Saturday before, and continues the whole of the following week. It is a season of holiday and joviality ; sports, games, and races take place at the villages on different days—at Middlesmoor on Monday, at Ramsgill on Tuesday, and Dacre Banks on Wednesday. Pateley Bridge is the great centre of attraction during the whole time. Feasting and hospitality prevail to an extent seldom witnessed in other places.

BISHOPSIDE,

So named from its owners, the Archbishops of York, is the most populous township in Nidderdale, and situate on the north-eastern side of the valley; south-eastward it is parted from Hartwith by Smelthouse Beck; the river Nidd forms the boundary along the south and south-west; on the north the moorland stream of Doubergill divides it from Fountain's Earth, and the eastern side abuts on the Skell rivulet.

This manor was given to the Archbishops of York by King Athelstane, probably in the year 939, after his great victory at Brunenburgh, when he granted many important privileges to the owners of the *Liberties* of the saints John of Beverley, and Wilfrid of Ripon; and this manor was among the benefactions conferred on the latter saint, and it continued an appanage of the See of York until the 36th of Henry VIII (1544), when Archbishop Robert Holgate, by indenture dated the 6th day of February in that year, surrendered to the King the manor of Ripon, and nine others belonging to the church, amongst which were Bishopside and Netherdale, which indenture was acknowledged by the King in Chancery the 2nd day of April in the following year, and was on the same day confirmed at York. These manors continued alienate until the year 1555, when Queen Mary, at the solicitation of Archbishop Nicholas Heath, restored them to the See of York. Notwithstanding the formation of the Diocese of Ripon in

1836, when much of the Ecclesiastical property in this neighbourhood was transferred to the latter, the Archbishops retained their jurisdiction over the manor of Bishopside. The courts are now regularly held twice a year, in the name of the Ecclesiastical Commissioners of England, at which surrenders are passed, and the duties of a copyhold manor performed. The greatest part of the old enclosed land is held by copy of Court Roll, subject to arbitary fines on alienation or decease of owner, or lease for lives, or for longer or shorter periods. A very small portion is freehold. The old enclosure of the township was something less than 2,000 acres, appendant to which was an extensive common of upwards of 4,000 acres of waste land, generally lying at an elevation of from 800 to 1,000 feet above the sea level; covered with ling, or heath, and and where damp with rushes. In some places the surface soil is peat, of considerable depth, in which are embedded timber trees of great bulk, those which have not been exposed to the air quite sound, even to the bark; the oaks are as black as ebony. This wild tract, generally level, or undulating, was the haunt of the red grouse, and other wild moorland birds. A few small, black-faced, hardy sheep were grazed upon it during the summer, and turves and peat for fuel were also obtained from it; but the annual value, upon the whole, was not great. The soil is not remarkably stony, yet in some places are fine masses of gritstone, upon which rock the whole rests. Many projects were started at different times for the enclosure of this waste, but without success, until the year 1857, when, on proper application being made to them, the Enclosure Commissioners of England issued a provisional order, dated December 17th in that year, for the enclosure of

BISHOPSIDE.

the same, on the following conditions :—That four acres, at a certain place, should be allotted for the purpose of exercise and recreation. That a piece of land called Blue Plain, another called Low Plain, another piece at the Knott, and four acres at another place, should be allotted to the labouring poor. That one-sixteenth part in value should be allotted to the Most Reverend Thomas Musgrave, D.D., Archbishop of York, as Lord of the Manor of High and Low Bishopside, in lieu of his right and interest in the soil of the said lands, exclusively of his right and interest in all mines, minerals, stone, and other substrata under the same—subject, nevertheless, to the right of the persons interested in any allotments at all times to get stone from their own allotment, and their ancient lands in the township, but not for sale. And that one-seventh part in value of all lands to be allotted in respect of copyhold lands, to be allotted to the said Archbishop, in addition to the said sixteenth, and that all allotments made in respect of such copyhold lands should be of freehold tenure. The Act of Parliament (21st Vict., c. 8), authorising the said enclosure, was passed March 26th, 1858.

The Archbishop's rights are now vested in the Ecclesiastical Commissioners ; and the common has since been surveyed, allotted, and partly enclosed. The ground set apart for exercise and recreation consists of ten acres near Howle Craggs, and three roods at Low Plain. The allotments to the labouring poor are 1a. 1r. 13p. on the Knott, 7a. 1r. near the Old Workhouse, and 1a. 1r. 38p. at Blue Plain. George Henry Strafford, valuer.

Besides the town of Pateley Bridge, Bishopside contains many small hamlets, amongst which is Wilsill, an old seat of

c

34 NIDDERDALE.

population mentioned in Domesday under the name of *Wives-hall*. It consists at present of a few farm houses and cottages, presenting no remarkable features of antiquity or otherwise. Near adjoining is Raikes School, of the endowment of Mrs. Alice Shepherd, of Knaresbrough; the following account of which is copied from a board in the Church of Pateley Bridge:—

"The late Mrs. Alice Shepherd of Knaresboro', in, and by her last will and testament, bearing date the 14th day of June, 1806, gave and devised all her real and personal property unto the Revd. John Tripp, Dr. of Laws, Watson Farside, Esq , and Robt. Stockdale, Gent:, upon divers trusts, and in particular that they should as soon as conveniently might be after her decease transfer the sum of £1000, Stock, in the Navy 5 per cent. annuities, then standing in her name, and place the same in their own joint names, to be applied for the purpose hereinafter mentioned, that is to say—that they, the said trustees, should yearly on the 2nd day of December, in every year, pay the Dividends, Interest, and produce of the said £1000, to the Minister and Churchwardens, and their successors for the time being, of the Church or Chapel of Pateley Bridge, in the county of York, to be by them, the said Minister and Churchwardens, applied and disposed of towards the teaching, and instructing 20 poor Children, either Boys or Girls or both, from 6 to 10 years of age, to be nominated and appointed by the said Minister and Churchwardens, out of the Children resident within the Chapelry of Pateley Bridge in Reading, Writing, and Accounts, by the Master of Raikes School in the said Chapelry; and her will was that the said Minister and Churchwardens should pay to the Master of Raikes School 20s. a year for each child which he should instruct by virtue of her said will; and also should yearly on Easter Sunday in every year provide for every boy to be taught under the said Charity, one full suit of dark drab clothes, with green collars and cuffs, a black Beaver Hat, and a pair of Shoes. And also shall in like manner provide for each Girl one round gown of dark Tammy Stuff, with green cuffs, and a black Beaver Hat, and a pair of Shoes;—which said articles she did direct should be purchased by wholesale, and at as low a price as they could be reasonably procured for; and if there should remain any surplus after paying the said Master, and purchasing such clothing; her will was that the same should be laid out in the purchase of Bibles and Spelling Books for the said Children, by, and at the discretion of the said Minister and Church-wardens; and further it was her will and mind that each child should be instructed three years from the time of his or her entrance.

Also the Revd. William Craven, Dr. in Divinity, Master of St. John's College, Cambridge, gave, by deed dated the 24th of August 1812, to the

BISHOPSIDE. 35

executors and trustees of the late Mrs. Alice Shepherd, the produce of £800, Navy Stock, 5 per cents, upon trust, to carry more fully into effect Mrs. Shepherd's will, and towards the repairs of Raikes School, or such Building as might happen to be erected, or used for that Charity."

The School having become ruinous, was rebuilt in 1816.

GLASSHOUSE MILL, situate between the river Nidd and the Railway, is a large flax spinning establishment, belonging to the Messrs. Metcalfe. Though it has not the magnitude of works of a similar kind seen in Leeds and other places, yet there is a cleanliness and elegance about it seldom seen in factories; the approaches are tastefully laid out, the reservoir, and everything connected with the works is made to assume an ornamental appearance. The machinery is driven by water and steam power, erected by the eminent firm of Messrs. W. Fairbairn and Son, of Manchester; the water wheel is of 120 horse power. The school belonging to the firm, in which the factory children are taught, is a beautiful decorated building. Very rarely do we see the useful and ornamental combined as at this place.

SMELTHOUSE MILL, lower down the valley, is a linen manufacturing and bobbin turning establishment, belonging to Messrs. Henry Kirby and Sons. It derives its name from its proximity to the lead smelting house of the Abbots of Fountains; the ore being brought thither from Greenhow on horses backs; a ford across the river Nidd, a short distance above, yet bears the name of *Lead Wath.*

FELLBECK is situate three miles east from Pateley Bridge, on the road to Ripon, and forms a hamlet of farm houses and cottages scattered over the sides of a shallow valley, through which runs a brook, known as Smelthouse Beck. A piece of land behind the Half Moon Inn bears the name of *Bollershaw*

Grange, which doubtless was the site of the Grange of that name, which belonged to the convent of Fountains, and which at the dissolution of that house was valued at 40s. per annum. It is now the property of the Greenwood family. *North Pasture House*, situate a short distance eastward, under the shadow of the rocks of Brimham, was another of the possessions of Fountains, and valued at the dissolution at 53s. 4d. per annum. The old Grange has been rebuilt ; over the entrance, cut on stone, are the initials M.L., and the date, 1657. On the garden wall are some hewn stones, which have formed an ornamental moulding in the old house. There are many houses in the neighbourhood of an age equal to the above, with carved and dated door heads, and mullioned windows.

FELLBECK HOUSE, situate on the hill side, on the left of the road leading to Pateley Bridge, was another of the possessions of Fountains, and valued at 20s. per annum. The monks appear to have obtained the greatest part of this corner of the township. They had also in *Pathlay-brig* property of the annual value of 29s. 5d. The waters of the beck immediately below this house give motion to the machinery of a corn mill. From the monks having possession of these lands, they probably never belonged to the Archbishops, but formed the half carucate of land which Gospatric held when the Domesday survey was made.

The mineral productions of Bishopside are building stone, of good quality and great variety, slates, but more especially flags, which can be obtained of almost any size and thickness ; they are extensively used for landings, and for the platforms of railway stations, where great extent of surface and durability are required. From their compact structure and hardness,

BISHOPSIDE. 87

they seem calculated to last for ever. The quarries are situate on the edge of the valley, below the upper bed of millstone grit, and extend from the Old Church, at Pateley Bridge, towards Yeadon. Coal has been obtained, but of inferior quality, near Smelthouse.

The manufacturing products are principally linen, linen yarns, and bobbins; the turning of the latter having become an important branch of industry in the dale during the last fifteen years; large quantities of wood growing on the slopes of the hills, and in the gills, being well adapted for that purpose.

The lands are chiefly of a pastoral kind, as will be seen from the following agricultural statistics, taken in 1854:—

TILLAGE.	a.	r.	p.	GRASS, &c.	a.	r.	p.	CATTLE, &c.	No.
Wheat	12	0	0	Clover	12	0	0	Horses	91
Barley	18	1	0	Pasture	1282	2	13	Colts	14
Oats	143	3	37	Houses, gardens, &c.	125	0	9	Cows	304
Vetches	0	1	0					Calves	205
Turnips	49	3	4	Waste attached to Farms	64	1	17	Other Cattle	105
Potatoes	19	1	20					Tups	10
Fallow	0	2	0	Woods	28	0	0	Ewes	500
				Small occupiers under 2 acres	52	2	0	Lambs	313
	244	0	21					Other Sheep	239
Grass, &c.	5759	3	19	Common	4195	1	20	Swine	186
Total	6004	0	0	Total Grass, &c.	5759	3	19	Total Cattle	1967

The annual value of property in this township, as returned by the Overseers of the Poor in 1857, was £4809. The value as assessed to the Property Tax in 1858 was £5780; and as assessed to the County Rate in 1859, £5312.

The population at the different decennial periods has been as follows:—1801, 1,487; 1811, 1,619; 1821, 2,072; 1831, 1,849; 1841, 1,987; 1851, 1,862; 1861, 2,052.

BEWERLEY.*

THIS township occupies the slope of the valley opposite to Bishopside, from which it is divided by the river Nidd; Stonebeck Down adjoins it on the north, on the west it extends to the confines of Craven and Knaresbrough Forest; Dacre forms the southern boundary. It has a very uneven surface, varying in height from 400 to 1,400 feet above the sea level, and presents many fine pictures of natural scenery. Bewerley Hall, with its beautiful and romantic grounds, including the glens and rocks of Ravensgill and Guy's-cliffe, Castlestead, Eagle Hall, Grassfield House, with the hamlets of Bridgehouse Gate, Bewerley, and Greenhow Hill are all within its limits.

During the reign of Edward the Confessor, this manor formed part of the possessions of the great Saxon earl Gospatric, who held extensive estates in this neighbourhood; after the Norman Conquest he was stripped of part of his lands, and Bewerley was given by the Conqueror to Erneis de Burun, one of his Norman followers; he was ancestor of the family of Byron, of whom the most illustrious member was the late distinguished poet. From De Burun it passed in a very short time to the family of Mowbray, Earls of North-

---

*The name is evidently derived from *Ber*, water, and *ley*, field—the watery field—an appropriate designation, as the river Nidd flows along one side, and many becks or gills intersect it from the west.

BEWERLEY.

89

umberland, and was by Roger, first baron of that name, given to the Abbot and Convent of St. Mary, of Fountains. The worldly wisdom of the monks was never more prominently displayed than in the care they took to make good their title to the lands thus bestowed on them; they obtained charter after charter renewing or confirming the respective grants, not only from the chief lords of the fee, but from every one who could be supposed to have any claim or interest therein. The grants of Mowbray were confirmed not only by the King, but also by the Archbishop, and Dean and Chapter of York, by Alice de Gante, wife of Roger de Mowbray, and afterwards by the successive barons De Mowbray, down to Thomas, who died an exile at Venice in the year 1400. These grants included not merely the surface soil, but also all mines of lead, iron, metals, and minerals beneath the surface. By one charter, Roger de Mowbray gave to the Abbot and Convent part of the Forest of Nidderdale, west of the river Nidd, with the use of the customary roads, and a new one thirty feet in width. This gift was confirmed by King Henry II. By another charter, he gave to them all the land between "Pateleigate and Iwdone.* Another charter confirmed to them the ownership of all mines of iron, lead, and other metals and minerals in the Forest of Nidderdale.

Nigel de Mowbray confirmed his father's gift of all that part of the Forest of Nidderdale west of the river Nidd, with the granges of Dacre and Bewerley, and right of road.

William de Stuteville confirmed to the monks certain lands

*This *Iwdone* is evidently not the place now called *Yeadon*, which is in Bishopside, and on the east side of the Nidd, whereas this is some place on the west side of that river.

40　　　　　　　　NIDDERDALE.

near Craven Keld. This is on the top of Greenhow, at the boundary between Knaresbrough Forest (of which Stuteville was lord,) and the Forest of Nidderdale.

Another charter from Nigel de Mowbray confirmed all the donations of Roger his father, Alice de Gante his mother, Adeline de Aldefield and Ralph her son, with the granges of Dacre, Bewerley, and *Rodley*.

John de Mowbray, son and heir of Roger (second of that name), quit-claimed to the monks all the bees, wild and domestic, which they had, or could obtain in Nidderdale, Dacre, Bewerley, Sixford, Burthwaite,* and Dalhaghe.

John de Mowbray, lord of the Isle of Axholme, gave them license to build houses and make enclosures within the free chace of Nidderdale. He also issued an order to his officers of the manor of Kirkby Malzeard, commanding that they suffer the Abbot of Fountains to make his profit of the lead mine within his portion of Nidderdale.

A charter from Thomas, Earl Marshal of England, Earl of Nottingham, Lord Mowbray and Segrave, confirms the grants of Roger de Mowbray, and all others his ancestors, to the monks, in full possession of all mines of lead, iron, and other metals and minerals, within their portion of Nidderdale.

The monks held possession of their lands, with an occasional dispute with their brethren of Byland concerning boundaries,

---

*From the enumeration of these names, it appears that Nidderdale was not such an extensive district as at present, but limited to the western side of the river Nidd; all the other places named (with the exception of the last, which is Dallah, or Dallowgill, where the monks also had possessions,) are now included within the limits of Nidderdale.

BEWERLEY.

41

until the general dissolution of the monastic orders in England, when

> "At last the earthquake came—the shock that hurl'd
> To dust, in many fragments dash'd and strown,
> The throne, whose roots were in another world,
> And whose far-stretching shadow awed our own ;
> From many a proud monastic pile o'erthrown,
> Fear-struck, the hooded inmates rush'd and fled ;
> The web, that for a thousand years had grown
> O'er prostrate Europe, in that day of dread
> Crumbled and fell, as fire dissolves the flaxen thread."

The grange of the monks at Bewerley at that time was valued at £16 16s. 8d. per annum. The chapel built by them yet exists. Coming to the crown this manor was soon granted out, probably Sir Lewis Mordaunt, Knight, was the first recipient, as he, along with others, sold the same in the year 1537 to Thomas Benson, Esq. In the year 1600 it was purchased by John Armytage, Esq., afterwards Sir John Armytage, who soon sold it again. At length, in the year 1674, it was conveyed to Dame Mary Yorke, widow of Sir John Yorke, by John Dove and others, in which family it yet remains.

The family of Yorke is of considerable antiquity in this county, and has held lands in Nidderdale for a long period.

Sir Richard Yorke, sometime Mayor of the Staple in Calais, was Lord Mayor of York in 1469, and again in 1482 ; and representative in Parliament for that city 12th Edward IV. His first wife was Jane, daughter of Richard Mauleverer, of Allerton Mauleverer, by whom he had two sons—Sir John Yorke, sometime Mayor of the Staple of Calais, and Thomas Yorke, who is presumed to be the person mentioned in Burton's Mon. Ebor. as *Presbyter de Myton*, and 27th Abbot of Whally.

42   NIDDERDALE.

By his second wife Joan he had another son named *John*, who was ancestor of the Yorke's of Gowthwaite and Bewerley. Sir Richard died in April, 1498, and was buried in the parish church of St. John's, at Ousebridge, in York,* where a table tomb yet remains to his memory.

John Yorke, third son of Sir Richard, married Catherine Patterdale, by whom he had three sons and one daughter. the youngest son, Sir John Yorke, Knight, Lord Mayor of London,† married first, Ann, daughter of Robert Smith, by

---

*At St. John's Church, Ousebridge, York, is a Chantry, called Yorke's Chantry, founded by Sir Richard Yorke, Knight, at the altar of Our Lady in this Church, to pray, &c., and help divine service in the said church: value £8 15s. 4d. a year. And in the north choir, on knots under the wooden roof, is depicted Ar. a saltire—Yorke ; impaling, gules, three greyhounds in pale, coursant, Ar. Mauleverer : Yorke, single, ut supra ; Ar. three bars wavy, az. on a chief, gu. a lion passant gardant, Ar. Merchants of the Staple. In the north-east choir was a man in armour kneeling ; on his breast his coat of arms, viz. Ar. a saltire, Az. behind them four daughters kneeling ; under this inscription is placed, " Orate pro anima Ricardi Yorke, Militis, bis Majoris civitatis Ebor, ac per   .   .   .   .   . Majoris Stapuli Callisie, et pro Johanne et Johanne uxorum, ac etiam pro omnibus liberis et benefactoribus suis qui   .   .   .   . die mensis Aprilis, Anno Domini MCCCCXCVIII." Under all these were four men and their wives kneeling, which Dods- worth supposes might be the daughters of Sir Richard, with their husbands.—*Drake's Ebor*, p. 279.

†Though styled Lord Mayor of London in all the printed pedigrees, his name does not occur in Stow's List of Mayors ; in the 3rd year of Edward VI. (1549), Richard Turke, and John Yorke, were sheriffs of that city, and Rowland Hill, mercer, Lord Mayor. " Sir John Yorke had been Under-Treasurer of the Mint. Together with other officers of the same he had a pardon for all manner of transgressions, &c. July 24, 1552." (Strype). On the accession of Queen Mary, Sir John Yorke was sent to the Tower, for what offence we know not. 1553. " The xxvij day of July the Duke of Suffolk, maister (Cheke) the kynges scolmaster, maister Coke (and) ser John Yorke, to the Towre."—The Diary of Henry Machyn, Camden Soc., 1848. On the 5th of November in the same year he was at large, and attended a sermon " at saint Sthevyns in Walbroke," where " dyd prych master Fecknam." On the 16th day of July, 1561, at the christening of Robert, son of Sir Gilbert Dethick, for whom the Queen was sponser, " and my lade Sakefield the quen's depute ; and after wafeers and epocrasse grett plente, and myche pepull ther, and my lade Yorke bare my lade depute's trayne ; and so hom to here plase, and had a bankett."

BEWERLEY.

whom he had two children—William and Grace. William appears to have died young, as he is never mentioned afterwards. Grace married —— Fanshawe. Sir John married secondly, a lady named Paget, by whom he had ten sons and three daughters,*—Peter, the eldest; Alane, William, Sir Edmund, Vice-Admiral in the British Navy; Henry, John and Robert. The daughters were Anne, married to Sir William Hilton; Catherine, and Margery.

Sir John was the first of his family who held lands in Nidderdale. On August 25th, 1546, he purchased the Forest of Nidderdale, by which we understand what is now known as the townships of Stonebeck Up and Stonebeck Down. Two years afterwards he purchased the manor of Appletreewick, in Craven. Sir John died in 1549, and was buried in the church of St. Stephen's, Wallbrook,† when he was succeeded by

---

*The pedigree of the Yorkes', given in *Clarkson's History of Richmond*, makes Ann Smith mother of the great number of children; he also makes them eleven sons and four daughters, and says that Alane, who died unmarried, was the eldest. Roland was the sixth son, of whom he says nothing: Was he not the Roland Yorke who served under the Earl of Leicester in the Netherlands, and had a command in the battle of Zutphen, where Sir Philip Sydney received his mortal wound? That fight is described by the Earl of Leicester in a letter to the Secretary Walsyngham, 28th September, 1586. "Theie were at the last, I thinke I may saye the most notable encounter that hath bine in our age, and will remaine to our posterity famous, the days fight, I meane, when our sonne was hurt, where these gentlemen were for hast driven to serve a foote, and sett themselves in the first rank (with) Mr. Rowland Yorke, who had the charge of that companie theie were in."—Leycester Correspondence, Camden Soc., 1844. On the capture of Zutphen, Rowland Yorke was made governor thereof, who betrayed his trust, and yielded the fort to the Spaniards, "for which good service he was afterwards poisoned by them." He is also said to have been the first who brought the rapier-fight into use in England. Whitaker, in his pedigree, also omits Sir Richard, a soldier, and knighted for his services. He lived at Ripon, was Justice of Peace for the West Riding in the 10th of James I., and also was Muster-Master.

†Stowe's Survey of London.

NIDDERDALE.

Peter Yorke, Esq., his eldest son, who married Elizabeth, daughter of Sir William Ingilby, of Ripley, Knight, by whom he had issue four sons—John, Thomas, William, and Richard. In his will, without date, made in London, he is described as Peter Yorke, of Gowthwaite, in the County of York, Esquire; he desires "to be buried in the church of St. Stevens, in Walbrucke, where his father, Sir John Yorke, and his mother was buried." He bequeaths to his second son, Thomas Yorke, one tenement, commonly called Psevells Farm, then in his own occupation. To his said son Thomas, and to his two younger sons William Yorke, and Richard Yorke, £200 each, to be paid out of the profits of his "mynes of lead over." For the performance of which said legacy he entreats his son John Yorke to have a special care and regard. Bequeaths to his brother William Yorke "one colte called Christopher," and to Thomas Spence "Bald Jackson." He gives to his brother William authority to bestow upon Thomas Spence "all my apparell that I have here at London, excepting my best cloak, which I give to my eldest son, and my ruby ring to my wife." Appoints his "dear and loving wife" sole executrix, and Sir William Mallory, of Hutton, in the County of York, Knight (to whom his best saddle, with the furniture), and his brother-in-law, William Ingilby, of Ripley, Esq. (to whom one of his "best nags," and the other to his brother Edmund Yorke), supervisors of his will. Also, "I will that x^{li} of the cc^{li} wch I appointed to my sonne Thomas Yorke shalbe bestowed upon & towards a tombe to be made for my $fath^r$ Sr John Yorke & me." Witnesses, Thomas Ingilby, gent., William Yorke, gent., and Thomas Spence. Proved 4th July, 1589. Administration granted to John Yorke, son and heir of the deceased, executrix having renounced.

BEWERLEY.

Sir John Yorke, of Gowthwaite, in the County of York, received the honour of Knighthood at Windsor in 1603. In 1611 he was involved in litigation with Francis, Earl of Cumberland, respecting free chace and warren in the manor of Appletreewick, Sir John claiming the above as appurtenant to his manor, which the Earl resisted, contending that Appletreewick was a member of the Forest of Skipton; that the inhabitants dwelling on the Prior of Bolton's lands there did, both in the Prior's time and ever since, yearly pay *foster oates* to the Bowbearer, or the Forester, of the Forest of Skipton; and did also pay *foster hens* and *castle hens*, and did suit and service yearly at the Forest Court of Skipton. Also that the said Earl and his ancestors have had their keepers at their wills, to range and view the deer within the town fields of Appletreewick; and set courses, and made general huntings on the commons, and through the fields and enclosures there.

Also that Sir John Yorke and his ancestors, never had any keepers there for deer; neither used to hunt there without leave of the Earl and his ancestors, except by stealing of them in the night time, or of courtesie, when the said Earl and his ancestors yearly bestowed deer on the said Sir John Yorke and his ancestors.*

From words this dispute came to blows, for some of Earl Francis' shepherds resorting to Appletreewick fair, for the purpose of buying lean sheep to be fatted in the parks, and refusing to pay the accustomed tolls at the town's end, were fallen upon by Sir John Yorke's bailiff and servants, and soundly beaten.

Whitaker's Craven, 2nd Ed., p. 439.

46 NIDDERDALE.

In another shape this matter came before the Star Chamber, which took cognizance at that time with severity of every instance of disrespect offered to a nobleman. From the records of that court—*Hilar. 1. Car. Comes, Cumbria, versus Yorke Equ. &c.*—we find that the defendant, Sir John Yorke, often gave directions to the defendants Fenton and John Yorke, to kill deer in Appletreewick Fields; and accordingley they, with others, 19 Jac. (1620), with a gun shot one of plaintiff's staggs, and pursued him with a blood-hound, and John Hunt said they would hunt and kill the deer at their pleasure; and Fenton, at another time, in Sir John Yorke's presence, shot with a gun at ten of the plaintiff's staggs in Appletreewick Fields; and Sir John, in a haughty manner, sent the plaintiff word he would kill and hunt deer there if he could; and for this hunting, and provoking speeches, they were committed to the Fleet, and fined—Sir John £200, Fenton £100, and John Yorke £50; but with the title, touching the bounds of the plaintiff's chace of Skipton and Barden, and the defendant's manor of Appletreewick, the court would not meddle, but left it to the law.

This may serve as a specimen of Star-Chamber justice, says Dr. Whitaker, from whom we have taken the above account. The title should, at all events, have been tried first; for, till that was decided, no proof existed that the defendant was not hunting in his own free warren, and his threatenings might amount to no more than a declaration that he would maintain his own rights.*

*Tradition tells a wild story about a treasonous play being acted in the great chamber at Gowthwaite Hall, for which Sir John was fined by government, and to raise the money was obliged to dispose of part of

Sir John married Julian, daughter and co-heir of Ralph Hansby, Esq., of Beverley and Tickhill, but dying without issue, was succeeded by his nephew (a son of his brother Thomas, by Frances, daughter of a Babthorpe, of Babthorpe).* He died at Sleningford; his will is dated 7th March, 1634-5, from which we make the following extracts† :—

"I Sir John Yorke, of Sleningford, Knight, now grown into yeares and beinge desirous in the time of perfect memory (though sicke in body) to settle & dispose of my temporall estate in such sorte as may both give content to myselfe and may make peace amongst my ffreinds after my departure hence. I doe hereby make this my last will & testament."

He desires "to be buried in the Chappell att Middlesmoore in Netherdale, where divers of my ancestors are formerly layde"—"that Julian now my wife shall first have her jointure, or what shalbe due unto her after my decease."

Bequeaths all the rest and residue of his lands, &c., and his wife's jointure after her decease, to his nephew John Yorke, his heirs and assigns,—"excepting one parcel of lands called the Bayle bancke beinge within the Manor and township of Bewerley in Netherdale," which he desires may be sold by William Norton the younger, of Sawley, gentleman, and his (testator's) servant Richard Beckwith, the proceeds being disposed of as follows :—To his servant Richard Beckwith £30, Jane Hardcastle £3, Isabel Driffield 40s., William Trees

his estate in Nidderdale. Certain it is that about this time, for a consideration, he granted long leases (some for 3,000 years) of his property in the township of Stonebeck Up. We think it far more probable that this measure was taken to pay the costs and fines incurred by this litigation, and unjust punishment, than for any real crime against government.

*Clarkson says by Frances, daughter of George Vavasour, of Spaldington, Esq.

†These extracts, so illustrative of the manners of a bygone age, have been furnished by the kindness of a gentleman, whose labours in this department of literature when published, will be a valuable mine of information to the genealogist, antiquary, and local historian.

NIDDERDALE.

50s., Margaret Aumond 50s. Residue as his wife thought fit. To Richard Beckwith he bequeathed his "old gray Barbary mare;" to his brother, Mr. Richard Yorke, his "black mare;" to his (testator's) "servant Francis Grainge the Gray Meare he rydes on called the lame mare." Bequeaths to his nephew, John Yorke, "the new sewt of Tables in the great Chamber at Goulthwaite and the three Turkee Carpitts," after the decease of his wife, whom he makes residuary legatee, desiring her to see him "honestly brought forth at his burial." The executors, Christopher Wandesford, Master of the Rolls in Ireland; William Norton the younger, of Sawley, gentleman; and Major Norton, of Richmond, Esq., to each of whom a piece of gold. "Lastly my will and mind is that my servant William Radcliffe be kept at my house at Goulthwaite, by my nephew, with meat, drink, and clothes for life." Proved 13th March, 1634-5. Administration granted to Major Norton.

According to his desire he was buried in the "Chappell at Middlesmoore."

John Yorke, Esq., of Gowthwaite, nephew of the above, married, first, Florence Sharpe, of Westmorland, by whom he had three daughters—Elizabeth, married to James Lesly, Lord Lindores in Scotland, to whom she was second wife; Frances, to Thomas Barney, of Dole Bank, in the County of York; and Jane, to Lieut.-General David Lesley, Lord Newark, in Scotland.

He married, secondly, Catherine, daughter of Sir Ingilby Daniel, Knight, of Beswick, in Yorkshire, by whom he had one son, who on the decease of his father succeeded to the estates.

BEWERLEY.

Sir John Yorke, of Gowthwaite, Knight,* married Mary,†
daughter of Maulger Norton., Esq., of St. Nicholas, near
Richmond, by whom he had one son, Thomas, who succeeded
him, and one daughter, Mary, who was wife of Sir Edward
Blackett, of Newby, Bart. Sir John was elected Member of
Parliament for Richmond in 1661. He died April 3rd, 1663,
at the early age of 29, and was interred in the chapel at
Middlesmoor, where the following inscription, on a brass
plate, yet remains to his memory :—

"HIC JACET JOHANNES YORKE DE GOWTHWAITE EQUES AURATUS, PRO
ANTIQUISSIMO RICHMONDIÆ MUNICIPIO IN COMITIIS PARLIAMENTI SILLUS
TRISSIMO REGE CAROLO SECUNDO DELEGATUS PRIMARIUS. OBIIT APUD
LONDINUM TEMPORE COMITORUM TERTIO DIE APRILIS ANNO DOMINI 1663.
ÆTATISQ. SUÆ VIGESIMO NONO, CUM SUPER ERANT UNICUS FILIUS THOMAS
ET UNICA FILIA.

HOC MONUMENTUM IN PERPETUAM EJUS MEMORIAM FIDELISSIMA CONJUX
MARIA MÆRENS POSUIT.

REQUIESCAT IN PACE."

*Aug. 3rd, 1660. Then received by the hands of Colonel Thomas
Daniel, the sum of £61 10s. for fees, due to the King's servants for the
honour of Knighthood conferred on Sir John Yorke, of Goulthwaite,
in the County of York. Geo: Owen, York Herald.—*Clarkson's History
of Richmond*, p. 330.

†This marriage took place 15th January, 1658, when Sir John was a
minor; when he came of age he settled upon his wife, as a jointure, all
his manors or lordships of Netherdale and Appletreewick, Gowthwaite
Hall, &c. It was by this lady that the property of the Nortons, at
Richmond, came into possession of the family of Yorke, as dower.
This was the Dame Mary Yorke, who during her widowhood purchased
the manor of Bewerley in 1678. In the year 1662, in the list of trained
horse for the Wapentake of Claro, Sir John Yorke, of Gowthwaite, was
rated at one horse and arms. In his will, dated 7th February, 1662-3,
he desires to be buried at Middlesmoor; bequeaths £200 per annum out
of lands and tenements in Netherdale and Appletreewick to Mary, his
wife, for her life; remainder to his son, Thomas Yorke, and his heirs
for ever. Appoints his wife sole executrix. Proved 15th July, 1663.

D

NIDDERDALE.

Thomas Yorke, Esq., of Gowthwaite and Richmond, only surviving son of the above, was born June 29th, 1658, elected M.P. for Richmond in 1695, 1698, 1700, 1701, 1702, 1705, 1707, and 1715. He married Catherine, only daughter and heiress of Thomas Lister, of Arnolds-Biggin, December 7th, 1680, by whom he had two sons and three daughters—John, his heir; Thomas, successor to his brother; Catherine, Mary Anne, and Elizabeth. He died November 16th, 1716, and was buried at Richmond. His eldest son,

John Yorke, Esq., of Gowthwaite and Richmond, succeeded to the estates. He represented the borough of Richmond in parliament from 1708 to 1757. He married January 5th, 1732, Anne, daughter and co-heir of James Darcy, of Sedbury, Lord Darcy of Navan, but dying without issue,* July 14th, 1757, was succeeded by his brother,

Thomas Yorke, Esq., of Halton Place, in the parish of Long Preston, in the county of York, who then became of Gowthwaite, and was elected M.P. for Richmond on the decease of his brother. He married November 4th, 1720, Abigail, daughter and co-heiress of William Andrews, Esq., of Barnes Hall, in Worcestershire, and had issue, John, his heir.

Thomas, of Halton Place, and of the Middle Temple, barrister-at-law, born June 5th, 1738, married at Newcastle, February 8th, 1774, Jane, daughter of Joseph Reay, Esq., of Newcastle-on-Tyne, and died July 3rd, 1811, leaving issue—

John, successor to his uncle.

Thomas Henry, M.A., Vicar of Bishop Middleham.

Edmund, M.A.; Margaret, and Anne.

Katherine, second wife of Lieutenant General Sir John

*He was found dead in his garden. Buried in Richmond Church.

BEWERLEY. 51

Clavering, K.B.; Mary and Anne, who both died unmarried in 1778. On his decease, March 26th, 1770,* his eldest son,

John Yorke, Esq., of Bewerley, lord of the manors of Bewerley and Ramsgill, in Netherdale, and of Appletreewick, in Craven, who served as High Sheriff of Yorkshire in the year 1788. He married, firstly, in 1763, Sophia, daughter of Sir John Glyn, Bart., of Hawarden, by whom he had an only child, who died in infancy; and secondly, 1769, Elizabeth Woodstock, daughter of John Campbell, Esq., of Fish River, in the parish of Hanover, Jamaica, by whom he had no issue.

His highly cultivated mind, well stored with ancient and modern learning, expanded by a long residence in foreign countries, was open to every liberal and humane idea, and the tale of distress, or any public improvement, ever met his attentive ear. The poor lost in him a most bountiful benefactor; nor will his name ever be thought of without uniting to it every virtue which can adorn human nature. Few have left behind them a character more distinguished for active benevolence and extensive charity, and long will his memory be cherished by a numerous and respectable acquaintance, who will never forget the facetious companion at his hospitable board. His humility of mind extended even to the grave, and his last request was, to be interred not among his own relations in the family vault, at Richmond, but in the most private manner,

*He was buried in London. On one of the communion flaggons belonging to Richmond Church is inscribed—"The gift of Thomas Yorke, Esq., to the Parish of Richmond for ever, 1762." April 6th, 1762, Thomas Yorke, Esq., purchased of the corporation of Richmond, for £276 5s. in fee, the foggage of Bell Banks, which previous to the year 1692, were uninclosed, Newbiggin Close, and several quit rents, two tofts, and two gardens, then thrown into one, and made part of his great garden."—*Clarkson's Richmond*, p. 330.

NIDDERDALE.

and without the least appearance of parade, in Hudswell Churchyard, where a plain stone, with a simple inscription, covers his much lamented remains—*

Requiescat in pace.

"In memory of John Yorke, Esq., of the Green, Richmond, and of Bewerley Hall, in the West Riding of Yorkshire, eldest son of Thomas and Abigail Yorke, formerly of Helperby, who died January 29th, 1813, aged 78 Years. R.I.P."

John Yorke, Esq., nephew of the above, son of Thomas Yorke, of Halton Place, succeeded to the estates. He was born on the 29th of February, 1776, and was High Sheriff of Yorkshire in 1818; married in 1821, Mary, eldest daughter of Icabod Wright, Esq,, of Mapperley, Nottinghamshire, by whom he had issue—

John Yorke, Esq., of Bewerley Hall, born March 28th, 1827, married September 5th, 1859, Alice, fifth daughter of James Simpson.

Thomas Edward, born August 4th, 1832, married February 17th, 1863, Augusta Margaret, eldest daughter of the Hon. and Rev. John Baillie, rector of Elsdon, and canon of York.

Frances Mary, born December 21st, 1828

Caroline, born August 11th, 1830, married the Rev. John Tyrwhitt, vicar of St. Magdalene, Oxford.

After a life spent in the improvement of his estate, and promoting the welfare of his tenantry, Mr. Yorke died February 5th, 1857, and was buried in a family vault in the church of Pateley Bridge, when his eldest son succeeded to the estates.

Arms—*Argent*. A saltire, *azure*. Crest—A monkey's head erased, proper.

*Such is the character drawn by one who probably knew him well in life.—*Clarkson's Richmond*, p. 333.

BEWERLEY.

Bewerley Hall, seat of the family of Yorke, adjoins the village of the same name, and is pleasantly situate in a warm and fertile spot, on a gentle eminence,   park, studded with timber trees, extending down to the river Nidd, sheltered on the western side by a range of hills and woods, and commanding beautiful views of the surrounding country—

"A happy rural seat of various view."

The house, with the exception of the round towers on the eastern side, which formed part of the old hall, is a modern building, erected by the late John Yorke, Esq., between the years 1815 and 1820; the most recent addition, near the principal entrance, was made in 1848. It is of a square form, fronting the east and south; the principal entrance is on the east, which front is flanked by two projecting round towers, embattled and surmounted by slender spires; the south front is also embattled, overlooks the lawn, and commands fine views of the woods and rocks of Guy's-cliffe and Brimham, whose shaggy sides and uncouth forms have a fine effect in the distance. The grounds around are tastefully laid out, and kept in admirable order; amongst the flowering shrubs the *Rhododendron* claims particular notice from its abundance and beauty. Behind the Hall is the Chapel of the old monastic day, plain and humble, yet bearing unmistakable evidence of its use, and also of its builders; the motto in large old English letters,

Soli Deo honor et gloria,

And the huge **M.H.** of Marmaduke Huby, abbot of Fountains, from 1494 to 1526, are yet conspicuous on the walls; the motto is on the east end, and the initials on the east, north, and south sides. It is a low building; the windows

NIDDERDALE.

are of three lights each under a square label moulding. The entrance is through an elegant little porch on the south. The bell turret yet remains at the east end. The walls are prettily overgrown with ivy, moss, and ferns. It is an interesting place, both from its present appearance and past history; built when the Romish religion was in the height of its prosperity,, within its walls,

> " The mass was sung,
> And the censer swung,
> And the incense rose on high."

It has since been applied to different uses, in 1679, it was fitted up and used as a school; of which the following particulars are recorded in the Pateley Bridge registers—

" 1679. Memorand. that the Lady Yorke was pleased to give the old Chappel and Chappell yard at Bewerley for the conveniency of a School and School house. And did by her Assignee Michael Inman, deliver the same to Mr. J. Beckwith of Bewerley, one of the Feofees named in her Deed of Gift.

Whereupon The Worshipfull Mr. Sam. Taylor of Wallingwells in the county of Nottingham, together with his now heir Hen. Rich. Taylor Esqe have been at the charge of building a convenient house, and repayred the other end for the school-house. And ye sd Rich. Taylor Esq. now patron of the sd School, hath entered Bond of 400li to me Tho. Furniss, and Anthony Wood of Bpside for the payment of Ten Pounds p. annum to a Schoolmaster, by him or his heirs to be chosen for the teaching of Twelve boys only in the Latine tongue &c. The same being also to be nominated by him, or his heirs &c. The Ten Pounds to be paid at Candlemas and Lammas, by equal porcons."

" 1680, Judith Darnbrook sepulta erat xxiij die Ap. Memorandum yt there was given by her towards the maintaining of two poor boys within Bewerley, at the School there with Learning Books wholly in English the sum of Twenty pounds, to be paid out of her estate, but the same gift was contracted to Eight pounds only, which was paid by Michael Inman her Administrator in right of his wife; for the interest of which one boy ought to be taught there &c."

Even to within living memory it was used as a school on week days, and as a chapel on Sundays; it is now a depository of garden implements; the inside of the east window contains a collection of fine specimens of minerals, spars, and petrefactions.

The gardener's house, a short distance south-east of the Hall is an antique Tudor building, said by tradition to have been the *priest's* house. The front windows are of six lights each divided by stout stone mullions; in the kitchen is the old fire place with its wide chimney; the staircase also preserves its original appearance; much oak, and one beautiful piece of walnut pannelling is preserved in the upper rooms; one of the chambers has a ceiling very elaborately ornamented, in the central compartment is a figure of a lady in an antique dress; the beams are adorned with vines and bunches of grapes; in one part is an armorial shield, charged with a fesse and three fleurs-de-lis. This house was once the property of the family of Darnbrook, afterwards of that of Inman.

The grounds attached to the hall are most beautiful and romantic, and were considerably enlarged and improved by the late John Yorke Esq. Leaving the smoothly shaven lawn with its beds of flowers and clumps of evergreen shrubs basking in the sunshine, the walk winds up the Fishpond wood, which is principally composed of beech, an exotic in this neighbourhood, the soil however appears suitable, as the trees have generally attained to a great height. In this wood is a fish-pond, a fine sheet of clear water formed by throwing a dam across the bottom of a narrow valley, and intercepting one, of the many small streams which run from the adjacent hills. It is a cool delightful spot on a summer's day, shaded by lofty trees, in which a colony of rooks have taken up their abode. Crossing the brook called Fossbeck, near its junction with Raven's beck, the hamlet of Middletongue, a cluster of half a score dwellings, almost hidden in the woody glen, is seen on the right, and the romantic Ravensgill is entered. On one side is a plantation of tall larches on the slope of a steep hill, on the other side, deep, down below, flow the waters of the brook Raven's beck; in summer they steal along almost unseen, though faintly heard, murmuring, as they twist around great moss-covered boulders, which appear to have fallen from the sides of the hills for the purpose of interrupting their course; in winter, or after heavy rains, the water rushes down all bubbles and foam, bounding from crag to crag, or twining around, or diving beneath huge blocks of stone; and such is the rapid descent, that in place of one grand fall, there are a thousand small cataracts.

> " Midst greens and shades the wild wave leaps,
>   From cliffs were the wood-flower clings ;
> All summer he moistens his verdent steeps
>   With the sweet light spray of the mountain springs :
> And he shakes the woods on the mountain side,
> When they drip with the rains of autumn tide."

The walk ever keeps winding upward, upward still—amid tall ferns and taller trees ; the restless brook ever murmuring and gleaming deep down below. Nearer the top of the glen grey crags, and lofty cliffs of gritstone rise abruptly from the hill. Seats are placed at intervals at particular points, where a view of more than ordinary beauty or interest is obtained : *the seat* under the shelter of a jutting crag discloses a view of the town of Pateley Bridge on one side and Brimham Rocks on another. Near the head of the glen, the trees are Scotch fir and spruce, some of them growing almost out of the rocks, the cliffs grow higher and darker, and the whole scene becomes more rugged and wild. A fissure in one clift bears the name of " Jackman's Shop," the traditional

BEWERLEY. 57

abode of a wild man; not unlike the occasional resort of a robber. The botanist may here revel amidst a profusion of mountain plants, ferns, heaths, mosses, and lichens; amongst which the whortle-berry *Vaccinium Myrtillus*, is abundant, and luxuriant; the more elegant cowberry, *Vaccinium Vitis Idœa* and the different kinds of heath or ling. Among ferns, the common Bracken is most abundant, covering the sides of the hills with the masses of its verdure; of rarer kinds will be found the tall and graceful *Osmunda regalis, Polypodium* in variety and abundance, *Ceterach officinarum, Lastrea Dilatata, Allosorus crispus, Filix Mas, Filix Femina, Crystopteris fragilis, Asplenium Ruta muraria, Asplenium Adiantum-nigrum, Blechnum spicante*, and many others. The top of the glen is wild and grand—

> " Down, down, precipitous and rude
>   The rocks abruptly go,
> While through their deep and narrow gorge
>   Foams on the brook below."

At the top of the gill is a dwelling which bears the name of the Raven's nest. Crossing the brook at the point where it descends from the moor, the opposite side is gained, which has a more easy slope and less grandeur than the other; it is also planted with trees, and belongs to another owner, and thus cuts asunder the two interesting pieces of mountain scenery Ravensgill and Guyscliffe, which if united by a bridge at the head of this ravine, and a more practicable walk through the *Skrikes* plantation, would form a promenade at once wild, grand, and unique. A mill race winds along the breast of the hill conveying water from Ravensgill beck to a corn and bobbin mill in the valley below.

NIDDERDALE.

A footpath leads through this plantation to the heath above, which is called *Nought Moor*, (a name of evil signification,) on the edge of which is a rock of singular form, called the Crocodile, from a fancied resemblance between projecting and receding parts of the stone, and the gaping jaws of the monster. The opening is about six feet in height, and the upper jaw projects considerably, forming a shade or a shelter as need may require. From this place the valley is seen to great advantage, the whole of its length from Whernside to Brimham Rocks, spread beneath the observer like a map, not like a dry skeleton, but blooming with life and beauty; every change of position produces a new picture, not one of those boundless ones which are seen sometimes from an eminence in more level countries, but one that the eye can take in with all its groupings, and always enclosed in a frame of brown or purple hills. While under the shelter of the upper jaw of this stone monster we can contemplate the scene below, to describe it in words is impossible; behold the scene in its present beauty and variety, the rich and cultivated vale, studded with human habitations, and alive with human industry,—and then carry back the thoughts to a remote period, when between this height, and the kindred rocks of Brimham nothing was seen but a lake winding among the hills; the observer may fancy that he hears the winds sweeping over it and the tides dashing against the rocks beneath his feet. Then let him pause in imagination, for perhaps a thousand years, and he will behold before him instead of the lake, lofty precipices, and hills shaggy with tangled woods, and in the valley below the river winding along, and the trees shedding and renewing their leaves, with no human eye to notice, or human heart to

BEWERLEY.

59

regret or welcome the change. Then he may behold the first settlers enter the region and become joint tenants with the wolf the boar, the wild bull, and the red deer—another pause— the din of arms is heard, and he beholds in the valley below a small square fortress with the proud bird of conquest, the Roman eagle, hovering over it. So may he, at his leisure, pause and review the different revolutions which have taken place in the valley until at length he sees the iron trackway and the fire-impelled chariots of the present iron age sweeping along under a cloud of smoke, reminding him that his reverie must be cut short, or the returning train will leave him behind.

Below this rock is a singular hollow called "The Trough," through which the road from Pateley to Otley passes; the hills rise abruptly from it on three sides leaving an opening to the main valley, and another very narrow one to the south- west; the sides are clothed with heath, and fern, " and many a hanging crag." In summer this wild spot is pleasant to look upon, when the sunshine is streaming over its dark craggy sides; but viewed on the eve of a winter's day, when dark masses of cloud are driving over the hills, it has a solemn almost awful aspect. In the centre of this hollow is the site of a Bale or Baal hill,* or place where lead was

*Such is the name given to these places all over the lead mining dis- tricts of Yorkshire,—the refuse left on them proves beyond a question what they have been. Some are of opinion that on these hills sacrificial fires were kindled to the god *Baal.* Though this may not be strictly true, it is not unlikely that they derive their name from their similar- ity of situation to the fires lighted on high places, to that, almost universally adored Deity. The worship of Bel, Baal, Belinus, or Balanos, prevailed nearly all over the east; and his places of worship were " groves" and " high places." It was to this God that the Hebrews so frequently apostatised, making " their children to pass through fire to this grim idol." The Baal of the eastern nations, and the Bel of the Druids were the same god. Eusebius says, the Jupiter of

60

NIDDERDALE.

smelted in very early times; this place appears to have been selected for the purpose of catching the blast rushing into the gorge from the south-west, as well as for the sake of fuel. These places are found nearly all over the dale, even where no lead has been raised near them; no vegetation grows upon them, the soil has been poisoned by the fumes of the lead; fragments of calcined ore, pieces of pure lead, and charcoal are found on most of them. In some places the matter has been smelted over again with profit.

On the opposite side of this hollow, on the top of Guyscliffe is a mock ruin, from which a most extensive view of the country around is obtained, far beyond the limits of the dale, over Knaresbrough forest, Harlow hill with its lofty tower, Harrogate, Knaresbrough, York Minster, and the blue outline of the distant Wolds—passing northward may be seen Crake Castle, the line of the Hambleton hills, as far as Eston Nab, near the mouth of the Tees. This distant prospect is visible all along the edge of Guyscliffe, which is 1,000 feet above the sea level, and upwards of 650 feet above the valley below.

the Romans was the same as the Baal of the Babylonians and the Phœnicians. The grand festival to this deity was on the eve of the first of May, when the sun entered Taurus, and Spring began: on that evening in all Druidical countries, fires were lighted on the *Cairns* and the mystic orgies of that religion celebrated. Though the practice has been long discontinued, yet the name remains, the Irish yet call the eve of the first of May *La Bealtine.* Though we do not believe that those parched and barren places were the actual spots, where fires to the god Baal were lighted, we are of opinion that they derived their name from them. The first were made on high hills, in order that they might be seen at a distance—the last were also made in high places that they might the better catch the wind, in order to fuse the ore, and from this similarity of position alone they had their name. Many places in Nidderdale bear the name, as Baal Crag, Baal Rigg, Baal Ing, Baal Bank, &c. Also when men or animals are poisoned by the fumes of lead they are said to be *Baaloned* or *Beloned.*

BEWERLEY.

> " Thou who wouldest see the lovely and the wild
> Mingled in harmony on Nature's face,
> Ascend our rocky mountain.   Let thy foot
> Fail not with weariness, for on its top
> The beauty and the majesty of earth,
> Spread wide beneath, shall make thee to forget
> The steep and toilsome way.
>
> > Thou shalt look
>
> Upon the green and rolling forest tops,
> And down into the secrets of the glens,
> And streams, that with their bordering thickets strive
> To hide their windings.   Thou shalt gaze, at once
> Here on white villages, and tilth, and herds,
> And swarming roads, and there on solitudes
> That only hear the torrent and the wind."

About midway of its range the cliff is broken by an opening called " The three Gaps," where it assumes the appearance of huge isolated crags with three openings leading through.   The sides of the rocks are worn into innumerable crevices and crannies as if by the waves of a sea washing away the softer parts.   At this point the observer will see another splendid picture of the valley, the whole of its length,

> > " The scene
>
> Is lovely round ; a beautiful river there
> Wanders amid the fresh and fertile meads,
> The paradise he made unto himself,
> Mining the soil for ages.   On each side
> The fields swell upward to the hills ; beyond,
> Above the hills, in the blue distance, rise
> The mighty columns with which earth props heaven."

On both sides of this opening the cliff is upwards of 200 feet in perpendicular height,

> > Shaggy and wild
>
> With mossy trees and pinnacles of flint,
> And many a hanging crag."

These rocks are of gritstone, in thick masses, with occasional beds of slaty shale, which in the lower part has been worked and flags obtained.   Near the eastern extemity, where

62 · NIDDERDALE.

a low straggling fence divides the estate of the Yorkes of Bewerley, from that of the Ingilbies of Ripley, the cliff is the highest, rugged, broken, and disjointed, every fissure bearing a plant, or tree, the oak, the holly, the birch, the mountain ash, the heath, and the whortleberry, all cling to the front of the precipice, and add greatly to its beauty. Some of the rocks have particular names, one enormous fallen mass, more than 20 yards in length by 8 or 9 in height is called "the Saw-horse"; it has more the shape and appearance of a gigantic cannon; a cave, covered with a large crag is "Katie's Parlour," and another "the Giant's Chair."

All along the face of the cliff are scattered enormous boulders in vast irregular masses, which have evidently fallen, or slipped down to their present position from the face of the precipice above, These are thickly clad with a profusion of mosses and lichens the growth of centuries. This rugged ground is a thick wood, principally of oak, mountain ash, and birch, with large patches of lofty breckons. What must strike every beholder is the luxuriance of the whortleberry plants and the mosses, the *Orthotricum* or bristle moss especially clothes the old, low branches of the birch with such an abundance of foliage as is rarely seen elsewhere. The Muscologist might wander in this solitude for many a day with pleasure and profit—

> " Where, to charm the curious eye,
> A host of hidden treasures lie,
> A microscopic world that tells,
>   That not alone in trees and flowers
> The spirit bright of beauty dwells,
>   That not alone in lofty bowers
> The mighty hand of God is seen,
> But more triumphant still in things men count as mean."

About 200 yards from the foot of the cliff, in a cup shaped hollow, formed for its reception by a landslip, is a beautiful piece of water, called Guyscliffe Tarn; about 100 yards in length, by half as much in breadth, of an oval shape. It is (surrounded by moss-grown crags, and trees nearly as moss-grown) well stocked with fish, supplied by two or three springs which rise near its margin, and kept at one uniform level by a *swallow* at one corner. It is reached by a carriage road formed through the woods, and is a favourite resort in the summer season. A ramble among these woods and rocks, with an inspection of the fine scenery around, to the inhabitant of a large smoky town is like a visit to another world, the contrast is so great.

> " Oh 'tis a joyous thing
>   Beside some moss-clad rock,
> That for uncounted centuries
>   Hath defied each tempest shock,
> Upon the scented heath   .
>   All carelessly reclined,
> To lie and listen joyously
>   To the murmuring mountain wind.
> Far from the busy world—
>   From heartless tumult far—
> Where nought deep silence can disturb,
>   Save the elemental war."

CASTLESTEAD is the name of the ancient Roman camp, now applied to the castellated mansion recently erected by Mr. George Metcalfe on its site. This house is of a square form of considerable architectural pretensions, with steep and gabled roofs, which, with other features remind the observer of the " stately homes " of England, during the 14th and 15th centuries ; although it is evident that the architect has aimed at no mere imitation of the work of past ages ; all parts being apparently designed to meet the wants of modern society ; the win-

64   NIDDERDALE.

dows being wider than in the usually understood style of that period, and differing also in the massiveness of the divisions or piers.   On the north, or entrance front is an open arched porch ; and over the Entrance Hall a tower, having at one angle a turret staircase, the slated spire of which is surmounted by a handsome vane.   The east, or Terrace front, is embellished with bay windows rising through two stories, between which are the lofty arched and coupled windows of the staircase.   The south front looks upon the flower garden, and the ground along the bank of the river is tastefully laid out with walks and planted with shrubs, which in the course of a few years will make this the most charming spot in the vale of the Nidd.

The design was by W. R. Carson, Esq., of Manchester, the building was completed in 1862, and is one of the most elegant pieces of architecture in Nidderdale.   The approach on one side is by a wrought iron lattice bridge of 100 feet span across the river, erected by J. and G. Joicey of Newcastle-on-Tyne ; and on the other, by a pleasant drive through the fields from near Bewerley Hall.   Standing on a gentle eminence in the centre of the valley, it commands beautiful, though limited, views all around.   What makes it more interesting is its situation on the site of the Roman camp or fort, which has long borne the significant name of Castlestead.✳ No stone work or foundations of buildings were found when the excavations were made for the erection of the new house,

---

✳ " Castle-stead, or Castle-steeds," says Gough in his Camden, " is the common name given to the *Castella* on the wall of Hadrian. There are two forts near Corbridge in Northumberland called Castle-steeds." To this name may be added two others equally significant, applied to places immediately adjoining—*Harefield* and *Harewell* the first syllable of both meaning soldier.

hence we may infer that the conquerors of the world were content with a fortress of timber and earth. The agger is now sloped a little and planted with shrubs or laid out as a flower garden.

This interesting piece of ground was formerly part of the Eagle Hall estate, and only recently purchased by its present owner, who has shewn judgment in the selection of the site, and fine taste in the erection of the house and the laying out of the grounds.

GRASSFIELD HOUSE, the seat of Hanley Hutchinson, Esq., is situate further up the valley, near the road leading to Ramsgill. It was built in 1810, and is a spacious and substantial fabric of stone, surrounded by gardens, shrubbries, and thriving plantations, pleasantly located, and withal a desirable place as a residence. A short distance further up the valley is a mill belonging to the same gentleman, for rolling sheet lead, and manufacturing leaden pipes.

EAGLE HALL is pleasantly situate on the side of a wooded glen, on the right of the road leading from Pateley Bridge to Greenhow, and along with a considerable estate in land, and the mineral royalty of the manor of Bewerley for a considerable time belonged to the family of White, of Wallingwells, and its maternal ancestors, the Taylors. At what time the estate was acquired we have no direct information ; the Taylors have been long connected with the neighbourhood in a manner honourable to themselves. In 1678, "The Worshipfull Mr. Samuel Taylor, of Wallingwells," and his heir Henry Richard Taylor, Esq., repaired the old chapel near Bewerley Hall, for the purpose of converting it into a school, and also endowed it with ten pounds per annum, "for the teaching of twelve

NIDDERDALE.

boys only in the Latine tongue." Also, in 1683, Richard Taylor, of Wallingwells, Esq., and his uncle Richard Taylor, of Newall, erected a gallery for their own use in the old church at Pateley Bridge. From the Taylors the estate passed to the Whites, by the marriage in July, 1698, of Thomas White, Esq., to Bridget, sole daughter and heiress of Richard Taylor, Esq., M.P. for East Retford, and Sheriff of the County of Nottingham, in 1699. John, their eldest son died unmarried; when Taylor White, Esq., the second son, succeeded to the estates. He was twice married—first to Ann, daughter of Thomas Errington, of Beauforth, Esq.; and secondly, to Frances, daughter and co-heiress of Major General John Armstrong, by whom he had issue :—Taylor, Thomas a lawyer, Stephen L.L.D., a Clergyman, Anne and Frances. On his decease in 1772, his eldest son

Taylor White, Esq., born in 1743, succeeded, who married Sarah, eldest daughter and co-heiress of Sir Isaac Woollaston, Bart., by whom he had issue :—Lydia, Thomas, Sarah, Elizabeth, Taylor, Frances, and Charles Lawrence. On his demise in 1795, his son

Thomas Woollaston White, Esq., succeeeded; who on Dec. 20th, 1802, was created a baronet, with remainders in default of issue male to his brothers, Taylor and Charles Lawrence White. He was born January 20th, 1767, married January 3rd, 1800, Elizabeth, daughter of Thomas Blagg, of Tuxford, Esq., and had issue :— Thomas Woollaston, Elizabeth, and Sarah. During the war with France, Sir Thomas raised, armed, and clothed, at his own expense, a corps, called the *Sherwood Rangers*. He died in 1817, and was succeeded by the present baronet,

BEWERLEY.

67

Sir Thomas Woollaston White, who was born at Wallingwells, in 1801; married in 1824, a daughter of George Ramsey, Esq., of Barnton, near Edinburgh, she died in 1825; when Sir Thomas married secondly in 1827, a daughter of W. Ramsey, Esq., a banker in Edinburgh. Educated at Rugby, he afterwards entered the army as cornet in the 10th Dragoons; in 1842, became ensign in the 3rd West India Regiment; was Lieut.-Colonel of the Notts. Militia from 1833 to 1852. Heir apparent Thomas Woollaston, born in 1828.

Arms-*Gules*, a chevron, vaire, between three lioncels rampant.

' Crest—An eagle, sable, rising with wings expanded, from a ducal coronet, argent.

This estate has recently come into the hands of other owners; by an arrangement of which we know not the particulars; Sir Thomas W. White only held one fifth part; the Rev. Taylor White one other fifth, and T. F. A. Burnaby, Esq., of Newark-on-Trent, the other three fifths. The last-named owner obtained possession of the whole, and shortly afterwards sold one half thereof to Hanley Hutchinson, Esq., of Grassfield House.

The Hall is a plain modern building, of no great size, nor remarkable for anything but its situation, and the fine prospect from its front; around are grounds neatly laid out and planted with shrubs and evergreens, sheltered on the North and West by groves of tall trees. A door head in one of the outbuildings bears the initials and date T. I. W.1689, which has evidently been above the entrance of a former house. The view embraces the valley of the Nidd, Pateley Bridge, Castlestead, Braisty Woods, Brimham Rocks, and is of great beauty and variety. The name is doubtless derived from the *eagle* crest of its owners.

68   NIDDERDALE.

About half-a-mile west of the hall, at the foot of a wooded hill, is the entrance to an abandoned lead mine known as the "Eagle Level," from which issues a body of water of sufficient strength to drive a mill, to which purpose it is applied at Bridgehouse Gate. This level extends upwards of a mile into the hill. Over the entrance arch is engraved on a large stone, the compass, level, pick, and other tools used in mining operations, surmounted by the *rising eagle* crest of the Whites, and the date July 13th, 1825. The slopes of the hills around are clad with native woods, with a slight intermixture of larches, and the whole glen is a choice spot for the botanist, as it contains great variety of plants, mosses, and ferns.

A short distance further up is Baal Bank, where some have supposed firey sacrifices were offered to the eastern god Baal— a type of the sun. It is a steep, dark, heathy, uncultivated hill side, fronting the north, where probably the earliest miners on Greenhow smelted their lead ore.

Bridgehouse Gate is a hamlet about a quarter of a mile from Pateley Bridge, where is a school, partly free, maintained by John Yorke, Esq., for the education of the children of Bewerley and Pateley Bridge ; and a chapel, with burial ground attached belonging to the Independents, built in 1816, which is a substantial building of stone, and will accommodate about 600 hearers. There is a small endowment for the maintenance of the officiating minister, consisting of land let for £21 a year, left by Martha and Dorothy Dale,* in 1844. The musical career of Mr. William Jackson, the eminent Yorkshire musical composer, was commenced at this place, in

* They were daughters of James and Hannah Dale, of Otley, and grand-daughters of Dorothy Wigglesworth, of Pateley Bridge. Dorothy died April 24th, 1844, aged 21 years ; and Martha died April 30th, 1844, aged 23 years. Buried in Pateley Bridge church-yard.

connection with the singers of this chapel. He had come to school here, but instead of devoting all his time to the acquisition of "book learning," he sought the more congenial society of the singers of this chapel. "They put into his hands the old sol-fa-ing gamut and drilled him into the reading of music, in which he soon became a greater proficient than in the reading of books. His progress astonished them all; and he returned from school full of musical notions." Since then his career has been one of successfully directed industry and talent; his productions have become standard works, and his name one, of which the music-loving population of Yorkshire is justly proud. His compositions have been, "The Deliverance of Israel from Babylon," an oratorio; "Isaiah," an oratorio; "The Year," a Cantata; "The 103rd Psalm," one or two Masses, and a variety of minor pieces, which have been more or less successful.

BEWERLEY VILLAGE is about half a mile distant, but does not present any feature of particular interest. The lead mines, Greenhow-hill, and Stump-cross Cavern will be described hereafter.

The mineral productions of Bewerley are principally lead, for which it is deservedly celebrated, the mines on Greenhow, and around have been worked from time immemorial—Limestone, composed almost entirely of fossil remains, which is burned into lime excellent for agricultural purposes—Gritstone, of good quality for building—Flags and slates, with a small quantity of indifferent coal.

The state of cultivation is shown in the following Agricultural Statistics taken in 1854.

NIDDERDALE.

UNDER TILLAGE.	a.	r.	p.	GRASS, &c.	a.	r.	p.	CATTLE, &c.	No.
Wheat	4	1	0	Clover	2	0	0	Horses	91
Barley	6	1	0	Permanent Grass	1859	3	18	Colts	9
Oats	82	0	20	Sheep Walk ..	161	1	35	Cows..............	287
Beans	5	0	0	Houses, Fences, &c. .... }	148	2	38	Calves	189
Vetches	2	2	0					Other Cattle	177
Turnips	35	0	0	Waste	153	1	33	Tups	6
Potatoes	15	1	0	Woods	358	0	8	Ewes	1085
Fallow	4	0	0	Common	2963	1	4	Lambs	674
				Occupiers under 2 acres }	50	8	24	Other Sheep	241
								Swine	114
				Total Grass, &c.	5717	3	0		
				Tillage	154	1	20		
Total Tillage ..	154	1	20		5872	0	20		2823

The population in 1801 was 1075; 1811, 1220; 1821, 1408; 1831, 1310; 1841,   ; 1851, 1269; and 1861, 1297. The annual value of property assessed to the poor rate in 1857, was £4112. As assessed to the county rate in 1859, £4453, and as assessed to property tax in 1858, £4973.

DACRE.

An excursion of about three miles eastward by railway from Pateley Bridge, will take the tourist to Dacre Banks station, whence he can easily reach Dacre, Hartwith, and Brimham Rocks. The township of Dacre comprises the villages or hamlets of Dacre, Dacre Banks, and Hayshaw; Harewell Hall, and Lacon, or Low Hall, are also within its limits. The river Nidd divides it from Hartwith and Bishopside on the north, Bewerley adjoins it on the west, the other boundary is formed by the parish of Hampsthwaite, formerly part of Knaresbrough forest, from which it was divided by a fence called the "Munk Wall," which was built in very early times by the monks of Fountains for the purpose of dividing their lands from those of the royal forest. This boundary, from Greenhow-hill to the river Nidd is thus described in a perambulation made February 26, 1577—" Over Monga-gill to a place where Craven Crosse stood, which is over against the end of Monga-gill; and soe from thence to Craven Keld by the high waye which leadeth from Hebden to Pateley Bridge; and soe following the same waye to Greenhow-hill; and then on the skirt of the south side of the same hill bie a certaine waye which leadeth towards Ripley, and by the same waye to the head of Greenhow-syke, being between Caud-stones and Redlysh; and soe descending downe the same syke unto Plompton Gate, and soe following the same gate unto Pallice

NIDDERDALE.

stone—and from thence unto the ende of a certain ould Dike in Brarthwaite, and soe unto Padside beck ; and from Padside beck, as the Munke wall leadeth upon the south syde of the water of Nydd, unto the water of Nydd, and soe directly over the said River of Nydd unto the sayd wall on the north side of the same water."

As already mentioned, during the reign of Edward the Confessor, Dacre belonged to the Saxon earl Gospatric :* after the Norman conquest it formed part of the possessions of Erneis de Burun, and in Domesday survey is entered amongst his lands, and said to contain three carucates, or about 360 acres. Afterwards it became part of the possessions of the family of Mowbray, and was by them and their subinfeudatories given to the Abbot and convent of Fountains.

Roger de Mowbray gave and confirmed to Bertram Hagett and his heirs, certain lands in Dacre belonging to his fee.

Bertram Hagett gave to the monastery of Fountains all his lands in Dacre, in wood and plain, meadow and pasture.

William Hagett confirmed to the said monastery the gift of his father.

Roger de Mowbray confirmed the gift of Bertram Hagett.

Alice de Gante, wife of Roger de Mowbray, also confirmed

* Gospatric was a noble Saxon, whose lands were not at first seized by the Conqueror ; he was even received into favour, and, on payment of a large sum of money was created count of all the country north of Tyne ; and appears to have demeaned himself with great servility ; but all was not sufficient to make William forget that Gospatric was an Englishman. Within less than a year he deprived him of the dignity for which he had paid, and made him no restitution ; the reason alleged was, that Gospatric had fought in defence of York, and taken part in the insurrection in which Robert Comine perished. Seized with chagrin and remorse the Saxon for ever abandoned his native land and settled in Scotland, where his descendants long continued to dwell in honour and opulence.

the same, with licence to the monks to remove their grange in Dacre at their pleasure.

Nigel de Mowbray also confirmed the gift of Bertram Hagett, with the grange of Dacre.

William de Mowbray confirmed the same, as his father and grandfather had done.

William de Castelia quit claimed to the said monks all claims which he had on lands in Dacre, which had belonged to Galfrid Hagett, and which were then held by the said monks.

On the dissolution of the monastic orders, the grange at Dacre was valued at £13 6s. 8d. per annum; and that of Hayshaw at £10 per annum. At that time the whole came to the crown, but was soon granted or sold therefrom; and after passing through the hands of different owners, the royalty, with a considerable portion of the soil came into possession of the family of Ingilby, of Ripley Castle, by which it is yet held.

Dacre, which gives name to the township, is a small village situate on a hill, about half a mile south of the Dacre Banks railway station. The old grange, which bore the name of the Hall, has been rebuilt, but none of its antique features are preserved.

The Independents have a place of worship here called Providence Chapel. It is a spacious building of stone, erected in 1827, at a cost of £280, and will seat about 400 hearers; there is a burial ground attached.

On the south-west of the village, near a farm house called Heckler Hill, is an ancient burial ground belonging to the Society of Friends; it is about fifteen yards long and fourteen

NIDDERDALE.

broad ; but is not used at present, the Friends having a burial ground at Darley, a village immediately adjoining. A stone wall surrounds the ground, the doorway into it is walled up, on a stone above it is the date 1682. There are two tombstones of coarse grit, laid flat on the ground, one of them bears in raised capitals, the following inscription :—

Wm. Clayton departed this life the 20 day of the 12 month Anno. Dom. 1706.

The other is close beside it, and bears in similar characters,

Ma : Bradley departed this life the 17 day of 12 month Æd, 68. Anno. Dom. 1730.

The Meeting House adjoining to it, built in 1696, was pulled down, and the materials sold to the late Sir William Ingilby, of Ripley, only a few years ago. From the remaining foundations, the fabric appears to have been eleven yards long by eight broad ; a stable attached at one end made the entire length about 14 yards.

Braithwaite school, situate on the open moor to the westward of this village, was founded by deed dated January 21st, 1778, pursuant to the will of Edward Yeates, dated January 22nd, 1774, for the free education of three children from the hamlet of Dacre, and all the children of four houses at Deer Ings, six at the Heights, three at Holebottom, and three at the Row. The endowment was a house, twenty-three acres of land and nine cattle gates.

Dacre Pasture was an open, stinted common comprising upwards of 1154 acres, until the year 1854, when it was surveyed, allotted, and enclosed ; since then it has been generally cultivated, and many parts of it rendered very productive. Amongst the allotments was one to the poor widows of Dacre, of which the Surveyors of the Highways of the said township were appointed trustees, and were to account for the disposal of the profits to the Jurymen, at the Court held for the manor of Dacre after Easter annually. It is described in the award as consisting of eight acres, and bounded on the east by an allotment awarded to Francis Thorpe; on or towards the west by one awarded to Sir William Amcotts Ingilby; and on or towards the north by the Dacre and West End road. The trustees to maintain the fence at the north end thereof. Daniel Seaton, was the sole commissioner or valuer, and the award was completed and signed on the 7th day of February, 1845.

Across the upper part of the Pasture a thin seam of coal has been extensively worked. Many Baal hills, or places where lead had been formerly smelted, were found in different parts of the pasture; they have been brought into cultivation by removing the upper stratum and substituting fresh soil. One near Dacre Banks church, of more than ordinary size, was found to contain so much unfused ore that it was removed, and smelted over again with profit.

Hayshaw is a district on the western side of the township, extending from Guy's-cliffe on one side, to Thornthwaite on the other; it consists chiefly of scattered farms and cottages.

At this place were found in the year 1735,* two Roman pigs of lead, with a stamp, or inscription on them, indicating that they had been smelted when the emperor Domitian was consul for the seventh time, a period equivalent to the year 81, of the Christian era. The ore had doubtless been raised on Greenhow, and probably smelted near the place where they were found.

* Pennant says in 1731.

76 NIDDERDALE.

The townships of Dacre and Bewerley were for a long time in a kind of union, by mutual agreement, for the maintenance of their poor; this union was dissolved in 1851, after much litigation, commenced on the part of Bewerley, and terminated in favour of Dacre, after an assize trial at York of six days' duration.*

Harewell Hall† is situate on an eminence overlooking the railway and the river Nidd, about a mile to the westward of Dacre Banks station; it is now used as a farm house, but at the time of its erection has been a building of considerable pretentions. It fronts to the southward, and consists of a centre and one projecting wing on the eastern side; this last appears to be the oldest part of the building; just below the apex of the gable is a large carved stone divided into three compartments, the central one charged with the *star* of the Ingilbies, of Ripley, between the initials **W. I.** accompanied by the date 1652; thus shewing that it was built by Sir William Ingilby in that year. The chimneys are projecting masses, rising from the foundation at the rear of the building; the windows are of five lights each, with stone mullions between. It is not unlikely that this place was occupied by some branch of the Ingilby family soon after its erection; not long afterwards it was occupied by Sampson

*For further particulars of this trial see Appendix.

†The name *Harewell* i.e. the soldiers well, seems to point to some remarkable spring, which may have supplied the garrison of the adjacent fort of Castlestead with water.

DACRE.   **77**

Lupton, gent., member of a family of some consequence in Nidderdale at that time.*

Near this place the railway crosses the river Nidd, by a bridge of five arches, four of stone, on the sides, and an iron girder in the centre of 90 feet span. Almost close to the Dacre Banks station is a deep cutting through a hill of rock, the upper beds being very hard and compact, the lower of a coarse

---

*Braisty Wood was the original home of this family, of whom William Lupton and Sampson Lupton were living in 1593, from whom descended John Lupton, of Braisty Wood, whose wife's name was Mary; he died in 1689, and was buried at Pateley Bridge; she died in 1698. Their son, Sampson Lupton, Senr., of Harewell Hall, gentleman, was buried at Pateley, February 16th, 1697-8. By his will, dated February 11th, 1697-8, he bequeaths to William Skaife, of Low Laith, Farmer, his son-in-law, and James Horner, of Whitehouses, all his moiety of tenements and messuages, at Appletreewick, in trust, to be sold to pay the principal and interest owing to Sir John Ingilby, bart., remainder to Margaret, his wife, to raise portions for his five daughters; personal debts and funeral expenses to be paid out of his Braisty Wood estate, by the said William Skaife and James Horner, to whom he gives one moiety of his messuages, lands, grounds, pastures, &c., at Braisty alias Braistow Woods, to pay his debts, and to raise £100 for his son John Lupton, to discharge a sum in which he was bound for his brother Sampson Lupton—when paid, the moiety of Braisty Wood, &c., to his son John Lupton, for term of 99 years, or his life, remainder to his grandson William Lupton—remainder to his grandson Sampson Lupton. The other moiety of Braisty Woods, then belonging to his mother Mary Lupton, after her decease, to his wife Margaret, remainders to his grandsons Thomas and Sampson Lupton. To each of his five daughters £50, out of Braisty Woods, and £50 out of the Craven estate. Margaret, wife of the above, daughter of William Skaife, of Braisty Woods, died November 2nd, 1718, aged 74, and was buried at Ripon, where the following inscription yet remains to her memory. "Here lieth the body of Margaret Lupton, late wife of Mr. Sampson Lupton, of Braisty Woods, in Netherdale, who departed this life the 2nd of November, Anno Domini 1718, in the 74th year of her age, and lived to be mother and grandmother to above 150 children, and at the baptizing of the first grandchild, the child had ten grandfathers and grandmothers then present."

For these hitherto unpublished particulars of the family of Lupton, we are indebted to Mr. R. H. Skaife, of the Mount, York, who has also furnished us with much valuable matter relative to other places within this district, to whom we take this opportunity of tendering our grateful acknowledgments.

78   NIDDERDALE.

gritstone, between which is a parting of shale a few inches in thickness.

Low Hall, sometimes called Lacon Hall, from a former owner of that name, is situate about half-a-mile eastward of Dacre Banks, close to the railway. The front commands a pleasing prospect down the green and wooded valley to the eastward. The Hall itself is of a square form, surmounted by a triple roof; the windows are of seven lights, divided by a transom. Over the front door are the initials M. W. and the date 1635. On one of the buildings is E. L. 1711. It is now the property of the Ingilbies, of Ripley Castle.

Dacre Banks is a small, well-built, but scattered village, situate between the river Nidd on the north, and the steep ascent of Dacre Pasture on the south; the houses are placed at random, without any order or regularity in reference to each other, a common method of arrangement in all the old villages of Nidderdale, but which does not appear to extend lower down than this. Many of the inhabitants are employed in the spining of yarn and the manufacturing of linen cloth. Tow was spun by machinery at Dacre Banks Mill, in this village, at the factory now occupied by Messrs. Grange and Bell, the first of any place in England. This was owing to the ingenuity of a self-taught mechanic, of the name of Charles Gill, who was born at this village in the year 1774, and employed in the above-mentioned mill in 1798, soon after which period he invented the *Tow Card*, a machine which has been extensively used in the spining of that article; he was also inventor of another machine employed in tow spining, called the *Porcupine* or *Porcipine*. An eminent maker of manufacturing machinery took out a patent for a machine called a *Porcipine*, which was found to be copied from that invented by Gill some years before, when the patent right was set aside. He was the inventor of many other machines used in different processes of manufacture, and had lucrative situations offered to him by manufacturers of machinery, but he always preferred remaining in his native valley, in which he died in the year 1851. Though his inventive talents did not acquire him great wealth or distinction, they yet, joined with industry, secured him a competence in his old age, and he had the pleasure of knowing that it was honourably won. One of his sons is now partner with Mr. J. Todd, in the Nidderdale Foundry.

The Church is a small building, in the early English style, consisting of nave and chancel, with a square tower, surmounted by a slender spire, built in 1837, at a cost of £750, which was raised by subscription, with the exception of £150, given by the Church Building Society. The Dean and Chapter of Ripon are patrons of the living, which is worth about £100 per annum. A neat parsonage was erected also by subscription, near the church, in 1838.

The district attached to this church is thus described in the reply of the Dean and Chapter of Ripon to the letter of the Ecclesiastical Commissioners, enquiring into the state of Cathedral Churches, dated April 8th, 1853.

" Dacre. Comprising that township or hamlet in the parish of Ripon, population 695 ; and the hamlets or places called New York and Summer Bridge, in the adjoining township of Hartwith, in the parish of Kirkby Malzeard, population about 720, together 1415. The incumbent states that these latter hamlets are ecclesiastically in Dacre, it being the express wish of the bishop, that he should take them under his care, being

NIDDERDALE.

close by, and at a considerable distance from Hartwith church, and ought to have been legally so, but by an oversight, neglected to be carried into effect. The extent of the district is four or five miles by five or six. Income, including a temporary donation by the Dean and Chapter of £20, per annum, £56 14s. 2d.; but from which must be deducted an annual payment of £5, on account of money borrowed. A house of residence.

In 1838, the Dean and Chapter gave £50, as a donation to the new chapel."

Dacre Banks school was founded in 1695, by William Hardcastle, who built the house, and bequeathed £100 to provide a salary for the master, and the money was paid in 1783, into the hands of Sir William Ingilby, Bart.; William Mountain, by will dated 28th December, 1778, left £100 to the school, which was received by the trustees of the same. It was intended to be free only to the descendants of the founder. The master now receives £20 per annum, from the Rev. H. D. Ingilby, of Ripley Castle, and a committee of eight gentlemen in the neighbourhood guarantee to him a certain salary; he also receives the children's weekly pence. The school is a plain building with square windows, and stone mullions, over the door is inscribed EX DONO. W.H. 1695. It is situate on the east side of Dacre Pasture, and has a play ground and garden attached.

The township contains 5381a. 3r. 34p. of land, including nearly every variety of soil.

The annual value of this township as assessed to the poor rate in 1857, was £3376. As assessed to Property tax in 1858, £4168; and to the county rate in 1859, £3798.

DACRE. 81

The population has been subject to considerable fluctuation, in 1801, it was 592; in 1811, 710; 1821, 777; 1831, 698; 1841, ; 1851, 673; and in 1861, 739.

HARTWITH.

This township is situate to the northward of Dacre, from which it is divided by the river Nidd for a part of its length, the remainder of the boundary on that side being the " Munk Wall" already mentioned, which divides it from the parish of Hampsthwaite, and the township of Clint in the parish of Ripley; on the other three sides it abuts on the townships of Bishop Thornton, Warsall, and Bishopside, in the parish of Ripon. Hartwith-with-Winsley constitute a chapelry in the parish of Kirkby Malzeard, from which they are 8 miles distant. The hamlets of Summer-bridge, New York, Low Laith, Braisty Woods, Brimham Rocks, Brimham Hall, and Lodge, Winsley, and Hardcastle Garth, are all within this township; which presents great variety of soil and scenery, but to the tourist the great attraction are the rocky wonders of Brimham.

Previous to the Norman conquest Brimham* was held by two Saxons, Gospatric and Gamelbar; after that event Gamelbar was entirely dispossessed, and Gospatric only held three carucates and two oxgangs; three other carucates which had

---

* Brimham is the high, or exposed home or dwelling, *Brim* being yet a common term in this neighbourhood for an elevated place exposed to wind and weather. *Hartwith* is not mentioned in Domesday—it means simply the wood or forest of the Hart. *Winsley* appears to be only the *Whinny field—Whin* being the name commonly used for the gorse plant, *Ulex Europæus.*

HARTWITH.

belonged to him, were held by Erneis de Burun, and two oxgangs which had been Gamelbar's, were held by Gilbert Tyson. The lands of these three lords were however soon swallowed up by the Mowbray fee, and in a short time afterwards again disposed of for religious uses. Roger de Mowbray gave this township to the abbot and convent of Fountains reserving for his own use a buck, a doe, a wild boar, and a kid annually, and what birds he thought proper to take. This reservation tells us what the principal inhabitants of Brimham at that time were, and from them we may infer the state of the country; an uncultivated region of

"Rocks, caves, lakes, fens, bogs, dens, and shades."

In the year 1280, Roger de Mowbray, third baron of that name, gave all the wild beasts and birds in the whole forest of Brimham, for the use of the Infirmary at Fountains, and allowed the monks to have their own foresters.

The monks held possession of their lands in this township until the dissolution of their house in 1539, when the whole came to the crown;* from which it was soon granted out, the soil passing to many different owners, while the royalty, with a considerable estate came into possession of the Nortons of Grantley, Lords Grantley and Markenfield, in which they yet continue.

---

* The valuation at that time was—The Lordship of Hertwith £18 18s. 10d. per annum; The Lordship of Wyndsley, £12 15s. 1d.; Logia Brimben, £11 13s. 4d.; and Hardcastle 40s. per annum. At the same time Richard Haxby was bailiff of Hartwith, whose annual fee was 20s. Miles Hardcastle was bailiff of Wyndsley, Brimben, and Warshall, whose wages were 26s. 8d. per annum, and Lawrence Smyth was receiver of the rents of Brimham, and received 40s. a year for his trouble.

BRIMHAM ROCKS.

These celebrated rocks, one of the wonders of Nidderdale, are situate on a piece of elevated ground, about sixty acres in extent, on the north side of the valley of the Nidd, about one and a half miles from Dacre Banks station, four from Pateley Bridge, nine from Ripon, ten from Harrogate by road, and upwards of twelve by railway. Placed at an elevation of nine hundred and ninety feet above the level of the sea, and exposed to the fierce action of the elements on every side ; these rocks present a most singular appearance at a distance, they have been compared to a ruined city of Titans, and the broken skeleton of a mountain —the last no inappropriate comparison. No description can do justice to them ; their grotesque singularity and rugged grandeur alike defy the pen of the poet, and the pencil of the artist. Produced by a violent disruption of nature, when the crust of the earth has been rent asunder, and these heavy masses of millstone grit upheaved and piled around in random confusion, afterwards washed and worn into crevices, and their forms rounded and smoothed by the waves of a sea beating on and around them ; the softer parts have yielded to the action of these elements, which the harder have resisted, hence their strange and uncouth forms, which fill all beholders with amazement. Thousands of years must have elapsed since

BRIMHAM ROCKS.

any material change has taken place in their forms, as they are thickly coated with mosses and lichens, and no process of waste is visible at present; many of their heads are crested with masses of heath or ling, growing out of a stratum of peat, in some cases fifty or sixty feet above the surface. The first person who had the ability to describe what he saw was Mr. Pennant, who visited these rocks in company with George Allen, Esq., of Darlington, in the year 1777. He thus describes his visit:—* " The celebrated *Crags*, the supposed aggregate of *Druidical* antiquities, are on the rude plain of the summit; beneath which is a vale, wooded with birch, holly, and hazel. The crags are dispersed in all parts, in groups of various extents, and frequently in single masses. They are often undiscribable, and require the best skill of the artist to give an adequate idea of their multiform singularity.

On my arrival on the summit of the hill, the seat of wonders, my astonishment was unspeakable; the whole was new to me; a flat, covered with stones of forms the most singular, and many of sizes most stupendous—My fancy could not create remains of the works of art, or relics of Druidical superstition. Like the philosophers in the court of *Brobdignay*, I sheltered my ignorance, that I had found nothing but *relplum scalcath*; which is literally interpreted *lusus naturæ*, the sports of nature: the coincidence of a multitude of stones, at the great event of the subsidence of the waters after the deluvian catastrophe, or which nature, in her frolics, caused to assume the variety of impressed forms 'we see on them. The stony part will retain them to eternity; they were left concealed in the soft or muddy part which subsided with them,

* Tour from Alston Moor to Harrogate, p. 118.

NIDDERDALE.

till the frequency of lesser deluges washed away the soft con-
cealing parts, and exposed to view these semi-miracles."

The next who described these rocks was Major Hayman
Rooke, in 1786, who could see in them nothing but Druidism;
conceiving that the hands of that cunning priesthood had
shaped the idol rock, balanced the rocking stones, and bored
the Cannon Rocks, for rites and purposes connected with their
mysterious faith : which it is easy to perceive is nothing but
the play of the wildest fancy. As from among the centre of
the rocks the visitor gazes around him filled with wonder and
amazement, he may exclaim with the only poet who has truly
described the scene :

> " Dark mountain desert, awful piles of stone,
> Like giant ruins I How ye seem to mock
> The puny efforts of such feeble things
> As we, frail mortals are I Far round I see
> Strange broken columns rise, shapelessly grand;
> As if some more than merely human race
> Had made their dwellings here. Through gloomy pass
> I wander, formed by none of Adam's sons;
> The work of Him, at whose resistless word
> The mountains melt, the valleys cleave,
> The rocks fall down. In all this wilderness
> I trace the power of His almighty hand.
> Above my head are masses hung, as if
> The affrighted earth had once disgorged and driven
> Them up on high, then, falling down, they lodg'd
> Thus strangely, where the sweeping breeze might seem
> Enough to dash them on my trembling frame.
> The rocking stone, on lofty column poised,
> Yields to my touch, and at terrific height,
> In mid air vibrates.
>
> Through perforated rock,
> The human voice proceeding, sounds unearthly;
> As if the very stone itself threw out
> The groans of some sad spirit warning men
> That there is an abyss of woe beneath,
> Where vengeance reigns, were mercy never shines."*

*Leisure Musings, by the Rev. James Holme.

BRIMHAM ROCKS.

In the year 1792, William, Lord Grantley, built a house and suitable offices in the centre of this wild region, for the accommodation of visitors. This house is generally the point whence visitors start to survey the rocks; near the house is the *Oyster-shell rock*, and the *four rocking stones*; these last form a group, two of them have rock basins on their upper surface, and are more easily moved than the others; one of them is thirteen feet in length, seven in breadth, and has been estimated to weigh fifty tons. Major Rooke claims the discovery of the moving of this rock, and thus describes it: " This is an extraordinary group of rocks, in which there seems to be a kind of uniformity preserved. On the top are three rocking stones; the middle one rests upon a kind of pedestal, and is supposed to be about *a hundred tons weight*; on each side is a small one. On examining the stone it appears to have been shaped to a small knob at the bottom, to give it motion; though my guide, who was seventy years old, born on the moors, and well acquainted with these rocks, assured me that the stone had never been known to rock; however, on my making trial round it, when I came to the middle of one side, I found it move with great ease. The astonishing increase of the motion, with the little force I gave it, made me apprehensive the equilibrium might be destroyed; but on examining it I found it was so nicely balanced that there was no danger of its falling. The construction of this equipoised stone must have been by artists well skilled in the powers of mechanics. It is, indeed, the most extraordinary rocking stone I ever met with; and it is somewhat as extraordinary that it should never have been discovered

88   NIDDERDALE.

before, and that it should now move so easily, after so many years of rest."

This writer could see nothing but Druidical skill and artifice in these rocks ; since his time another stone here has been found to move, and, if carefully examined, doubtless others might be found to do the same.

The view from the rocking stones is at once singular and extensive, including the rocks in every variety of grotesque shape and position, and taking in the country far beyond, even to the towers of York Minster, and the blue summits of the wolds eastward ; the rich plain that skirts the Hambleton Hills is spread before the eye in variegated beauty ; northward the view is not so extensive, being closed by the long ridge of land which bears at its eastern extremity the Roman camp of Nutwith, marked by a clump of dusky firs.

On the verge of the precipice which girdles the mass of rocks on this side, stand the *Baboon's Head, the Pulpit Rock,* the *Serpent's Head,* and the *Yoke of Oxen* ;* near this last is the *Idol Rock,* one of the most singular masses, and one of the greatest wonders of the place.

> " Amid this wondrous scene,
> Strangest of all, the Idol Rock appears,
> Stupendous mass ! on pedestal so small
> That nothing save the most consummate skill
> Could thus have placed it."

The base is an elongated conical piece of rock, at the bottom three feet seven inches in diameter, diminishing upwards,

---

*These names are frequently changed by the innovating, garrulous guide, who has changed the *Baboon's Head* to the *Gorilla's,* and the *Yoke of Oxen* to the *Bulls of Babylon,* which unsettling of nomenclature he calls keeping pace with the times. Unique as the rocks are amongst the freaks of nature, there is nearly as much originality about the *guide* but infinitely less grandeur.

until at about two feet from the ground the diameter is only twelve inches; above this the stone bulges or swells out all around in an irregular kind of circle until it is forty-eight feet in circumference; above this is another stratum of a softer stone, which is worn away until it is considerably less in circuit than the lower mass; above this comes another stratum of a harder grit, of a circumference nearly equal to that below; above this, the mass contracts, and then again towards the top expands, and is finally covered with a waving crest of heath, at a height of twenty feet from the surface. The form of this rock is such as easily to lead to the belief that art has been employed in its formation, and that it has been shaped in this wise by the cunning of Druid priests as an Idol. Some even pretend to see the marks of the tool upon the slender pedestal, but "this is pure imagination all." We do not believe that art had anything to do with this most singular rock, it is all natural, and really surprising it is to see such an enormous weight of stone so nicely balanced on such a slender stem, and which has preserved its upright position through the unnumbered ages that have elapsed since it assumed its present shape; besides it has been exposed to tempests which have made

> " Castles topple on their warder's heads,
> And palaces and pyramids to slope
> Their heads to their foundations."

It yet maintains its equilibrium as steadily as on the first day it stood above the receding tides which helped to shape its present form. From near this rock, the eye wanders over a wide expanse of heathy moors, dark and bleak, extending to the north-west, as far as Whernside at the head of the valley of the Nidd. Hardly anything else is seen in this direction,

90

NIDDERDALE.

one ridge of wave-like heath rising behind another. In August and September it appears covered with a vast carpet of purple, and when the sun shines hot upon it, the surface appears to have a wavy oscillating motion—

> " The Moors—all hail ! Ye changeless ye sublime,
> That seldom hear a voice save that of Heaven !——
> Here all is sapphire light, and gloomy land,
> Blue, brilliant sky, above a sable sea,
> Of hills like chaos, ere the first command,
> ' Let there be light !' bade light and beauty be."

South-west of the house the crags form a lofty irregular precipice, apparently piled in the greatest confusion and disorder ; amongst these is the *Chimney rock*, so named from a funnel-like perforation passing through it. From the top of this a fine view is obtained of the valley of the Nidd, as well as of the country far to the south and west. Amongst the most conspicuous mountains may be distinguished Beamsley-Beacon, Kexgill Moor, Roggan Hall, Simon's Seat, and Lord's Seat, all in the forest of Knaresbrough or immediately adjoining. Near this place is the *Boat rocking stone*, supposed to weigh upwards of 40 tons, placed on the verge of the precipice, and so nicely balanced that it vibrates with only a slight pressure, and so considerably that we might imagine it possible without any great exertion of force to hurl it into the valley below ; but such is not the case, no merely human strength can dislodge it. We cannot perceive anything artificial about its formation, nor is there sufficient evidence to induce us to believe that it was thus nicely balanced by Druidic skill for oracular purposes—else might we exclaim

> " behold yon huge
> And unhewn sphere of living adamant,
> Which pois'd by magic, rests its central weight

BRIMHAM ROCKS. 91

> On yonder pointed rock : firm as it seems,
> Such is its strange and virtuous property,
> It moves obsequious to the gentlest touch
> Of him, whose breast is pure ; but to a traitor,
> Though even a giant's prowess nerv'd his arm
> It stands as fix'd as Snowdon."

An opening in the rock, on the top of the precipice, with three large crags piled arch-wise above it, is called The *Lover's leap*, a leap from which would be likely to cure not only the pangs of slighted love, but all the ills that flesh is heir to. We are not aware that any of the love lorn nymphs or swains of Brimham have ever tried the experiment ; and the name is like many more purely imaginary—like those of *Tom Taylor's Chamber, The Druids Cave, Pulpit, Parlour,* and *Bedroom,* applied to a series of caves or dens in the rocks, which might afford cold and uncomfortable dwellings for the " sages skill'd in nature's lore" whose names they bear. *The Giant's head and neck rock* looks from this cliff over the valley beneath. An opening in the girdle of crags gives access to the plain below, where the face of the cliff can be seen to great advantage in all its rugged grandeur. Here is *the Great Split rock*, a mass of stone about one hundred yards in circuit, through which an opening about four feet wide has been rent by some sudden shock, as the indentations, projecting and receding parts on each side, if brought together would fit into each other. On the upper side of this rock, is a low crag of a circular form, from opposite sides of which have grown an holly and an oak, neither of them of great bulk, but only inferior in age to the rock on which they grow. The group called the *Middle Crags* is seen to great advantage from this point. A heath-clad hillock near this rock is probably a barrow, it is of a conical form, and apparently artificial.

NIDDERDALE.

The Cannon rocks are large masses of rock perforated through their entire thickness, upwards of twenty feet by a circular hole about twelve inches in diameter, of nearly uniform width from end to end, and having the appearance of a shot hole—hence the name of the rocks;—a shorter one through a part of the same rock is called the *Druid's Telescope.* Perforations of a nearly similar kind are visible in many of the rocks, and have *probably* been caused by the decay of some gigantic fossil *Lycoped* or *Equisetum*, from its harder matrix of gritstone, the sides are rugose or indented, and the softer vegetable matter having been wasted by the action of the elements, left its place unoccupied. These holes have also been impressed into the service of Druidism. Hargrove, the historian of Knaresbrough, says—" To a person stationed at this side, the voice of another placed at the mouth or lower extremity of the cylinder sounds most dismal. Immediately above the orifice of the cylinder, and on the very summit of the rock, are two small grooves, about two feet asunder, and of equal dimensions; they are perfectly circular, of about two inches in width, and the same in depth, and might serve for the insertion of two pedestals or props, which it is not improbable, may formerly have supported the form of some oracular idol; for these tubes, which are internally rugose, were capable of augmenting the sound of the voice and giving its tone a degree of almost supernatural vehemence and terrible solemnity; and by the artful management of the Druid priests, might occasionally become instruments for the promulgation of oracular decrees.

It would much improve the pleasure of a ramble among

BRIMHAM ROCKS. 93

these rocks, could we possess but a firm faith that they were the veritable abodes of Druidism ; and see the places where

> " The Pagan's myths through marble lips were spoken,
> And ghosts of old beliefs still flit and moan
> Round fane and altar overthrown and broken,
> O'er tree-grown barrow and grey ring of stone."

The *Crown Rock* is a stone of large size somewhat in the shape of a crown, the angles are nicely rounded and smoothed ; on one side is an opening called the *Druid's Oven*, and on the other, another called the *Courting* or *Kissing Chair*.

The *Cheese Wring* is so named from a resemblance to the celebrated Cornish rock of that name. Great numbers of the isolated crags have names, generally modern and unmeaning, as *Stelling Crag*, an uncommonly large detached rock ; the *Porpoise Head*, the *Sphinx's Head*, the *Boar's Snout*, *Hawk's Crag*, so named from a pair of hawks regularly building their nests there ; the *Flower Pot Rock*, the *Aerial Altar*, the *Foxholes*, the *Elephant Rock*, the *Rhinoceros Rock*, &c.

What is called the *Druid's Circle* is almost close to the house, it consists of a group of stones in their natural state, which art *might* form into a circle, but which have only a very remote resemblance to one at present.

The *Mushroom Rocks* and *Hares' Heads*, are groups detached from the main mass, the former on an eminence a short distance to the north-east.

> " Which were it not for many a rude rock nigh,
> Rising in lofty ranks and loftier still
> Might well themselves be deemed of dignity."

The *Boat Rock*, is a lofty crag, so named from its shape, which resembles a boat ready for launching. Not far from which is the largest rocking stone known to exist here, supposed to weigh upwards of 100 tons ; it is placed on the top of another crag, and is not easily accessible. It is close to the Cannon Rocks, which with the *Crown* and *Porpoise Head* form one group.

A small lake covering about half an acre south of the main mass of rocks is called Brimham Tarn ; part of it is of considerable depth. On the opposite side of the road about a quarter of a mile distant, on the moor below, a dam has been thrown across the bottom of a narrow valley, and the water running down it damned and thrown back, so as to cover an area of about ten acres in extent. The dam yet remains only broken in the middle, which might be restored at no great cost, and would add another attraction to the many already existing at Brimham. There cannot be any doubt but that it was formed by the monks of Fountains, for a fish pond ; for they were men who loved dainty cheer.

Graffa Crag and the *Beacon Rock* form a group on the southern boundry of the rocks, close to the house called Graffa House, they are grand and lofty, and the latter had its name from being the place where a beacon was erected when the first Napoleon Emperor of France threatened to invade England ; the steps which were put up at that time yet remain on the north side of the crag. Graffa plain *the place of graves*, adjoins Graffa Crag to the eastward, and is generally said to bear three or four large barrows, which on examination appear to be nothing but natural hillocks. A short distance to the south-west, also detached from the main mass of rocks, is an upright stone, about thirteen feet high and four broad, resembling at a distance a small tower, called by the inhabitants the *Noonstone*, from the sun shining upon one of its sides at that time of the day.

The soil among the rocks is generally dry and sandy, formed from the decomposition of their substance, and full of water-worn fragments of quartz. On the summit of many of the highest rocks is a considerable thickness of peat, generally covered with heath. Is that the place of its formation? or, how has it come there? The vegetation is of the hardiest kind, the oak, the birch, the holly, the mountain ash, the white thorn, and the hazel occasionally grow out of the fissures of the rocks, but they are of dwarfish size; and a straggling wood of the same girdles the foot of the precipice towards the west. Mosses and lichens abound among and upon the rocks, but not in great variety. The three British varieties of heath may be found; and the Whortleberry, (*Vaccinium Myrtillus*,) the Cowberry, (*Vaccinium Vitis Idæa*,) and the Crowberry (*Empetrum Nigrum*) are very abundant, growing in the crevices and on the crests of nearly all the crags; the Pettywhin, (*Genista Anglica*) occurs among the heath. Ferns are not particularly abundant, except the common Bracken; and occasional tufts of Polypody on the rocks; the Spleenwort (*Ceterach Officinarum*) and *Hymenophyllum Tunbridgense* are also occasionally met with. Club mosses are also found among the heath, so that the botanist will find ample amusement for a summer's day in this high region.

Hartwith Chapel is situate about a mile in a south-easterly direction from the rocks, and nearly in the centre of the township. It is a plain, unpretending fabric, consisting of nave and chancel, with a small wooden bell turret on the west gable; the side windows and doors have pointed arches, the

NIDDERDALE.

east window is of three lights under a depressed arch, yet it belongs to no acknowledged style of architecture. It was originally built by the subscriptions of the land owners* and tenants, and consecrated in the year 1751; enlarged in 1830, by adding to the east end, a recess for the communion table, a vestry and a sexton's room; and by erecting a gallery on the north side, two hundred and fifty additional free sittings were obtained. The cost was defrayed partly by the land-owners, aided by a grant of £230, made by the Church Building Society in London. The chapel yard was enlarged, and reconsecrated in 1827; the additional land was given by the Rev. John Swire, Vicar of Manfield, one of the patrons of the living.

The Parsonage House, buildings and garden, were originally built, given and devised to the curate of Hartwith in perpetuity, by Miss Margaret Dougill, of Dougill Hall, in the year 1796; but have since been improved and remodified by the Rev. J. E. Robson, the present incumbent† in the year 1832, at a cost of £200, given by the Governors of Queen Ann's Bounty towards the augmentation of the living.

The endowment was begun by the benefactions of four individuals, Mrs. Elizabeth Whitay, her two grand-daughters Miss Margaret and Miss Elizabeth Dougill, and Mr. Thomas Danson, of Winsley, amounting to the sum of £600; which

---

* At Hartwith, was founded about fifty years ago a chapel of ease to Kirkby Malessart, the erection of which was retarded for some time by a very singular impediment; namely, a contest between two principal freeholders, one of them an unmarried lady of a very benificent turn of mind, in order to determine which of the two should contribute all the timber; a privilege which each demanded, and neither would share with the other."—*Whitaker's Richmondshire*, Vol. ii. p. 113.

† We are indebted to this gentleman's kindness for much information respecting the chapel, which we thankfully acknowledge.

HARTWITH. 97

being met with a like sum by the Governors of Queen Ann's Bounty; amounted to £1,200; which was by the patrons of the living, laid out in the purchase of a farm at Easington, in the parish of Slaidburn, in the year 1788. In the year 1826, a further augmentation of £800, was made to the living by the said Governors from the Parliamentary grants. The farm at Easington was sold in 1857, under a commission from the proper authorities, and the proceeds, amounting to the sum of £2,156, was again invested in the funds of the said Governors of Queen Ann's Bounty; so that there is now in the funds of the said Governors the sum of £2,956, belonging to the living of Hartwith; the interest of which at £3 per cent. per annum, is payable half-yearly to the incumbent; who is also in receipt of £2 per annum, being a rent charge out of an estate in Hartwith, now belonging to the Greenwood family, originally given by Mrs. Mary Midgeley; and, also of £1 per annum, payable out of an estate in Darley, given by Thomas Atkinson. There has recently been a further augmentation from the Ecclesiastical Commissioners of about £13 a year. The present annual value is about £116. The patronage was vested in the Dougill and Roundell families; the consecration deed gives power to Elizabeth Dougill and Margaret Dougill, both of Hartwith, spinsters, and their heirs for ever, to nominate one fit priest; and also to Danson Roundell, of Marton, in the county of York, Esq., and his heirs for ever, to nominate another fit priest to officiate and perform divine offices in the said chapel; one of which priests the vicar of Kirkby Malzeard may elect and appoint.

On boards within the chapel are recorded the different benefactions which have been granted towards the endowment,

G

NIDDERDALE.

which have been already mentioned; one states in whom the right of nomination to the living is vested, and that the chapel was consecrated August 7th, O. S., 1751. Rebuilt and enlarged, 1830. The Reverend Matthew Metcalfe, A.B., of St. John's College, was first minister of Hartwith Chapel, Ano. Dom. 1752. The Charities belonging to the Chapelry are enumerated on another, of which the following is a copy—

" Mr. Robert Haxby, of Hartwith, built the school and endowed it with a small estate in Lands, situate in Darley: the trust is vested in the Dougill Family, of Hartwith. He also left the interest of £20, to be distributed yearly at Christmas, to the poor of Hartwith-cum-Winsley. Mrs. Hardisty, of Winsley, left the interest of £200 to be distributed yearly at Christmas, to the poor widows of Hartwith-cum-Winsley. Mrs. Mary Midgley, of Winsley, left 10s. to be distributed yearly at Easter, to the poor of Hartwith-cum-Winsley. Mrs. Mary Hardcastle, of Hartwith, left 10s. to be distributed on St. Andrew's Day, O.S., to the poor of Hartwith-cum-Winsley."

On a marble tablet at the east end is inscribed—

" To the Memory of the Reverend Edward Capstack, who was for more than 30 years the respected Minister of this Chapel. He died on the 20th May, 1822, aged 79 years. In conformity to his desire he was interred at Dent, the place of his nativity."

A board in front of the north gallery states that it was erected and the chapel enlarged in the year 1830—another on the west states—

" This gallery was built for the use of the singers at the expense of the late Mrs. Elizabeth Whitay, Ano Dom: 1754, Æ tates suæ. 84."

In the burial ground, a range of altar tombs against the west wall, belongs to the families of Dougill, Skaife, and Hebden, of Dougill Hall and Braisty Woods. Near the middle of the ground an upright stone bears the following inscription—

" In Memory of William Darnbrough, who for the last forty years of his life, was the Sexton of this Chapel. He died October 3rd, 1846, in the 100th year of his age.

HARTWITH. 99

'Thou shalt go to thy fathers in peace; thou shalt be buried in a good old age.'—Gen. XV. 15.

> The graves around for many a year,
> Were dug by him who slumbers here,
> Till worn with age he dropped his spade,
> And in this dust his bones were laid;
> As he now mouldering shares the doom,
> Of those he buried in the tomb,
> So shall he too, with them arise
> To share the judgment of the skies."

On an examination afterwards made in the Pateley Bridge register, it was ascertained that Darnbrough was 102 years of age and a native of Hayshaw. Another stone commemorates Francis Robinson, of Hartwith, who died October 28th, 1852, aged 94 years. At the west end of the chapel, a stone bears on the upper part, the reclining figure of a female with a book in one hand, and below

"Sacred to the Memory of Mary Jane, daughter of Thomas and Mary Skaife, of Darley, who died August 1st, 1858, aged 21 years.

> The victim of the murderer's blade
> Beneath a gory corse was laid;
> •Her soul, we trust, to realms has flown,
> Where theft and murder are unknown."

To make the meaning of this inscription clear, it must be stated that she was murdered by her lover, a young man named James Atkinson, on Sunday evening, the 1st of August, after they had attended service together at this chapel, supposed in a fit of jealousy. He was tried at York Assizes for the crime, and acquitted on the ground of insanity. The place where the deed of blood was done, a lane in Darley, on the opposite side of the valley, can be seen from the place of her burial.

THE SCHOOL is almost close to the church on the north. Over the door is the date and initials of the founder,

100 NIDDERDALE.

R. M. H. Ex Dono. 1719. It was founded and endowed by Robert Haxby, with lands in Darley, the rent of which is received by the master. It is free only to the children of the tenants of three farms then belonging to the founder.

At Hedge Nook, about a quarter of a mile north of the school is a public-house, at which resided a few years ago, John Winterburn and his wife, who had a family of twenty-three children, all of whom arrived at the age of maturity. Should the same rate of increase be continued in the family for only a few generations they would people a kingdom.

BRIMHAM HALL is about a mile eastward of the rocks, now used as a farm house, is situate in a slight valley, close by the side of a small brook, and occupies the site of the old monastic Grange or Lodge, belonging to the abbey of Fountains; the original fabric has been pulled down, and the large, carefully-dressed stones used, in the erection of a barn and outbuildings attached to the farm; even those which have borne inscriptions have been separated and placed indiscriminately in the walls, some outside and some inside. There appears by the fragments yet visible to have been three inscriptions; some of the letters are a foot in height, in a kind of Longobardic character, part are the old black letter, and others are in bold Roman capitals, all in alto-relievo. No complete inscription can be made out, but SOLI ES ORIA which can yet be seen, have formed part of the sentence "Soli deo honor et Gloria," which the Monks engraved around their tower at Fountains, and which may have had a conspicuous place on the walls of their chapel here. Of the meaning of the other letters no correct idea can be formed. **NORE S OHN SNO TVSE COR M** are to be seen on various stones in the walls, some of them inverted. Hargrove in his history of Knaresborough, says : "tradition informs us that this was originally a Roman fortress, and afterwards converted into Brimham Grange, a dairy house to Fountain's Abbey." Grave doubts may be entertained about the Roman fortress, and that it was something more than a mere diary house to Fountains is evident from the remains, as well as from the inventory and valuation of goods here at the time of the dissolution. At that time its annual value was £11 18s. 4d.; at the same time were stored here 9 quarters of rye, 20 quarters of oats, and 100 loads of hay ; here was also a service of plate, consisting of a goblet of silver and gilt, weighing 11¼ ounces, valued at £2 9s. 10d. One silver salt, weighing 8 ounces, £1 7s. 6d., and seven silver spoons, weighing 9¼ ounces, valued at £1 10s. 10d. Here was also a chalice of silver for the use of the chapel, weighing 11 ounces, and valued at 26s. 8d.; rather costly furniture this for a mere diary house. The hollows of the two fish ponds yet remain, of a rectangular form, near the house, on the east side ; they were supplied by a reservoir, which also yet remains on the hill above, close to the east side of the turnpike road.

BRIMHAM LODGE is situate about half a mile to the eastward of the Hall, and is one of the most stately and venerable buidings in the township, it is perhaps also the most desirable as a residence, being situate on a fertile soil, surrounded on three sides by a grove of lofty sycamores, in which a colony of rooks have made their abode. The house is three stories in height, the windows are of many lights each, divided by stone mullions. Over the door is inscribed DEO FAVENTE, T. B. 1661. The walls are adorned with masses of ivy, and the garden is in accordance with the style and age of the house. The front commands a beautiful view of the valley to the south and east.

A short distance eastward the waters of the slender rivulet Lurk Beck join those of Shaw Beck, and form the stream which afterwards divides the township of Bishop-Thornton from that of Clint, and then flows through Ripley Park. In the wood called Low Eppage is a sulphur spa.

WINSLEY HALL is a well-built and respectable house, near the road leading from Burnt Yeates to Brimham, about half a mile distant from the former place. This estate was purchased in 1801, for the sum of £2,000, by the trustees of the Burnt Yeates School, to which it now belongs.

SPRING HOUSE, situate on an eminence a short distance west of Winsley Hall, was formerly the residence of the family of Danson, which held a considerable estate in this township for a long time, of whom was

Laurence Danson, of Winsley, who was possessed of lands in Birstwith and Winsley, 16th, Henry VIII; purchased lands in Winsley of William Hardcastle, March 17th, 20th of Elizabeth; and in 1575, had a pardon of alienation for purchasing lands in Winsley, of Sir Lewis Mordaunt and others. He died in 1590, as appears from a general livery, granted to his son Laurence Danson, of his house and estates in Winsley, by Lord Treasurer Burleigh, and Richard Kyngsmyll, Esq., surveyor.

Laurence Danson, gent., of Spring House, held lands in Winsley, by Knight's service; he married Margaret Brown, by whom he had two sons, Laurence and John, and four daughters, Isabel, Margaret, Anne, and Jane. His eldest son

Laurence Danson, of Spring House, gent., possessed lands

HARTWITH. 103

in Winsley and Knaresborough Forest. Administration of his effects was granted to his widow, September 5th, 1664. His wife's name was Elizabeth, by whom he had two sons, Laurence, his heir, and William Danson, of Stripe, in Hartwith, who was buried at Hampsthwaite, June 1st, 1684 ; he appears to have died without issue, as on November 1st, 1694, his brother, Laurence Danson, his executor, and Laurence Danson, Jun., gent., convey Stripe House, &c., to Robert Askew.

Laurence Danson, eldest son of the above, was appointed for all his lands in Yorkshire, principal for one musket, on July 12th, 1677, and for a soldier armed with a musket, October 15th, 1703. He was twice married, first to Sushannah Holdsworth, of Kettesmoor, in September, 1656, by whom he had no issue ; secondly to Jannett, daughter of John Dougill, of Hartwith, in May, 1678, by whom he had two sons and one daughter. Laurence Danson, the eldest, died unmarried, and was buried at Kirkby Malzeard, January 19th, 1688. Thomas Danson, of Winsley House, born in 1678, married Sushannah Brooksbank, of Birks, in Ovenden, in 1709, by whom he had no issue. On May 1st, 1708, he released to his father all claim to legacies from his grandfather, Laurence Danson, and John Dougill, late of Hartwith, deceased. Both the sons dying without issue, and the father dying also February 24th, 1729-30, the estates passed to the two daughters, co-heiresses, Jane, wife of William Roundell, of Scriven, who was baptized at Hampsthwaite, January 20th, 1680 ; married at Trinity Church, in York, November 8th, 1702, and buried at Knaresborough, May 19th, 1758; and Elizabeth, born in 1684, who married Gregory Elsley, of Patrick-Brompton,

NIDDERDALE.

from whom the present family, represented by Charles Heneage Elsley, M.A., Recorder of York and Richmond, is descended.

At the lower part of this township the river Nidd is crossed by a narrow arch, about six feet wide, and seventy feet in span, called New Bridge. It has been built merely for the accommodation of foot passengers and pack horses. A bridge existed here called New Bridge, built of timber, in Leland's time, about the year 1536; the narrow arch of stone succeeded, which having become somewhat ruinous, was rebuilt on a new site, about forty years ago. It is mentioned in a rustic rhyme current in the neighbourhood :—

> " Up Swincliffe, down Swarcliffe,
> And ower't New Brig into Hartwith."

Monk-wall, one of the boundaries of the forest of Knaresbrough, passed close to the north end of this bridge, leaving the whole of the river within the forest, and sometimes a strip of land on the northern side. Its course is thus described in the perambulation of 1767 :—" Monk-wall leadeth in some Places by the edge of the said River, and in others at some distance from the same, to Haxby-Bridge, otherwise New Bridge, and from the said Bridge, proceeding on the north side of the River, to the now apparent remains of the said Monk-wall, in a Dwelling-House, belonging to Samuel Moorhouse, part of which House is built upon his Majesty's said Forest, and the other part upon the lands in the Township of Hartwith-with-Winsley; and from thence following the said Monk-wall, by the north side of a certain parcel of Land, near the said House, called Wreckholm, to a corner of the said Monk-wall, bearing on or towards the south-east, and following the said wall as it turneth Northward to Burnt Yeates."

The house which stood on the boundary, and through which the perambulators passed, has entirely disappeared; the railway has also cut up the old wall, and the clearings consequent thereon, have done much to efface it in this neighbourhood.

HARDCASTLE GARTH is an ancient hamlet situate on the slope of the hill, about half a mile above New Bridge, and was in early times a small grange, or farming establishment belonging to the monks of Fountains Abbey, valued on the dissolution of that house at 40s. per annum. One of the old houses, now converted into a stable, appears to have been built during the monastic age; over the entrance of another is the date 1666. Here is also, what is seldom seen in those days a cider or crab mill in working order. Here is also an ancient burial ground belonging to the Society of Friends.

> " Ye, who sometimes, in your rambles
> Through the green lanes of the country,
> Over stone walls gray with mosses,
> Pause by this neglected graveyard
> For awhile to muse, and ponder."

It is of a square form, about sixteen yards in breadth by twenty-two in length, surrounded by a stone wall which is partly overgrown with ivy, a few trees grow near the wall inside; the mounds over three graves are quite distinct. The last funeral took place here in 1859; some surviving relative has planted a laurel at the head of one, and a lilac at the feet; the half worn away mounds over half a dozen more are also visible. This was set apart as a burial ground at a very early period in the history of the Friends, during the life time of George Fox himself. In the Kirkby Malzeard registers are a few entries relative to this place—

106   NIDDERDALE.

"1678. A child, son of Peter Stott, of Pateley Bridge, dyed suddenly, by Williamor John Ripley last seen of Ketsmore, the 2nd day of 7 mr. Noe notice given to the Minister.   Enquire of Thomas Horner, who made the coffin, for affidavit, and affidavit of Sir William Ingilby, buried in Hardcastle Garth the 4th of 7 br. his name, Abraham Stott."

"1701. William Bradley, of the parish of Hampsthwaite, was buried at Hardcastle Garth, within the parish of Kirkby Malzeard, August the 4th, 1701."

"Isabel Emmot, Quaker, of Westsike, in *Hampstead* Parish, was buried ye 25 of March, in Hardcastle Garth."

"Robert, the son of John Hardcastle, of Hardcastle Garth, was buried in Hardcastle Garth, 23rd of September, 1705."

"Hardcastle Garth, Sarha Whittioar, bur. 21 May, 1711."

THE STRIPE, already mentioned in connection with the family of Danson, is situate on the right of the road leading from Hardcastle Garth to Hartwith Chapel. It is now a respectable farm house, belonging to the Rev. Danson Richardson Roundell, M.A., of Gledstone, near Skipton-in-Craven.   The situation is pleasant, among fertile meadows, commanding a fine view of the valley of the Nidd to the south and east.

DOUGILL HALL, so named from its builder and owners, is a short distance below Summer Bridge, between the turnpike road and the river Nidd.   It is a large building, three stories in height, with a double roof; the front windows are square. divided into four lights each by a mullion and transom. Over the entrance are the letters D. and the date 1722; the I. E time when it was built and the initials of John Dougill and his wife. Over the door of the old house is R. D. 1612, and above the door of another building in the yard G. D. 1696. In front of the house, which looks to the eastward, is the garden, in which is a number of yew trees clipped into fantastic forms.   The premises are surrounded by a fine

HARTWITH. 107

grove of large sycamores, among which are an aged yew, a remarkably fine beech, and a large walnut, which last is a scarce tree in this valley. This estate passed from the family of Dougill to that of Swire, by the marriage of Roger, eldest son of Samuel Swire, Esq., of Cononley, in Craven, with Elizabeth, daughter and co-heiress of John Dougill, Esq.* She was born in 1730, and died July 18th, 1773, and was buried at Kildwick ; her husband, Roger Swire, died January 22nd, 1778. They had a family of eight children, five sons and three daughters. It now forms part of the estate of their descendant, Samuel Swire, Esq.

Above the Hall, towards the north, on a hill

> " Crowned with a peculiar diadem,
> Of trees in circular array so placed
> Not by the sport of nature but of man,"

Is an ancient well, of which no one knows the origin or use. Its situation on the crest of a hill makes it the more singular.

* " Hartwith burials—1744. Mr. John Dougill, buried August 20th, 1744."

Kirkby Malzeard Par. Reg.

Margaret Dougill, of Dougill Hall, by will dated 6 November, 1801, devised all her freehold and copyhold messuages, &c., in the parish of Kirkby Malzeard, Ripon, Ripley, Hampsthwaite, or elsewhere in Great Britain, unto the Revd. Samuel Swire, and William Day, Esq., their heirs and assigns for ever. Upon trust for her niece, Elizabeth Swire, of Melsonby, spinster, for life, remainder to said trustees, to preserve remainder to first, and other sons of said Elizabeth Swire in tale male, in strict settlement—remainder (except a farm in Hartwith), to John Swire, of Hull, for life, remainder to first, and other sons—rem. to daughters—with rem. to Mary Swire, of Hull, for life ; the ultimate remainder to Richard Henry Roundell, Esq., of Gledstone House in fee. She died July 31st, 1803, aged 71, and was buried in Hartwith Chapel yard, where an altar tomb yet remains to her memory.—Also of Jane Dougill, of Hartwith, who died February 1st, 1793, aged 85 ;— and another Margaret Dougill, of Hartwith, who died May 13th, 1768, aged 71.

108 NIDDERDALE.

Summer Bridge is situate close to the bridge of that name across the river Nidd, and within a few years has grown into a village of substantial stone-built houses, ranged along the sides of the road leading from Pateley Bridge to Ripley, and also down to the river. This enlargement and increase of population has arisen from the successful prosecution of manufacturing enterprise in the neighbourhood. The taste of the inhabitants appears to have improved as their number increased; they have a Mechanics' Institute, founded July 1st, 1841, with more than 100 members, who have a reading-room attached, and library containing upwards of 1,900 volumes. This educational and literary institution speaks well for the inhabitants, who are principally employed in the adjoining manufactories.

The Wesleyan Methodists have a chapel here, built in 1827, which will seat about 500 persons; a school-room was added in 1860.

New York adjoins Summer Bridge on the west, and is chiefly situate between the turnpike road and the river Nidd. It has increased in population and importance during the last thirty years, principally from the extensive flax spinning, and linen thread manufacturing establishment of Messrs. Thorpe being located here, which gives employment to a considerable number of the inhabitants, whose dwellings are ranged by the sides of the road. This firm was raised to its present importance chiefly through the exertions of the late Mr. Francis Thorpe,[*] who was a self-made man, possessed of

* In Knaresbrough church yard is a ridged tombstone of white marble, with the following inscription to his memory—" Sacred to the Memory of Francis Thorpe, Esqre., of New York Mills in this county, who died at Lanark House, Surrey, on the 29th of September, 1854, aged 64 years, and was interred here the 6th of October following."

business qualities in an eminent degree, which led to the acquisition of wealth in trade, at the same time he was respected by all in his employment for his urbanity and kindness.

Low LAITH is another hamlet near the road from Ripley to Pateley Bridge, a short distance west of New York. The Primitive Methodists have an elegant place of worship here called Belle Vue Chapel, with minister's house and school-room, built in 1859, at the cost of Mr. Richard Pullan, of New York.

A branch of the family of Skaife held property here for a long time—John Skaife, of Low Laith, was living in 1598 ; he had three sons, of whom William resided here, whose wife's name was Margaret, by whom he had two sons and three daughters ; he died in 1625—6, and was buried at Kirkby Malzeard ;* when his son, John Skaife, succeeded to Low Laith, whose wife's name was Hellen, by whom he had

---

* The following extracts from the wills of William Skaife, and Margaret his widow are curious, as illustrative of the manners of the times in which they lived. 21 March, 1625. I William Skaife of Lowlaith in Braistie wood Yeoman—To my son John Skaife, and Margaret my wife " all such sawen wood as is nowe upon, or within the messuages and houses, and groundes, where I nowe dwell, & wch I occupie provided that they shall make two Cubberts forth of the same, one for my daughter Marie, and another for daughter Anne, such a one as I promised her, provided also the said Cubbert stand in parte of her brideswaine I promised my said daughter Anne."—"Item. I give unto the ffatherlesse children & poore widdowes aboute Paiteley briggs five shillings, and penny Doale to be delte at Kirkeby Malzeard to the poore there."

8 Jan. 1641. I Margaret Skaife, of Lowlaith, widow—"To my sonne William Skaife, one arke in the chamber, one pair of sameron sheets, my great kettle, and dripping pan—To my daughter Maria Marshall, my other cloak and safeguard, and one arke in the house—To my said son William a table, and my lesse speete, four beefe-flitches and one bacon flitch, and all my mault and husbandrie instruments."

three sons; he died in 1649, and was buried at Pateley Bridge—William Skaife, his son, married Frances, daughter of Sampson Lupton, of Braisty Woods; he had one son, Thomas, who survived him, who on his father's decease in 1719, was of Low Laith and Padside, born in 1687, and living in 1720, at which time he had a family of two sons and one daughter.

BRAISTY WOODS* is a rural hamlet on an eminence near the old road from Pateley Bridge to Ripley. The situation is lofty and pleasant, commanding beautiful views of the valley of the Nidd east and west, as well as to the southward over the cliffs and woods of Guy's-cliff, Ravensgill, the Hall and grounds of Bewerley, and far beyond towards Greenhow. The lands are held principally by Miss Hebden and Mr. Thomas Skaife; over the door of the house belonging to the latter, are the letters T. S. and the date 1656. This family appears to have been the root or main stem whence all the other families of the name of Skaife in this neighbourhood, (and they are many) have proceeded; they were originally of Ingerthorpe, near Markington, of whom was

Thomas Schayf de Ingerthorpe, who by charter *sans* date (temp. Hen. III.) granted an annuity of 2d. to the poor coming to the gate of Fountains Abbey.

John Scayf held lands under the Abbot of Fountains at Ingerthorpe in 1336; the family afterwards migrated to Braisty Woods, where

---

* *Braisty* appears to be derived from *Brae*, a short, broken or irregular hill, or river bank, and *Stey* a north country word for steep.
  " The *steyest brae* thou wad ha'e fac'd it."
BURNS.

HARTWITH.   111

Robert Skayff was keeper of the cattle for the monastery of Fountains in 1481, and also in 1484.

William Skayff was also keeper of cattle at the same place in 1493.*

. John Skaife married Margaret Hardcastle, April 12th, 1562, and had a son

Thomas Skaife, born in 1563; who, in 1601, purchased a lease of an estate at Braisty Woods, for the term of 999 years, from Sir William Ingilby, Knight, of Ripley, which is yet held by his descendants, and what is most singular, the owner for nine generations in succession has borne the name of Thomas.

Thomas Skaife, son of the above, by his wife Alice, had a son

Thomas Skaife, born in 1616-7; he built the present house in 1656, and by his wife Ann, with other issue, had a son named

Thomas Skaife, born in 1651-2, who married Jane, daughter of John Lupton, of Braisty Woods, by whom he had a son named Thomas, who on his father's decease in 1708, succeeded to the estate.

Thomas Skaife, of Braisty Woods, gentleman, born in 1688, married in 1715, Ann, daughter of Laurence Allanson, of Littlethorpe, near Ripon, by whom with other issue he had

* In a survey of the possessions of Fountains Abbey, taken immediately after the dissolution, is the following entry relating to this family and this township—" Ther be ij Tenements parcel of the manor of Brymbem callyd Bangorhouses at lxxiiijs by yere; and Brasty wod at lxxiijs iiijᵈ with all lands, medows, pastors, comons, and wasts thereunto belonging in the tenure of Robt. Skafe and Willm. Skafe, and rents by yere. vijˡⁱ vj viijᵈ."

112   NIDDERDALE.

two sons, Thomas and Allanson ;* on his decease in 1766, his son

Thomas Skaife, succeeded, who was born in 1716-7, he married Elizabeth Eaton, of Harewell Pastures, died in 1789, and was buried at Hartwith, when he was succeeded by his son

Thomas Skaife, born in 1755, who married in 1778, Hannah, daughter and co-heir of William Hardisty, of Hardisty Hill, in the parish of Fewston, by whom, amongst other issue, he had two sons, Thomas and Joseph. He died at Littlethorpe, in 1836, when the estate came to his son, another

Thomas Skaife, of Braisty Woods, born in 1780, married in 1808, Elizabeth, daughter of Edmund Brown, of Cracoe, in Craven ; he died at Manchester, in 1855, and was buried at Hartwith, when the paternal estate came to the present owner,

Thomas Skaife, of Braisty Woods, now residing at Ripon, of which city he is a common councillor.

Joseph, brother of the above Thomas, married Elizabeth,

---

* He was murdered and robbed on Sawley Moor, February 23rd, 1765, when returning from Ripon. The tradition is, that he had been collecting his rents at Littlethorpe, and was returning home on horseback, when he was waylaid, murdered, and robbed of all valuables, excepting his silver buckles. His horse returned to Braisty Woods without its rider, which alarmed his household, when a party went out in search, and his dead body was found, carried home, and buried at Hartwith, where an inscription on an altar tomb yet remains to his memory. The murderer was not discovered at the time. Some years after, the notorious Tom Lee of Grassington Wood End, was, with a young accomplice, arrested for another murder. The accomplice turned King's evidence, and it came out on the trial that the said accomplice assisted Lee in the murder of Allanson Skaife.

This, along with much information relating to the families of Skaife, and the neighbourhood generally was furnished by Mr. R. H. Skaife, of York.

daughter of Mr. Peter Davies, of York, by whom he had issue

Robert Hardisty Skaife, of the Mount, York, Gentleman.

Previous to the recent enclosure a great part of Hartwith Moor had been cultivated, but at such a remote period that the heath had again resumed its dominion, and clad the whole with a dark brown robe. The tradition is, that it was ploughed during the reign of king John, when the Pope having placed the kingdom under interdict and cursed the soil, the inhabitants deeming that the curse extended only to the enclosed lands, cultivated the commons to evade its effects. Baal hills or old smelting places were numerous on this moor, though no lead ore was ever raised in the township, the miners finding it easier to bring the ore to the fuel, than to convey the fuel to the ore. The moor, containing 862a. 1r. 12p. was enclosed five years ago; the award was signed January 9th, 1858, Ralph Lodge, of Bishopdale, in the parish of Aysgarth, sole commissioner or valuer. Amongst other allotments was one containing 3a. 1r. 16p. to the Churchwardens and Overseers of Hartwith, in trust as a place for exercise and recreation for the inhabitants of the said parish and neighbourhood, subject to a right of road through the same. This exercise ground lies by the sides of the road leading from the chapel to the Ripley and Pateley Bridge turnpike road.

The Mineral productions of Hartwith are gritstone in abundance, well adapted for building purposes, slates and flags; near the Chapel is a bed of rock composed entirely of fossil shells, some parts of it similar in appearance to the mountain limestone, to which it has some slight affinity; it

NIDDERDALE.

forms an excellent material for the making of roads. Coal, but of a thin seam and indifferent quality has been obtained in Winsley. The state of cultivation will be seen from the following agricultural statistics taken in 1854.

TILLAGE.	a.	r.	p.	GRASS.	a.	r.	p.	CATTLE.	No.
Wheat	228	0	20	Clover	142	2	0	Horses	126
Barley	129	2	0	Grass	2270	3	34	Colts	60
Oats	417	3	20	Sheep Walks	24	0	0	Cows	347
Beans and Peas	2	3	20	Houses, Fences, &c.	275	3	33	Calves	248
Vetches	15	3	26					Other Cattle	234
Turnips	174	2	20	Waste attached to Farms	224	2	30	Tups	24
Potatoes	20	3	24					Ewes	468
Flax	0	1	10	Woods	379	1	32	Lambs	580
Fallow	130	1	12	Commons	724	0	4	Other Sheep	271
				Occupiers under 2 acres	11	1	23	Swine	190
				Total Grass, &c.	4052	3	36		
				Tillage	1120	1	32		
Total Tillage	1120	1	32	Total	5173	1	28	Total Cattle	2545

Since the above were taken the moor has been enclosed, and the amount of cultivated land consequently increased, and that of common diminished. The soil is of great variety, and some of it near Brimham Lodge and the Stripe, of excellent quality, some on the contrary is cold, clayey, and poor. The annual value of the township as assessed to the poor rate, in 1857, was £4,900; as assessed to Income tax in 1858, £6,320; and as valued to the county rate in 1859, £5,737. The population in 1801, was 449; 1811, 480; 1821, 675; 1831, 943; 1841, : 1851, 1162; and in 1861, 1227.

STONEBECK DOWN.

The upper part of Nidderdale is divided into three townships, Stonebeck-Down, Stonebeck-Up, and Fountains Earth, which before the formation of the district parish of Ramsgill, constituted the chapelry of Middlesmoor in the parish of Kirkby Malzeard. From Pateley Bridge upwards, the valley has generally a north-westerly direction, though to use a bold illustration, it is as crooked as a flash of forked lightning. The first of these townships that we enter on ascending the dale is Stonebeck-Down, which is bounded on the south by Foster Beck, where it falls into the Nidd, and further up by Merryfield Beck, which divide it from Bewerley; the river Nidd forms what may be called the north-eastern boundary in the centre of the valley; How Stean Beck divides it from Stonebeck-Up on the north, and a range of lofty heath-clad mountains, generally the summit of drainage between the valleys of the Nidd and Wharfe, divide it on the west from the parishes of Linton and Coniston in Craven.

A small portion of this township is entered in Domesday survey under the name of *Hegrefeld*, now Heathfield, as having, during the reign of Edward the Confessor, belonged to Gamel; then to Berenger de Todeni, who had here three carucates of land; a very small part of what the township

116 NIDDERDALE.

contains. Soon afterwards it came into possession of the family of Mowbray; at which time it was known as the forest of Hyrefield, in which Roger de Mowbray gave to the abbot and convent of Byland, pasture for eighty mares and their foals, in pure and perpetual alms; which gift was confirmed by Nigel and Robert, his sons. Afterwards the same Roger and Nigel gave to the same convent, a part of their forest of Nidderdale, within certain metes and bounds, for the maintenance of thirty sow pigs and five boars; the monks paying by way of acknowledgment one mark of silver annually. These gifts plainly indicate that the state of the valley at that time was purely pastoral.

In the year 1172, Roger de Mowbray and his sons Nigel and Robert, borrowed from the aforesaid monks the sum of three hundred marks of silver for the term of ten years, upon mortgage of a certain part of the forest of Nidderdale, upon condition that half a mark should be deducted from the three hundred every year, for rent of the said land; and, if the whole sum, with the exception of the five marks, was not paid at the end of the ten years, the lands were to remain in the occupation of the said monks until it was paid. This sum was not repaid at the time stipulated, nor even during the life time of Roger de Mowbray, nor of his son Nigel; and was subsequently the cause of much ill feeling between the family of Mowbray and the Monks, and led to frequent contention and suits at law; sometimes the monks, sometimes the barons gaining the advantage. At length the monks obtained a charter from Roger de Mowbray, second of that name, in the year 1251, which confirmed to them for ever, the forests of Hyrefield and Middlesmoor, within the follow-

STONEBECK DOWN. 117

ing boundaries, viz.—" As Hyrefield beck comes from the boundaries of Craven and falls into Nidd, so upwards by their midstream of Nidd as far as Stean, and so upward by the wall and ditch, which divide between Middlesmoor and Lofthouse, as far as Douter, and so by Douter as far as Durrandpot, and so upwards by the waters of Nidd as far as the hedge which divides the lands of the Abbey of Fountains from those of Byland, on the south part of Nidd; and so by the hedge and ditch, likewise the boundary between the lands of the same abbeys, as far as the boundary of Masham at Brumehill, and from thence to Nidderhows, thence by a straight line to Little Quernside, from thence to Great Quernside, and so by the boundaries of Craven as far as Minhow, and thence to the head of Hyrefield beck."

Within these limits (though some of the places are now difficult of identification), is included the whole of the two Stonebeck townships, comprising nearly 27,000 acres of land. The reservations were, to the barons the chase of the buck in the proper season; while the monks were exempted from entertaining the said Roger, his heirs or successors at their houses at Ramsgill or elsewhere, as they had previously been bound to do; they also obtained the right to dig, and plough any part of the said forests, and to dispose of their cattle within their pastures at their pleasure; and also a right of road for their men, cattle, and carts, going and returning through the forest of Kirkby Malzeard to their lands in Nidderdale; and the privilege of passing through the same forest with their horses, dogs, nets, bows and arrows, when going to hunt in their forests of Hyrefield and Middlesmoor.   For

118 NIDDERDALE.

this charter and the valuable privileges contained therein they paid the sum of one hundred marks.

The monks held possession of this domain until the dissolution of their house (1540) when it passed to the crown. In the same year it was granted by king Henry VIII. to William Pickering for the term of twenty-one years, at a rent of £50 per annum. In the year 1546, the whole of the forests of Middlesmoor and Hyrefield were purchased from the crown by Sir Richard Southwell, Knight, one of the king's surveyors. In the same year, the said forests were sold to John Yorke, Esq., of the city of London, and Anne his wife for the sum of £300; the said John Yorke paying to the king at the same time a certain sum of money for which Sir Richard Southwell stood bound; and from that time to the present the royalty and the greatest part of the soil has been held by the family of Yorke, the present owner being John Yorke, Esq., of Bewerley.

Heathfield, Gowthwaite Hall, Ramsgill, and Stean are the principal places in this township, which with these exceptions consists principally of scattered houses, each of which has a distinct name.

Heathfield is a hamlet, situate on an eminence near the south corner of the township, and was at one time the most important place in it, as it was of Saxon foundation, and is styled *Hegrefeld* in Domesday; at the present time it does not possess any features of interest. The hills to the westward attain considerable elevation, rising by easy gradations, though not of a mountainous character.*

* Heathfield Rigg is 1191 feet above the sea level; Flout Hill 1425; Burngill-head Moss 1600; Broadstone Rigg 1391; Mark Hill 1506. One mile to the west of it 1636; Swinebeck Knotts 1200; Ramsgill Bents 1200; Brown Hill, on Ramsgill Moor 1527.

STONEBECK DOWN. 119

In passing up the valley from Pateley Bridge, by one of the pleasantest of roads, in the summer season, New Bridge is to be seen on the right, a narrow, single arch crossing the river into the adjoining township of Fountains Earth. It is of considerable antiquity, only intended for foot passengers, or pack horses, and, in conjunction with a few old oaks, on the southern side, has a pretty pictorial appearance, and is withal a pleasing momento of a past age.

Gowthwaite Hall is the next object deserving of notice along the road, situate in an indentation of the valley close to the foot of the hills, at the opening of a woody glen called Burn Gill. Overshadowed by lofty groves of ash and syca-more, this antique mansion is a highly interesting feature in the landscape. Although no longer the seat of the family of Yorke, its builders and owners, and divided into three farm-houses, it yet preserves its original external appearance, without mutilation and addition. It was probably built, on an old monastic site, by Sir John Yorke, early in the seventeenth century, and was the occasional residence of that family for one hundred and fifty years. The general plan is an oblong square, with projecting portions north and south; the principal front is to the southward, and consists of two parts, one presenting the side wall, the other the gable to the observer. The greatest part of it is only two stories in height; the windows are large and square, of six, seven, and eight lights each, divided by transoms; at the east end is a large window, now blocked up, of nine lights, similarly divided, some of the original glazing yet remains. The en-trance, low and plain, is very singularly placed near the south-east corner. The whole building is of stone, and the

120

NIDDERDALE.

covering of thick slates, grey with age and coated with lichens,

> " The living stain, which Nature's hand alone,
> Profuse of life, pours forth upon the stone."

The disposition of apartments in the interior has been broken up since the division of the house ; the most easterly part, occupied by Mr. Joseph Weatherhead, possesses most of the original features. The kitchen yet preserves the old chimney, four yards wide, up which the blazing fire of logs has roared merrily in days of yore. The beam, supporting the floor above is of solid oak, of immense thickness ; the window occupies nearly all the southern side, which with its height, seem almost to realize the idea of the old hall of the feudal day—when

> " Knight and page and household squire,
> Loitered through the lofty hall,
>   Or crowded round the ample fire ;
> And stag-hounds weary with the chase,
>   Lay stretched upon the rushy floor."

The staircase has undergone but slight modifications; being upwards of six feet wide, with the steps of solid oak, two inches in thickness. The large room upstairs at the east end is the place where the treasonous play* is said by tradition to

---

* Dr. Whitaker relates this story—" The family at this time appear to have been catholics : and there still remains a large upper room in the house which retains the name of Hall, and to which the following tradition is attached. That a masque was acted in the adjoining apartment, which seems to have been the great parlour, or the principal chamber of the house, by the family and their servants, under the respective characters of protestants and catholics ; the catastrophe of which was, that the latter drove the former into an adjoining room, which no doubt was properly solemnified for the purpose. Remote as the place was, and surrounded by none but dependents of the family, this insult on the established religion of the country soon reached the jealous and inquisitorial Star-Chamber ; in consequence of which the

STONEBECK DOWN. 121

have been performed; and the same authority also mutters indistinct stories of murder committed here, and midnight ghosts stalking their solitary rounds, and the room being ever after kept closed; mere idle tales,

> "A woman's story at a winter's fire,
> Authorized by her grandam."

The ghosts have disappeared, the tradition becomes vague and disjointed, and the room itself is a clean and comfortable place, the best in the house; when the great east window was open it would be nearly all light on two sides, until a recent period there was no ceiling, the naked rafters of the roof being visible; it is divided from the staircase by a pannelling of carved oak. The adjoining room yet preserves its original fire place, with the stone fender, and no grate, quite open to the roof as it was in the days when its occupants wore the belt and spur of Knighthood. The other parts, occupied by two farmers, have been more modernized, and are less interesting.

In some one of the many rooms of this house Eugene Aram taught a school, having under his care some youths who were afterwards distinguished in the world, as Dr. William Craven, and the brothers John and George Horner; these were of the most respectable and wealthy families in the dale, and the Hall itself was then occupied by Richard Craven. It was here that Aram found his deficiency of knowledge, and where he sought to remove by the most

Lord of Netherdale was so severely fined as to be compelled to enfranchise many of his estates. There is a basis of truth in this story I have no doubt; but do not know how far it is confirmed by the records of the court, or indeed whether they exist."

Richmondshire, Vol. ii. p. 111.

NIDDERDALE.

ardent application to study ; nor can a more appropriate place for the hermit student be easily found.

At this place in the year 1730, was born William Craven, D.D., he was son of Richard Craven,* who then occupied the Hall as tenant under the Yorke family. He received the rudiments of his education at home, afterwards at Sedburg Grammar School, and was entered at St. John's College, Cambridge, where he took his Bachelor's degree in 1753; and was fourth Wrangler as well as Chancellor's Medallist. He succeeded to the Arabic professorship in 1770, which he resigned in 1795. He was elected Master of his College in 1789, and died in 1815.. He published "Sermons, on the Evidence of a Future State of Rewards and Punishments," and "The Jewish and Christian Dispensations compared ;" this last was in answer to Hume. Bishop Watson, speaking of this work says—"The subject is treated with great prespicuity, and Hume's objections solidly refuted." He was a munificent patron of different charitable and educational establishments ; by Deed dated August 24th, 1812, he gave £800, Navy Stock, 5 per cent. towards the better endowment of Raikes' School, near Pateley Bridge ; and on the 4th of December, in the same year, he gave the sum of £2,000, in aid of the Charity founded by Mrs. Alice Shepherd, at Knaresbrough, for

---

* All the biographers of Dr. Craven appear to have been in error as to the time of his birth, some stating that he was born in 1728, others in 1731 ; the following entry from the register of Middlesmoor chapelry will settle the point—

"Gowthwaite. William, Son of Richard Craven, bap. Feb. 16th, 1730."

Previous to their removal to Gowthwaite, the Craven family resided at Colthouse, a hamlet about a mile further up the valley. Richard Craven, father of the Dr., died when his son was only two years of age.

"Gowthwaite. Richard Craven, buried April 24th, 1732.

STONEBECK DOWN.

apprenticing boys and relieving widows and indigent old people. From which actions he is better known to the world than from his talents or learning. Dr. Whitaker says " to the attainments of a profound scholar, he added the humility of a saint, and to the manners of a gentleman the simplicity of a child."

The farm buildings around the Hall appear to be all modern; the waters of the mountain stream which flows down Burn gill give motion to a corn mill close adjoining.

The sides of the valley are frequently and deeply cleft by narrow glens called gills, each with its picturesque wood-clad sides,

> " And one sweet brooklet's silver line."

Amongst which in this township, are Burn-gill, Riddings-gill, Colthouse-gill, and Rams-gill, which are all full of fine romantic scenery; the most beautiful perhaps is Riddings-gill, which is about half a mile from Gowthwaite Hall; it does not come quite down to the road, as it ascends the hill it grows deeper and deeper, until in some places the sides rise in rapid slopes, or precipices to more than one hundred feet in height, at times thickly clad with verdure, at times a naked cliff, disclosing the different strata as they rest upon each other, the upper rocks are gritstone, below are shales of various kinds. It is one of those wild-wood glens, which it is easier to conceive in imagination than describe, where

> " Boon nature scatters free and wild,
> Each plant or flower, the mountain's child;
> Here eglantine embalms the air,
> Hawthorn and hazel mingle there;
> The primrose pale and violet flower,
> Find in each cleft a narrow bower;
> Aloft the ash and warrior oak,
> Cast anchor in the rifted rock."

124 NIDDERDALE.

The outsides are planted with larches, and a slender stream, in summer, tumbles rather than flows along the bottom, twisting and turning round many a moss-grown root, and rock, which have fallen from the sides and impeded its course. About midway of the deepest part of the gill, a petrifying spring trickles down the rock on the north side, turning leaves, mosses, sticks, and all that it touches into stone, or rather encrusting them with a stony coat. A road winds up the gill close to the water, though frequently interrupted by old trees and masses of rock, and from which the beauties of the glen can be seen to advantage. In spring time when the woods are in fresh foliage, and the birds in full song, it is a delightful spot, and at any season of the year a choice nook for the botanist or the artist.

Colthouse is another hamlet on the western side of the road; it consists at present of two farm houses, both modern, though it was a grange of the abbey of Byland, and the name appears to indicate its use, taken in connection with Roger de Mowbray's grant to that convent of pasturage here for eighty mares and their foals. Like most of the hamlets and even single houses, it is situate at the junction of a lateral gill with the main valley.

Ramsgill, which may be called the capital of Stonebeck Down, is five miles from Pateley Bridge, situate near the junction of Ramsgill Beck, with the river Nidd; over the last is a substantial bridge of three arches. At this place was one of the granges of the monks of Byland, where they built a small chapel, that their shepherds and servants might attend divine service, and which remained entire until a very recent period.

STONEBECK DOWN. 125

About six o'clock in the evening on the 4th of July, in the year 1764, a sudden and remarkable flood occurred at this place, caused by the bursting of a thunder cloud or water spout on the hill above; the torrent came down the gill with such rapidity, that in less than two minutes, the stone bridge over the brook in the village, a butcher's shop, and a peat house were carried away; and in many of the houses the water was breast deep. No lives were lost, but there were some narrow escapes :— two children named Tobias and Thomas Harrison were tied together with *paddling strings*, and thrown upon a thick thorn edge for safety; a farmer riding through the village was overtaken by the sudden flood, and feeling, as he thought, his horse going down the stream with him, and that his latter end was near, cried aloud, as if making his will " *Ralph, Robin, an' Rebecca all alike! all alike!* which has since become a proverbial saying in the dale when equal division of anything is concerned.

The village consists of a cluster of ancient thatched cottages, some of them "so old they seem to have outlived a world's decay," two or three farm houses, a mill, a good inn, church, and parsonage, the latter pleasantly located on an eminence, a short distance south of the main village. The houses are placed without any arrangement with regard to each other, as though they had fallen at random from the clouds; many of them are at least two centuries old, a few have been re-built in a modern style. The inn was re-built about twenty years ago; in the open space in front is a fountain, erected in 1844, which yields an unlimited supply of pure water to the inhabitants.

The church was built in 1842, and consists of a nave with

NIDDERDALE.

a small portion at the east end enclosed as a chancel, and a tower at the west end, through which is the principal entrance. The style is early English, the windows single lancet lights, with the exception of the east, which is of two lights, and contains some stained glass. In 1860, three bells and a clock were placed in the tower, at a cost of £160, which was raised by subscription and the profits of a bazaar; the sittings are open stalls; the font is an octagonal pannelled shaft, with moulded base and cornice.

The living is a perpetual curacy, worth about £140 per annum, in the gift of the Vicar of Kirkby Malzeard; the district appropriated to it includes that portion of the valley situate between Foster Beck and Blayshaw Gill, in Stonebeck Down, and from Douber Gill to Backstone Gill, in Fountains Earth; the whole of which was formerly in the chapelry of Middlesmoor.

Two upright gravestones in the churchyard record : Charity King, deceased Jan. 24th, 1859, aged 95 years, and Ann Smith, who died April 16th, 1846, aged 90 years.

In a corner of what is now the churchyard stood the ancient chapel, which was pulled down when the church was built, in 1842, the east gable yet remains in the churchyard wall, it is of considerable thickness, pierced by three small lancet lights, each about three feet in height by a foot in width. When complete it was a long low building about 45 feet in length, by 18 in breadth, while the side walls were only about 5 feet in height; the roof was consequently of a high pitch. The chapel did not extend the whole length, a part at the west end being occupied as a dwelling. For some years previous to its demolition it was used as a barn. A small cross of jet

STONEBECK DOWN. 127

about an inch in length, by three-quarters of an inch in breadth, was found upon the site soon after it was pulled down.

Here is a school, but without endowment: John Yorke, Esq., pays a yearly sum to the master for the education of six free scholars. The annual court of the Lord of the Manor, John Yorke, Esq., of Bewerley, is held on the 29th day of October,* and is also the day when servants are hired for the ensuing year, and, altogether, a festival for the more youthful part of the population, ending with singing and dancing, smoking and drinking, and sometimes squabbling and fighting.

Ramsgill is best known to the world as the birth place of Eugene Aram, and pilgrimages have been made to it solely on that account; so true is it, that the birth, or even the coming to reside within the precincts of a secluded locality, of a genius, brings the remote country spot before the world, and when that genius has passed away, even under a cloud of shame, as in the case of Aram, the memory of his merits earns for it a reputation of lasting endurance; and however retired and humble the spot, as long as it exists, the glory of its great man rests with it, it is enriched with the legacy of his fame. The common flock of way-farers come not, but it boasts visitors of a higher class, of those pilgrims, who bend their steps in reverence towards the shrines of departed genius, and who love to linger near the landmarks that are left of men who were giants in their time.†

* Mr. Yorke, being Lord of the three Manors of Appletreewick, Bewerley, and Ramsgill, the courts are held on consecutive days, commencing with Appletreewick, on the 27th October, Bewerley next, and Ramsgill last. If the 27th falls on a Saturday, then Bewerley and Ramsgill courts are held on the two previous days.

† Burke's Vicissitudes of Families, vol. 1.

128 NIDDERDALE.

The particulars of the life of Aram have been made the subject of biography, romance, and song, and are consequently so well known, that it is useless to repeat them here ;—suffice it to say, that he was born in this village in the year 1704,* from which he was removed, along with his father's family, when very young to Skelton, a village between Ripon and Boroughbridge ; his father being at that time gardener to Sir Edward Blackett, Bart., whose seat, Newby Hall, was near to Skelton. Shortly afterwards, his father having purchased a house and premises at Bondgate, close to Ripon, removed his family thither about the year 1710. There Eugene went to school, where he says he was made capable of reading the testament, which was all that he was ever taught, except about a month, a long time after, with the Rev. Mr. Alcock, of Burnsal. When about thirteen or fourteen years of age, he went to assist his father at Newby, and continued there until the death of Sir Edward Blackett, when his intense love of books and literature first manifested itself; at that time mathematics were the chief objects of his studies. At the age of sixteen he went to London to act as bookkeeper to Mr. Christopher Blackett, merchant. After a year or two's abode there he took the small pox, from which he suffered so much that he was obliged to return home. He resumed his studies with increased avidity, in the departments of poetry, science and antiquities. Soon afterwards he was invited into Nidderdale to take charge of a school ; although this is generally said to have been at Ramsgill, it was more probably at Gowthwaite Hall.

* His baptism is thus entered in the register of Middlesmoor chapelry " Ramsgill. Eugenius Aram, son of Peter Aram, bap. ye 2nd of October, 1704."

STONEBECK DOWN.

129

In the year 1731, he married at Middlesmoor Chapel* Anna Spence, of a respectable, though not wealthy family, then residing at Lofthouse. About this period he was devoting all his spare time to the acquisition of Latin and Greek, and reading the best authors in these languages. In 1734, he removed with his family to Knaresbrough, where he taught a school, and studied the Hebrew tongue. In January, 1745,

* Their marriage is thus entered in the Middlesmoor register :

"Loftus. Eugenius Aram and Anna Spence married May 4th, after banns thrice pub. 1731."

The baptism of his wife is thus entered in the same register :

"Lofthouse. Anna, daughter of Christopher Spence bap. yᵉ 1st of March, 1708."

The baptism and death of their first child are thus recorded :

"Low Loftus. Anna, Daughter of Eugenius Aram bap. Jan. 23rd, 1732."

"Low Loftus. Anna, Daughter of Eugenius Aram buried June 3rd, 1732."

On the same day that Aram and his wife were married, a brother of his wife's was married, the entries follow each other in the register, and they are the first of the kind in that year.

"Isaac Spence and Jane Feart married May 4th, 1731, after Banns thrice published." Aram's wife had two brothers Abraham and Isaac, and one sister Rebecca, their father's name was Christopher, and their mother's Ann. The father was dead before the marriage of his son and daughter. On the 6th of January, 1730, the two brothers and sisters assign, or sell to Ann Spence of Loftus, their mother, for the sum of £15 10s. 0d. a dwelling house or cottage, together with a little garth or garden adjoining, and also one dresser, two bedsteads, and all the loose boards in the said house ; for the remainder of a term of 2000 years, granted by Mann Dowson, late of Lazenby Hall, gentleman and Ann his wife, to Christopher Spence, late of Low Lofthouse, blacksmith.

The signatures of the parties are appended to this document, (now in the possession of Mr. W. Beckwith, of Stean), beginning with Isaac Spence, who forms every letter separate from the rest, almost like print.—Anna Spence signs next, and her style of writing is very like her brother's.—Abraham Spence comes next, and is the readiest penman. Rebecca last, who writes an open, plain hand, but spells her name *Rebcah Spence.*

The family afterwards settled at Stean, where they held a small estate of about fifty acres of land, which continued in the representatives of the family until the year 1850, when it was purchased by Mr. W. Beckwith. The family now exists only in the female line.

I

130 NIDDERDALE.

Daniel Clark was murdered, and in the month of April in the same year Aram left his family at Knaresbrough and went to London; where he was engaged to teach Latin and writing, and where he acquired a knowledge of the French language. He remained in that situation upwards of two years; and was afterwards engaged as writing master at Hayes in Middlesex, with the Rev. Anthony Hinton, where he continued between three and four years. He was afterwards employed in transcribing the Acts of Parliament to be registered in Chancery. After this he was engaged at the free school of Lynn; where, in the month of August, 1758, he was arrested on the charge of committing a murder more than thirteen years before. The result is well known, he was tried at York; an accomplice, more likely a principal in the crime, was admitted evidence against him, (in which he certainly committed perjury), and Aram was sentenced to be executed ·and afterwards hung in chains in Knaresbrough forest near the place where the murder was committed. Much has been written and said about the defence he read on his trial, which is certainly a masterpiece of eloquence,* but not such as a

---

* This defence has been highly commended—*Bulwer Lytton* styles it " that remarkable defence, still extant, and still considered as wholly unequalled from the lips of one defending his own cause." *Scatcherd*, " That beautiful oration, which will ever delight the man of taste, the antiquary, and the scholar." *Smollett*, the historian, " A very artful and learned defence." *Bigland*, " An ingenious and eloquent defence." " The address, which he delivered on his trial in his own defence, is an extraordinary specimen of the curious learning with which his mind seems to have been stored."—*Pursuit of Knowledge under Difficulties.* Attempts have even been made to rob him of the honour of this, the last in March, 1863, at a meeting of the Bath Literary and Philosophical Association, when Mr. Hopkinson, of Stamford, F.S.A., stated that the defence was written by Mr. Mauleverer, " the head of the family at that time who resided in the family house,' who had been brought up to the law and travelled the northern circuit, and ' who, when in practice

STONEBECK DOWN

skilful advocate would have made in his behalf; for, while urging the improbability of his committing the crime, he entirely overlooks the manifest weakness of Houseman's evidence against him; and we think we may safely say that no jury could be found at this day who would condemn a man upon such slender proofs.   Though we believe the evidence insufficient to convict him of murder, we cannot acquit him of participation in some frauds in which the parties were previously concerned.   The greatest mystery is, why Aram, " whose days were honestly laborious, and whose nights were intensely studious ; a man who was such a greedy epicure of knowledge, in all its various departments ; a man, who appears to have lived only for the single purpose of enriching his mind with the treasures of literature ;" should make the acquaintance of such wretches as Terry and Houseman, that he was their associate cannot admit of a doubt.

" The whole affair is enveloped in mystery, and it will ever remain so ;—the truth will never be unfolded—but is it not possible, after all, that Eugene Aram, fell a victim to a vile conspiracy, got up by a set of designing and unprincipaled

---

was notorious for the ingenuity and astuteness with which he conducted a weak case; but if he had a good case, for his maladroitness and indifferent management of it.   In Aram's case, Saint Robert's Cave and the opportunity of exercising his talents in describing the mode and places of ancient sepulture, tempted Mr. Mauleverer to write the defence which was adopted by Aram.   I had the above account', he states in conclusion, ' from my father, who when a young man at college visited some friends of Mr, Mauleverer, then alive, about fourteen years after the trial of Aram, and they always believed and confidently asserted that Mr. Mauleverer was the real author, and that in fact Aram was not up to it."   To the man who made this statement we would ask—was there a head of the family of Mauleverer living in the family house in 1772, fourteen years after Aram's trial ? or in 1759, the year of his trial ? and, did not the last head of the family of Mauleverer die in 1720 ?

NIDDERDALE.

villains, with whom in the unsuspecting simplicity of his heart, he had occasionally associated."*

On the night before his execution he wrote these pathetic and philosophical lines—

" Come pleasing rest ! eternal slumber fall,
Seal mine, that once must seal the eyes of all ;
Calm and composed my soul her journey takes,
No guilt that troubles and no heart that aches !
Adieu thou sun ! all bright like her arise,
Adieu fair friends ! and all that's good and wise !"

It is needless to say that the sentence was carried into effect with all its brutal severity.

" The gibbet clasped its victim fast,
And his bones bleached in the wintry blast :
His passions brought a death of shame,
His learning gave him endless fame."

The house in which he was born has long since been destroyed to its foundations ; the site is however pointed out on a piece of unoccupied ground in the rear of two new cottages. In one of the latter is a relic, which tradition invariably attributes to him, a carving in stone of a large human face, with something of an Egyptian cast of countenance ; on the sides are two rolls, resembling ram's horns, as if the sculptor had intended it for a figure of Jupiter Ammon. The nose is broken, and it is otherwise slightly mutilated ; for a long time it was kept in a peat house, it is now placed for better preservation above the fire place in the kitchen of one of the new cottages.

Nothing is more evident, even to a superficial observer, than that the bottom of the valley of the Nidd, at no very remote geological period, has been the bed of a long narrow

* Life of Aram, published at Richmond, 1832.

crooked lake, or estuary ; all along from Birstwith to Loft-house, are ranges of terraces or old water margins at different levels, and rounded hills of sand and gravel which have been deposited in water. Above Lofthouse, towards the head of the dale, they are less obvious, or do not appear. Between Pateley Bridge and Ramsgill, they are very conspicuous close to the road, occasionally on different sides. The bed of this lake is the only real level land in the dale.

The glen that joins the main valley at Ramsgill presents some fine pictures of mountain scenery, and extends a considerable distance into the moorlands. Raygill House is an isolated hamlet close to the moors. Above Ramsgill the valley bends to the westward to Blayshaw and the hamlet of Stean. On Blayshaw Bents is a range of pit dwellings, nearly a mile in length, extending in a crooked line along the breast of the hill ; the pits are of various sizes, varying from 4 or 5, to 30 feet in diameter, and have evidently from their number formed the abode of a considerable colony of ancient Britons, probably not less than 1800 years ago ; but on this subject conjecture must supply the place of fact, for at that time written history they had none ; the dwellers here, and their actions are alike

> " Wrapt in the veil of time's unbroken gloom,
> Obscure as death and silent as the tomb,
> Where cold oblivion holds her dusky reign."

Similar pits are frequently to be met with both in this and the adjoining counties, always in uncultivated places, for the plough and spade have levelled them elsewhere ; they are generally of a circular shape, three, four, or five feet in depth, but varying considerably in diameter, with a raised border,

134 • NIDDERDALE.

through which is generally an opening on some side for an entrance ; above this was placed something like the spars of a roof, meeting in a point at the top, over which was laid a covering of heath or sods, forming a conical roof. Window or chimney we do not suppose existed ; the smoke from the fire kindled in the centre found its exit by the low doorway. Some of these were probably used as stores for their winter's food ; were they all occupied at one time they would accommodate a population of many hundreds. Their situation is such as to command an extensive prospect on the north and west, over the two upper forks of the valley and the hill between them. At one end is an enclosure, of a square form, about 28 yards in length by 24 in breadth, which bears the name of " the Roman Camp;" the surrounding barrier has been formed of stones and earth. Immediately adjoining these pits are large heaps of slag, or the refuse of iron smelting works, called "the cinder hills"; shewing that the ironstone, which is abundant in the neighbourhood, has also been won and smelted in very early times ; it might be by the Romans, but more probably by the Monks of Byland. The tradition is that these pits were the dwellings of the iron smelters, though it is evident that they belong to a far more distant age. This is the only place in the dale where these relics of its early inhabitants can be seen in such perfection, and these are not accompanied by tumuli, as is the case with similar works in other places. The ridge of rocks above the pits called Blayshaw Crags, rises to the height of 1100 feet above the sea level, and 600 above the river Nidd, in the valley below.

Blayshaw Gill is another of those wild mountain glens which cut deeply into the sides of the valley, with its wild

STONEBECK DOWN. 185

stream tumbling, and dashing down shelves, and precipices, fringed with crags, cliffs, and hanging woods.

STEAN is a small hamlet further west, situate in a slight hollow, on the southern slope of the valley. The Common called Stean Pasture was enclosed in the year 1775. George Jackson, and Christopher Watson, commissioners. Much of the land in Stean, as well as in the adjoining township of Stonebeck Up is held on long leases, granted by Sir John Yorke, and Dame Julian, his wife, very early in the 17th century, for the term of 8000 years. These leases were granted for the consideration of a sum of money in hand, and a reserved rent for the future. In one particular case, that of the farm now held by Mr. William Beckwith, the money in hand was £70, and an increased rent from 17s. 5d. to £5., annually, always reserved thereout. On the conditions—to the tenant, housebote, and firebote, with liberty to get slate and stone within and upon the said demised premises, and the moors and commons belonging to the same, for the sufficient and reasonable building, repairing, fencing, or manuring the said premises ; always reserving thereout unto the said John Yorke and Dame Julian, his wife, their heirs and assigns, the royalties of hawking, hunting, fishing, and fowling, and free liberty for their deer to feed and depasture upon the premises. And all hawks, &c., and all mines of lead or copper, ironstone, coals, freestone, slate, and other mineral metals in the premises, (other than slate and stone as above,) with free liberty, power, and authority to find, dig, and search for, and get the same lead ore, &c. ; and to cut down and carry away all woods and underwoods standing and growing there, to the only use and behalf of the said John Yorke and Dame Julian,

136   NIDDERDALE.

his wife, for the whole term of 3,000 years. The rent to be
paid by even portions, at the feast of St. Martin, the bishop,
in winter, and Penticost.   And also the yearly rent of
2s., at the feast of St. Martin, instead of Boons; also two
hens in kind at the feast of the Nativity; and after, or upon
the change of tenant by death, or alienation of premises 17s.
5d., by the ancient rent, over and beside the rent before
reserved.   And all fines, boons, dues, and services thereupon
due and accustomed.*

At the time when these leases were granted, timber was
probably abundant in the dale, which led the lord to reserve it
to himself; and the tenure under which the lands are held, easily
accounts for the scarcity of either natural or artificial woods
upon them, as the occupier has no motive for encouraging the
growth of one, or planting the other.

The mountain limestone here comes to the surface, and
many of the farmers have lime kilns on their lands, in
which they burn what is needed for their own farms.   Lime
is a favourite manure with the dalesmen, for their grass lands;
they spread it on in large quantities, covering the surface as if
with a coat of mortar, which effectually destroys the mosses,
and produces a heavy growth of the richest and most succulent
herbage.   This mode of tillage has long been pursued, and
with the most beneficial effect. In a lease, dated the 9th Feb.
1672, between Sampson Scowthrop, of Moorhouse, in Netherdale, and Christopher Paley, of Studfold; for certain lands
called the West Ing, the tenant agrees " to burn or cause to
be burned Twoe Sufficient Lyme Killnes within the said Tearm

---

* This deed is dated Sep. 16th, 1609, others are a few years earlier.

STONEBECK DOWN. 187

of ffoure years, and lye them in and upon the above demised primesses."*

The mineral productions of this township are many and valuable consisting of lead ore, which has been extensively mined on the south side near Merryfield Beck, and also partially at Lolly Scar, near Ramsgill, and attempts are now being made to obtain it in Blayshaw gill. Ironstone is abundant, disclosed in the strata in many of the mountain glens, and only used for the repair of the roads; that it has been smelted to a great extent in early times is evident, from the heaps of refuse found in many places; want of fuel was probably the reason why the works were discontinued. Coal is obtained near Ramsgill, and slates and flags near Raygill house, and in other places. The mountain limestone appears about Stean, and being composed entirely of fossilized remains of organic bodies, forms an excellent manure when burnt. Gritstone, though not so abundant as on the opposite side of the valley is found in sufficient quantities for building.

The moors yield turves and peat, which are the principal fuel of the inhabitants. From the following agricultural statistics taken in 1854, it will he seen that there is a great

---

* The same agreement introduces a few local terms which are not yet obsolete in the dale—the tenant agrees not to "plow, digg, hack, nor grave aney more than two sufficient dayes plowinge with a draught, in or upon the said premises." *Grave* and *dig* are synonymous terms, the former yet in common use. To *grave* the garden is to dig it. To grave peat is to dig it. A day's ploughing or mowing is yet a common measure of quantity of surface. The tenant also agrees to pay "all rents, casts, layes, gavels, dues, assessments and impositions," and also, "not to cut, fell, or twist the wood standing and growing thereon." Twist is a term yet used for pruning or lopping the branches of trees.

138

NIDDERDALE.

extent of waste land, and that much of the remainder is devoted to pastoral purposes.

TILLAGE.	a.	r.	p.	GRASS.	a.	r.	p.	CATTLE.	No.
Wheat	18	1	0	Pasture	1315	8	8	Horses	70
Barley	5	8	0	Meadow	858	2	0	Colts	21
Oats	186	1	0	Sheep Walks	2661	0	0	Cows	265
Turnips	68	2	0	Houses, Fences, &c.	24	0	0	Calves	277
Potatoes	21	8	0					Other Cattle	865
Fallow	4	8	0	Waste attached to Farms	192	1	0	Tups	50
								Ewes	2650
				Woods	182	0	0	Lambs	1726
				Commons	7171	1	0	Other Sheep	1872
Total Tillage	295	1	0	Occupiers under 2 acres	10	0	0	Swine	120
Grass	12414	8	0						
Total	12710	0	0	Total Grass, &c.	12414	8	0	Total Cattle	6915

The annual value of property in the township as assessed to the poor rate in 1857 was £2269. Assessed to Income Tax in 1858, £3750; and to the county rate in 1859, £3430.

The population at the different decennial periods has been in 1801, 434; 1811, 451; 1821, 568; 1831, 494; 1841, ; 1851, 385; and 1861, 400.

STONEBECK UP.*

This is the highest, and also the largest township in the dale, including all the upper part of the valley, extending to the " heaven water boundary" on the lofty range of heights, which separate it from Wharfedale on the west; towards the north it abuts on the parishes of Masham and Coverham, the boundary being formed by imaginary lines drawn across extensive moors, in some places the watershed on the hills forms the line of division; this line is also the boundary between the north and west ridings of the county; on the east it extends to the river Nidd and the township of Fountains Earth; on the south How Stean Beck, divides it from Stonebeck Down. With the exception of the village of Middlesmoor, the population is scattered in single houses on the sides of the hills, along the courses of the two principal streams, the Nidd and How Stean Beck. As these are of almost equal magnitude, and flow through the best portions of the township, we shall begin our topographical survey by a description of them, and the scenery on their banks, from their rise until their union below Lofthouse, when their joint streams may be said to constitute the Nidd proper.

* This, and the neighbouring township of Stonebeck Down, have their names from the How Stean, or Stone Beck, which runs in a remarkably stony channel between them—the *Up* and *Down* being relative to their situations in reference to its course.

140 NIDDERDALE.

The head of the vale is wild, grand, and desolate, surrounded on three sides by lofty heathy mountains, the two most prominent being Great and Little Whernside, which stand at the head, with ridges of lesser altitude on each hand; the summit of Great Whernside, bent like a bow, or the segment of a circle, extends for two miles at an altitude of 2200 feet above the sea level, the highest point at Long Crags being 2310 feet,* yet this elevation is attained by no very steep slopes or precipices, but can be ascended without much difficulty on all sides. The river rises on the eastern side from a spring called *Nidd Head*, at a height of 2000 feet. The first increase of water is received from small runnels in the peat; about a mile from its source it receives Craven Sike on the left, and Straight Dike from Black Fell Scar, on the right. Longhill Sike, and Crook Dike, both from the left,

---

* "In Great Whernside we have 500 feet of plates, flagstones and solid grits, above the lower millstone grit and coal of Parkhead. The uppermost rocks in Great Whernside may be referred to the upper plates and grits of Nidderdale —"*Professor Phillips' Geology of Yorkshire*, Vol. ii.

In his "Mountains, Rivers, and Sea Coast of Yorkshire," the Professor thus describes the Nidd—" The few tourists who penetrate the upper part of Nidderdale, above Angram, find the expansion of the remote fingers of this dale upon the broad slopes of Whernside extremely grand; the still fewer who have the resolution to pass over these slopes to the limestone pass between Great Whernside and Buckden Pike, will experience great enjoyment.

Between Angram and Govden Pothole, the river runs in a contracted partly limestone channel, having on the left bank very bold edges of gritstone, with coal strata interposed, between Govden Pothole and Lofthouse, the nearly dry channel is enclosed in rocks of limestone and woods, overhung by lofty gritstone hills. A similar description applies to How Steane Beck, which here enters the Nidd. Below Lofthouse, the emerging river flows in a picturesque woody dale, sheltered by gritstone summits 1000 and 800 feet high, by Ramsgill, Gowthwaite Hall—the house of Eugene Aram—to Pateley Bridge and Bewerley; and it preserves this character, with lower margins of gritstone to Ripley."—p. 70.

are the only further augmentations it receives worthy of
notice, until it reaches the region of cultivation and human
habitation among the meadows of Angram; when it receives
from the right the waters of Stean Beck, a stream equal in
magnitude to itself, which has drawn its waters from Herders
Edge, and the many small streams known as Little Cross
Gill Beck, Great Cross Gill Beck, Red Scar Dike, Skitter
Gill Dike, West Gill Dike, Blowing Gill Dike, East Gill
Dike, Blowing Gill Beck, Maiden Gill Beck, How Gill Sike,
and Wissing Gill Sike.   The situation of the farm-stead of
Angram is secluded and lonely, the last house in the valley,
standing on a tongue of land between two brooks, and fenced
around by bleak heathy mountains; on the west Great
Whernside, on the north Little Whernside, (1983 feet high),
and on the south Aygill Pike, and hills ranging from 1600 to
1700 feet in altitude.   The plough has not ascended so high
as this place, and the country is nearly destitute of trees, the
only exceptions being a few lonely alders by the sides of the
streams.   Below Angram the valley contracts, and the hills
rise more abruptly from the river, especially on the southern
side; limestone appears at the bottom, black and hard, above
which are thick beds of millstone grit and shale, with coal;
which last is worked on both sides of the valley, at Woogill
on the left, and Scarhouse Edge on the right; the seam is
little more than a foot in thickness, and the quality the best
in the dale.

The Lodge is the name of a couple of houses on the left,
and Heathen Car, the significant name of another on the
right—the first undoubtedly takes its name from one of the
hunting Lodges of the forest of Nidderdale; the other would

142   NIDDERDALE.

almost tempt one to think that it had been named by some
poor erring monk from Byland having been sentenced to pass
his time here "in penance dree," for some slight breach of
monastic rule, and deeming in his vexation of spirit that he
had been driven beyond the pale of civilization gave it the
name of *Heathen Car.**

Woodale is on the northern side, where is a fine avenue of
trees and a rookery, things of rare occurrence here; this part
of the dale being almost destitute of timber of any bulk, a
few sycamores near the houses, and a thin line of indigenous
trees by the sides of the river, constituting nearly the whole.
There are many patches of underwood consisting of thorns
and hazels (gorse is rare), scattered along the hill sides;
small plantations of larch occur lower down, but planting
has not been carried to any extent, even where it would have
been the most profitable use to which the lands could have
been put; besides clumps of timber would have sheltered the
enclosed lands, and greatly improved the natural beauty of
the valley. This scarcity of trees is owing chiefly to the
tenure under which the land is held, being long leases, which
reserve all woods and even underwoods, to the use of the lord
of the fee, with the exception of what may be necessary for
repairs on the premises. Woodale was the original home and
for a long time the residence of the family of Horner,† which

* Pronounced in the neighbourhood *Hadencar,* and found in nearly
a similar form in ancient maps. In Blome's Britannia, 1673, it is
Hathenker. In Spelman's Villare Anglkcanum, 1655, it is *Hatherker,*
and Newhouses, which is the name of the next hamlet is *Newthoas.*

† The name of Horner is very common in the dale; the Middlesmoor registers from their commencement are nearly half filled with
them. If they have all been derived from one family it must have

STONEBECK UP.

148

held a considerable estate, and have at different times been liberal benefactors to the township. George Horner was the owner of this place very early in the 17th century, from whom descended Simon Horner, who founded the school at Middlesmoor, in the year 1803. He married Elizabeth, daughter of Thomas Wickstead, of Nantwich, in Cheshire, and settled at Sunderlandwick, near Driffield in the East Riding; he attained the patriarchal age of 93 years, died July 29th, 1829, and was buried at Middlesmoor.

Below Woodale the hard black limestone disappears, apparently depressed by a *fault*, and the river flows occasionally over a bed of coarse gritstone, until it reaches Newhouses, when the limestone again appears at a considerable height on the south side. Numerous small streams pour into the river from springs on both sides, though none of them are of much importance; a current derived from the levels of the Woogill coal-pits enters from the north above Newhouses, and stains the stones in its bed of a dark ochery hue, indicative of the presence of iron. The hills on the south are short uneven slopes, rising rapidly from the river, sometimes broken into scars, which disclose the beds of gritstone, plate, and shale. On the north the slopes are easier and of greater length; the

been at a distant period. The following extracts will show their distribution at the beginning of the 18th century :—

"Lodge. George, son of Thomas Horner, bap. 2nd Nov. 1701."

"Middlesmoor. Alice, daughter of John Horner, Curate, bap. ye 13th of Jan. 1703."

"Woodale. George, son of John Horner, bap. ye 1st of Oct. 1704."

"Westhouse. Mary, the wife of Thomas Horner, buried the 24th Feb. 1716."

"Sykes. Ann Horner, buried July ye 20th, 1719, widow.

"Bouthwaite. William Horner, buried the 19th of February, 1711."

"Stean. Mary, daughter of Roger Horner, bap. ye 1st of March, 1712."

144   NIDDERDALE.

enclosed land of greater extent and value ; the meadow fields
have generally in some part of them a small barn, in which
the hay is housed to be eaten by cattle in the winter.   Some
patches of arable land begin to appear, but rarely a whole
enclosure.

Behind Woodale rises Deadman's Hill,* the boundary of
Nidderdale in that direction; a short distance from which, on
the moor are two small lakes, bearing the names of Woogill
Tarn and Coverdale Tarn. Newhouses is a very small hamlet,
situate almost close to the river, over which is a bridge of a
single arch, the first by which it is crossed.   Notwithstanding

* The ancient name of this hill was probably *Nidderhow* or the *lower
hill*, in contradistinction to the Whernsides, which it nearly adjoins on
the east.   The present name is said to have been given it, on the
discovery of human bodies, found embeded in the peat, in a perfect
state of preservation, due to the properties of the matter among
which they were buried. The tradition is, that these were the bodies of
three Scotch pedlers, who were in the habit of travelling through the
dales with drapery goods twice a year, occasionally carrying large sums
of money with them ; and that they were murdered for the sake of
their money in a house in the upper part of the dale, and the dead
bodies conveyed on a sledge to this place and buried at midnight, on
the boundary line between two parishes and two divisions of the
county ; the actors in this "most foul and bloody murder" deeming
that by so doing they would baffle the ends of justice, should any discovery
or judicial enquiry be made. No legal enquiry ever was made ; the friends
of the missing men some time after made search for them, they could
be traced into Nidderdale and even to a certain house there, but no
further.   Nothing was known to directly criminate any one, and
enquiry was dropped.   Many years afterwards these bodies were found
by workmen digging peat, when rumour again told the tale of the
murdered Scotchmen, and even pointed to the place where the deed
was done, declaring that there were stains of blood on the stairs which
could not be effaced.

> " Aged matrons shake their withered heads, and say
> That nothing, save the final judgment day,
> That stain of guilt can ever wash away."

All accounts concur (and it is nearly in the mouth of every one), that
more than one hundred years have elapsed since the deed was done,
consequently the actors must have gone to their final account long ago.

STONEBECK UP.

145

the name this spot has long been inhabited, and, though in Stonebeck Up, and consequently in the forest of Middlesmoor, at the general dissolution of the monastic orders, belonged to the Abbey of Fountains, and in a *valor* of the estates of that house, is styled "Logia de Newhouse in Nedderdale," and stated to be of the annual value of 60s. No vestige of the old lodge is visible, the present buildings are all modern.

The Nidd, from its rise to a short distance below this place, flows in an easterly direction, and thence southward until it passes Lofthouse, and joins How Stean Beck. The valley here is deep and narrow, on the right the Mountain limestone, in Thedra Wood, forms a lofty mural precipice, and on the left, close to the river is Beggarmote Scar, a lofty, ragged, weather-beaten cliff, above which, on the steep hill side, is a tangled brake of underwood. Here the township of Fountains Earth comes down to the water on the eastern side. Near the foot of Beggarmote Scar, a swallow in the bed of the river, called Manchester Hole, absorbs a large quantity of the water at all times, and in very dry seasons the whole of it. On the eastern side, about ten yards distant from the ordinary river bed, are two gaping fissures in the earth ; at the bottom of which the water can be heard, and occasionally seen. The sides of these openings are clad with mosses and ferns, and appear to be a favourite habitat of the Hart's tongue, or *Scolipendrum Vulgare*, the fronds of which attain a large size. About a quarter of a mile lower down is the great natural curiosity called

Goydon Pot,* a subterraneous cavern in the rock, which,

---

* Professor Phillips derives the name from the Celtic *Gof*, *Ogof*, a cavern. Is not the very significant word *Gob*, mouth, from the same

J

146 NIDDERDALE.

(except in great floods, or on extraordinary occasions,) swallows all the water of the river, leaving the ordinary bed quite dry, until it is replenished by fresh feeders from the sides of the valley. The mouth of Goyden Pot opens at the corner of an angular cliff of mountain limestone, and is about nine feet in height, by twelve in breadth; the upper part forms a kind of irregular arch; the bottom at the entrance has a descent of four or five feet, down which the water rushes with great fury over some huge fragments of rock, which appear to have fallen from the face of the cliff above. The rocky sides of this "long flexuous cavern" are composed of projecting shelves and indentations, crossed by innumerable joints and fissures, in which are firmly wedged fragments of trees, that have been brought down and driven in by the current; the face of the rock is worn quite smooth by the action of the water, no stalactites depend from the roof, as would have been the case had it been partially dry. This cavern continues for upwards of two miles; in dry weather it can be explored for about two hundred yards from its mouth, when further progress is stopped by the descent of the upper rock to the surface of the water. During floods the whole of the water cannot pass through this channel, when it flows along another upon the surface, which otherwise is generally dry; before it can reach the latter it rises five or six feet above the top of the Pot. The pressure of the water rushing through the cavern at these times must be enormous, enough almost to

source? and has it not also had some share in the naming of this capacious mouth? "It is also called Gowden and Cowden." Pot appears to be a common addition to the name of such places as *Hurtle-pot*, *Gingle-pot*, *Alum-pot*, *Dicken-pot*, &c., are names applied to similar objects in Craven.

STONEBECK UP.

rend its flinty sides asunder. The cliff above the orifice is about twenty-five feet in height, partially covered with ivy, and fringed at the top with a slight thicket of trees composed of the oak, the ash, the hazel, and the wild service, here called *heckberry*. The bed of the river curves round the hill, which its waters have entered, until it reaches Limley, (the Lime field), round which it suddenly bends in a different direction ; here a stream enters on the right, of a dark orchery hue, from the coal pit at Fogshaw, which is speedily lost again among loose stones at the bottom of the dry bed.

Limley consists at present of two farm-houses, on a hillock, moated on three sides by the bed of the river ; the present buildings are modern, an older house has stood on the hill behind, which was once the residence of the family of Bayne, now Baynes, in early times the most numerous and influential in the upper part of the dale. They are traditionally said to be descended from Donaldbayne, a Scottish king, or chief, who left his native land and settled here,

> " In the unremembered ages,
> In the days that are forgotten."

However obscure, or remote their origin, in 1484, when the chapel of Middlesmoor was consecrated, we find John Bayne, Ralph Bayne, sen., Miles Bayne and Ralph Bayne, jun., agreeing with the vicar of Kirkby Malzeard, on certain conditions to be observed by the inhabitants of the then newly constituted chapelry, towards the vicars of the mother church. In 1536, we find Marmaduke Bayne, bailiff of Nidderdale for both the houses of Byland and Fountains, and receiving 40s. a year from each as a reward for his services. The earliest registers of the chapelry abound with entries

148   NIDDERDALE.

belonging to members of the different branches of this family, who appear to have been located all over the dale.

Christopher, eldest son and heir of Walter Bayne, of Limley, born in 1603, was the first of the line, who about the year 1675, began to write his name Baynes.   He married, first, Margaret, relict of James Baynes of Raventhorpe, by whom he had one son and three daughters; and, secondly, Elizabeth Dawson, by whom he had one son and four daughters.   William Baynes of Kilburn, Esq., only son by the second wife, born in 1661, married in 1719, Tabitha, daughter of George Prickett, Esq., of York, Sergeant-at-Law, and had one son William, born Jan. 19th, 1729, who became one of the Gentlemen of the privy chamber to George II. and III.; and married Mary, second daughter of Christopher Roberts, of London, and had, besides other issue—Christopher, born August 6th, 1755, created a baronet June 29th, 1801; who married Nanny, daughter of William Gregory, Esq., of Ryde, in the Isle of Wight, and besides other issue, had William, the present baronet, born in 1789, married in 1815, to a daughter of General John Smith, of the royal artillery, and succeeded his father in 1837.   Residence, formerly, Harefield Place, Middlesex, now 25, Portland Place, London.*   Notwithstanding this branch leaving its native vale, and attaining to honours it never could have reached there, numbers of the same " kith and kin" were left behind,

---

* The arms are *sable*, a shin bone in fesse, surmounted by another in pale, *argent* on a canton of the last a vulture proper. Crest—a cubit arm vested, *azure*, cuffed *erminois*, the hand holding a jawbone, *argent*. Supporters—Two savages, wreathed about the head and waist, with clubs over their arms, all proper. Motto—*Furor arma ministrat*. These are engraved on a stone over the entrance of the old Hall at Kilburn.

STONEBECK UP. 149

and the blood of Bayne is yet extensively diffused through many families in the dale.*

Immediately below Limley the mountain limestone is again thrown down by a fault, and a mass of coarse gritstone appears in the bed of the river. In this gritstone, lead ore has been found in considerable quantities, at different times, as is evident from the old workings, and attempts are being made to reach it at a greater depth. The sides of the partially dry water course are fringed on both sides with native wood. Several small streams leap into the naked bed, and at length succeed in covering it, which adds much to the beauty of its appearance. The gritstone continues till within half a mile of the bridge at Lofthouse, when the limestone again resumes the ascendant; near the place where it rises is a very pretty fall, called Padkin Foss, (the demon haunted waterfall)

+ The following extracts from the Middlesmoor Registers will sufficiently shew their numbers and distribution :—

"Stean. Thos. son of Robt. Bayne, bap. 11th of March, 1701."

"Westhouses. Thos. son of William Bayne, bap. 18th of Jan. 1703."

"Thrope. Ellen Bayne, widow, buried, the 4th of July, 1714."

"Colthouse. Ann, daughter of Richard Bayne buried ye 21st of Novem. 1714,"

"Middlesmoor. ffrancis Bayne buried 31st of Decem. 1711."

"Herefield. ffrancis, son of Robt. Bayne bap. the 26th of March, 1713."

"High Woodale. William Bayne buried 1725."

"Rough Close. John Bayne buried 27th of March, 1752."

"Thwaite House. Isaac Bayne buried September 28th, 1732 "

"Thwaite House. Thos. son of Thos. Bayne
          Henry Son of Thos. Bayne bap. ye 9th of Jan. 1748-9."

At the east end of Middlesmoor Chapel are headstones to the memory of

William Bayne of Thwaite House, who died Jan, 7th, 1763, aged 65.

Thomas Bayne of Thwaite House, who died Jan. 25th, 1766, aged 62.

John Bayne of Limley, who died Nov. 17th, 1802, in the 98th year of his age.

about twelve feet in height, down which the water generally runs in streams, rather than flows in a single sheet; when viewed from below it appears to issue from a verdant arcade. Near Lofthouse, another swallow in the bed of the river drinks up the water, except in freshes, and the dry bed continues through the level meadows until it meets How Stean Beck coming from the west, and Blayshaw Gill tumbling from the south, where they all form a junction at one point.

The water which disappeared in the gaping jaws of Goydon Pot appears to keep in its subteranean course on the eastern side of the dry bed, and at length emerges at the foot of a low cliff of limestone in front of the parsonage, rather less than half a mile below Lofthouse, by three mouths, two of them close together, the smaller does not run at all times, the opening of the other can be ascended a short distance; the other mouth is about two hundred yards to the eastward; in dry weather the water comes murmuring from a mass of loose stones, but in floods issues boiling and foaming out of a rugged rocky orifice. The streams from these mouths flow along the sides of a triangular piece of ground and meet before they have run three hundred yards, and soon afterwards form a junction with the main stream. The subterraneous course is preserved at a higher level than the open one by many feet, as is obvious by the rapid descent of the waters after leaving this rocky prison.

How Stean Beck.—— This stream which joins the Nidd below Lofthouse is of equal magnitude both as regards length of course and quantity of water, and excelling it in the scenery through which it flows. Deriving its water from numerous gills, becks, dikes, whams, and sikes, on the long dark slopes

STONEBECK UP.

between Great Whernside and Meupher Fell, (the last 1887 feet high), and falling eastward with a generally quick descent, it enters the limits of enclosure and cultivation at High Riggs, where is a fall of about sixteen feet in height called Park Foss. This fall would form a fine subject for an artist, on the right the moor sweeps down to the water's edge, a dark heath-crowned rock rises above the stream on the left; the rock down which the water falls, is uneven and broken, and in summer the greatest quantity descends on the left side, but in winter, or in wet weather it plunges down in one grand irregular sheet of foam, bubbles, and spray, dashing against, and rebounding with a deafening noise, from the huge boulders beneath.

Below the fall, the banks are fringed with native wood, the ground generally rugged and steep. About a mile lower down, the stream is fenced on the south side by a lofty precipice of millstone grit, alternating with beds of shale, coated with a profuse growth of mosses, lichens, and ferns, and on the top with an abundance of native wild flowers; along the bottom of this cliff the water sweeps swiftly onward, over a succession of rapids, which have a fine effect, especially during freshes, when

> " Each wave is crested with tawny foam,
> Like the mane of a chesnut steed."

Further down is another fall, but only about six feet in height, called Cliff Foss, or Force; immediately below which a considerable affluent enters from the left, called Armathwaite Beck, from a gill of the same name, which is not without its sylvan beauty, more especially in the summer season, when

NIDDERDALE.

" Endlang the hedges thick, and on rank aiks,
Ilk bird rejoicand with their mirthful makes."

The mountain limestone now appears forming grand mural precipices near the stream, and gradually closing it in on both sides, until at length the troubled water is compelled to flow between walls of perpendicular rock. A foot path leading from the hamlet of Stean to Middlesmoor crosses the ravine by a narrow stone arch, in as picturesque a spot as artist or botanist would wish to behold on the calm eve of a summer's day.

" Where're we gaze, around, above, below,
What rainbow tints, what magic charms are found !
  Rock, river, forest, mountain, all abound,
And bluest skies that harmonize the whole :
  Beneath, the distant torrent's rushing sound,
Tells where the volumed cataract doth roll,
Between those hanging rocks, that shock, yet please the soul."

From this bridge to another bridge, on the road leading from Lofthouse to Stean, a distance of about a mile, the singularity, grandeur, and beauty of this stream and its attendant banks, reach their climax. The rock which here appears at the surface is the mountain limestone, locally called Stean marble, and through a narrow cleft in this hard substance flows the rapid mountain torrent, at a depth of from thirty to sixty feet, and sometimes more.

" Where *Stean* full many a fathom low,
Wears with his rage no common foe ;
For pebbly bank, nor sand-bed here,
Nor clay-mound, checks his fierce career,
Condemned to mine a channel'd way,
O'er solid sheets of marble grey."

This opening has been probably formed by some crack or fracture in the rock, for even imagination itself cannot conceive the idea that

" This mighty trench of living stone,"

could be worn by the attrition of water, rapid and powerful though the current be, from even the period when the Saurian was a monarch on earth to the present time. Access is only obtained to it at the lower end, where it can be entered at an opening partly made by the industry of man, who has quarried and taken away the stone to burn into lime. Here the picture presented is one of wild grandeur, of which all description must fail in conveying an adequate idea. At a depth of 70 feet flows the stream, generally of a brown colour, indicative of its origin from the peaty moors; tortuous, rugred, and uneven in the extreme is the path the troubled waters have to travel; at times noiselessly gliding over the smooth and slippery marble, then making a sudden dash down a slight fall, and chafing with angry murmurs against obstructing boulders; sometimes sweeping with arrowy swiftness along its polished bed it suddenly looses its rapidity, and rests dark and gloomy as midnight in pools which the sunshine never brightens. In winter, when the waters come down in heavy floods, black and turbid, imagination may picture to itself—

"Sad Acheron of sorrow, black and deep."

The sides are of rock entirely, not a perpendicular wall, but a series of projecting ledges, shelves, cavities, niches, cracks, and crevices of every imaginable variety of size and form. As high as the water reaches even in the winter season, the rock is naked and bare; above high water mark it is clad with mosses and lichens, in great abundance and luxuriance. From the crevices of the rock. spring many varieties of fern, amongst which are the beautiful tufts of the Black Maiden Hair, Maiden Hair Spleenwort; the Prickly Shield fern, and

154

NIDDERDALE.

above all others in abundance and luxuriance, the Hart's
Tongue, whose long fronds appear to hang pendulous in air;
with many others.*   The ivy trails its dark green foliage over
the rocks, and hangs in festoons down their sides.   Nearer
the top, where soil has lodged on the shelves, the mountain
ash, the elm, the oak, the birch, the hazel, and a variety of
indigenous shrubs have taken root, some of them appearing to
grow out of the rock itself, and contribute greatly to the
beauty and variety of this interesting spot; hanging over it
on both sides and partially hiding it from the observer above; ·
who, but for the thicket of wood, and the roar of the torrent
beneath his feet, would never suspect himself upon the brink
of such an awful abyss, for the sides descend for the most
part abruptly, and the breadth is never great, seldom exceed-
ing ten yards, and frequently narrowing to half that distance.
As if to give the idea of bridge building, a tree in one place
has fallen across from side to side, and yet continues to vege-
tate vigorously.   A view from the brink into the gulph below
is at once surprising and grand, while a sense of danger with
which it is attended gives it a touch of the sublime.   A host
of wild flowers in spring and summer bloom on the top of the
cliffs. On the southern side, a stream called Stean Gill enters
in a most peculiar manner; until within about 100 yards of
their junction it flows in a crooked channel, of its own formation, when suddenly an impassable barrier of rock rises in

* This part of the dale also yields *Grammatis Ceterach, Polypodium
Phegopteris*, different varieties of *Polypodium Dryopteris, Polystichium
Aculeatum, Polystichium Angulare, Crystopteris Fragilis, Lastræ
Oreopteris*, varieties of *Scolipendrium*, and most of the common kinds,
some of them in profusion. This notice of the ferns was communicated
by the Rev. Mr. Hairby, curate of Middlesmoor, to whose kindness we
are indebted for much information relative to the chapel and chapelry.

STONEBECK UP. 155

front, and it must either seek a new course, or accumulate and form a lake, until it runs over ; when, as if to prevent such an occurence, the accommodating rock opens a passage, at first by a double arch, at the distance of a few yards, the dividing column disappears, and the waters pass through the "mountain's marble heart," along a single rugged passage into the deep gulph already mentioned. This passage bears the name of Stean Gill foot. In other places small streams from the fields jump from the sides into the chasm, forming at times fine cascades, at others dripping and trickling down the rocks ; one spring, at least, that runs down the southern side is possessed of petrifying qualities, which it evinces by turning the mosses into stone in its descent. On the southern side, a fissure of the rock opens into a large gloomy cavern called "Tom Taylor's Chamber," in which numbers of bats hybernate during the winter. On the same side, about 200 yards from the river, in a meadow field at the foot of a small scarp of rock, is the mouth of a subterraneous passage, known as ELGIN'S HOLE, or Cavern ; it is of unknown length and extent ; some say that it has been explored to a distance of two miles from the entrance ; others, that it extends under the village of Middlesmoor ; both statements may be true, but no authentic account appears to exist of its thorough exploration. The roof and sides in the more distant parts are ornamented with stalactites of great beauty, and the floor crusted with stalagmite. In the parts near the entrance it has been dispoiled of its choicest ornaments, which is much to be regretted, as such objects never look so beautiful in any other place, as they do when glittering on the sides of their native rocks.

NIDDERDALE.

After passing the chasm, which we have attempted to describe, the waters of How Stean Beck pass downward in an easterly direction until they meet those of Blayshaw Gill, near the dry bed of the Nidd, as already mentioned, and a little lower down those of the Nidd itself, escaped from confinement in the gloomy recesses of the Goyden Pot; when the united streams pass downward with an easy descent, giving beauty and fertility to the valley, and motion to the machinery of numerous mills and manufactories, until they finally mingle with those of the more majestic Ouse, at Nun Monkton.* The principal fish in the Nidd and its tributaries are trout and grayling, more especially the former. Salmon used to ascend the stream about 60 years ago, since then the erection of mill dams has completely stopped them.

MIDDLESMOOR,+ which gives name to the Chapelry, and is the only village in the township of Stonebeck Up, is pleasantly situate on an eminence, the projecting point between the two valleys of the Nidd, and the How Stean Beck, at a distance of eight miles north-west from Pateley Bridge. It consists of a cluster of houses, placed in the same random manner with

* The two head branches of the Nidd, one (the Nidd) descending from Great Whernside, the other (Stean Beck) from Meugher fell, run with the dip of the strata north-east. After this union the Nidd runs due south-east, till it has passed the Greenhow anticlinal ridge, and then it turns due east, to encounter the magnesian limestone at Knaresbrough. The slope of the valley is rapid in the higher parts, and moderate in the lower region. Angram Ford 850 feet, Gowden Pot Hole 640, at Lofthouse Bridge the coral bed of limestone 540, Pateley Bridge 400 feet, Ripley 240 (estimated.)".—*Geology of Yorkshire, vol. 2. p.* 58.

The measures as given in the same direction by the ordnance survey are—Crown Inn, Lofthouse, 559 ; where the waters meet below Middlesmoor Parsonage, 500 ; Ramsgill Bridge, 461 ; New Bridge, 400 ; Pateley, near the bridge, 381 ; Glasshouse Mill, 350 : Low Mill, site of Lead Wath, 325 ; Summer Bridge, 311.

+ The name is evidently derived from its situation on the moor, in the middle, or between the two valleys.

STONEBECK UP. 157

regard to each other, that we have described as existing at Ramsgill, and the other villages in this valley; they are all substantially built of stone, amongst which are two inns. and a small chapel belonging to the Wesleyan Methodists; the others are farm-houses and cottages, with a large house, occasionally the residence of the owners of an extensive estate in the township.

The School was endowed by Simon Horner, Esq., who, by Deed, dated December 9th, 1809, granted £20 a year, to be paid out of his estate in this township, for the teaching of twenty poor children of Stonebeck Up, reading, writing, and arithmetic; who were to attend the chapel every Sunday, and be taught the catechism. The School-house also built by him, bears the following inscription on a stone fronting the village street—

" This school was endowed in the year MDCCCIII, by Simon Horner, Esq., of Sunderlandwick, and built in MDCCCVII."

The chapel is situate on the south-east of the village, on the verge of the hill. It is a plain, unpretending, yet venerable structure, built, and consecrated in the year 1484; the following account is inserted in the register—

In Registro Thomæ Rotheram, Fol. 217. Consecratio & Compos : Capellæ de Middlesmoor, remanet in Archives Arch : Ebor: in Anno 1484. & in Secundo Ricardi tertji.

Middlesmoor Chapel was consecrated in ye year 1484, by Dromorend Bishop of York,* in ye Second year of Richard the third.

* Thomas Savage was at that time Archbishop of York. " 15th Nov. 1484, a commission was issued to William, Bishop of Dromore, to consecrate *capellam et cimiterium in valle de Mydlesmore, infra*

158   NIDDERDALE.

Middlesmoor Chapel was a second time visited by yᵉ Bishop, at yᵉ request of yᵉ Inhabitants of yᵉ Vale of Middlesmoor, & yᵉ Chapel Yard enlarged & Consecrated for a Burying place, with all Holy Offices to be done at yᵉ Chapel, by contract & agreement made between John Blith, Prebend of Masham, John Mountforth, Vicar of Kirkby Malzeard, of yᵉ one part; & John Bayne, Ralph Bayne senr., Miles Bayne, & Ralph Bayne Junr., with yᵉ rest of the Inhabitants of yᵉ Vale of Middlesmoor on yᵉ other part——The Prebend & Vicar allow on their part to yᵉ Inhabitants yᵉ above privilege, on yᵉ Inhabitants representing yᵉ distance from yᵉ Church, & yᵉ difficulty of yᵉ Road to convey their Children to be Baptized, & their Corps to be buried. The Inhabitants bind themselves for ever to pay Tithes and Offerings, & all other Customary dues & demands, to yᵉ Vicar, for yᵉ Repairs of yᵉ Church, with Bread & Wine & Clerk dues, as have been formerly done and paid by yᵉ said Inhabitants of the Vale of Middlesmoor; and not to keep back, or prevent yᵉ gifts for souls, from yᵉ aforesaid Vicar & Prebend, and their successors. Also yᵉ Inhabitants, if any request it, may bury their dead at the mother church of Kirkby Malzeard.

Search being made at York, yᵉ 20th day of September, 1748, at yᵉ charge of yᵉ Chapelry, the above account of yᵉ consecration of this Chapel &c. was found in the register, and

circuitum de Nidderdale." Fabric Rolls of York Minster, p. 241. Surtees Society.—From Presentments made at the Visitations of the Minster, and of the churches dependent upon it, given in the same work, we find the following pertaining to this place.—" 1510. Nydderdaill. Mᵈ Yᵗ we of Nydderdayle has commond togeyer, & we fynd no thyng to shewe. Item. j. schalas, yt is rewyn in ye hedge. Item, ye conope. Item. j. box for ye sacrament.

" 1510. Middylesmore. Pressentantur ut defectiva calix revyn in ye edge, una pixis pro sacramento, unum canopeum." p. 264.

placed down for the satisfaction of the curious. The Rev. Wm. Firth, Minister."

As originally built, the roof of the chapel on the north side was not more than two feet from the ground, and it continued in that state until the 7th of June, 1775, when it was unroofed, and the walls raised to their present height. It consists of nave, chancel, porch, and a low square tower at the west end. On the south side are four windows of two lights each, with trefoil heads; at the east end are three windows, two of them of three lights, the other of two, similar in form to those on the south. The interior is one large room, with a flat ceiling, divided into two aisles by the pews. There are galleries on the north side and west end, which, as well as the pews, were built at different times by different parties at their own cost, for their own use, as is noted in the registers.

" The Honorable John Yorke, Esq. erected his Gallery of his own proper charge in the East end of the Chapel, December the 30th, 1751."

This, which must have obstructed the light, as well as being an unsightly object, has since been removed. The erection of others is noticed afterwards.

" The Gallery over the Belfry was erected September the 23rd, 1752, for the benefit of the Singers, that then were, or hereafter shall be, & for no other purpose."

" Matthew Bland erected the Pew, or Seat adjoining to the Belfry on the west of the Churchwarden's Pew, or Seat, and on Thomas Stoney's Seat on the North, of his own proper Cost and Charge ; by the Consent of the Minister, Churchwardens, and other principal inhabitants. June 6th, 1767."

160 NIDDERDALE.

A small tablet against the south wall states, that "these pews numbered as under 1, 2, 3, 4, were erected by George Horner, late of Woodale, in the year 1770."

Another memorandum states that the gallery in front of the chapel warden's seat, was built by the Rev. Thomas Lodge, George Watson, Joseph Kirtley, Richard Rider, Christopher Atkinson, and John Kirtley, in 1798.

The font is large and massive, in the shape of a cup with a short stem; the height is about two feet six inches from the ground, and the bowl about the same in diameter across the top; the stem is only about 6 inches in length; the capacious bowl is large enough for baptism by immersion. From its appearance we might suppose it more ancient than the present chapel.

Near the chancel entrance are two sepulchral inscriptions to members of the Yorke family, now of Bewerley,—one to Sir John Yorke, who died in 1663, already given in the pedigree of that family; the other is only E. Y. 1622. The following are on tablets against the walls: on the south

"Sacred to the memory of Simon Horner Esqre of Sunder- landwick near Driffield, third son of George Horner and Alice his wife of Woodale in this chapelry. He married Elizabeth, daughter of Thomas Wickstead Esq. of Nantwich in Cheshire, and endowed the school in Middlesmoor. Died July 20th 1829. aged 93."

On the north, near the east end—

"Near this place lies the body of the Rev. John Horner of Sikes, who died May ye 4th 1715, aged 52; and Jane his wife, who died August the 13th, 1754, aged 94 years. Also Alice their daughter, wife of George Horner, of Middlesmoor,

STONEBECK UP. 161

who died September the twenty-seventh, 1770, aged sixty-seven years."

The following statement of the charities belonging to the Chapelry, is copied from the board within the chapel—

" John Topham gave to the poor of Sikes and Lofthouse Granges ten shillings yearly, now payable out of some land called Holmfoot annually for ever on Decbr 2nd. Mr. G. Horner, and his successive order, Trustees. Mr. Robert Inman and heirs in trust for ever, for the payment of twenty shillings to the poor of Fountains Earth, to be paid at Bowthwaite on Whitsunday Monday yearly out of lands at Longside. Margaret Spence gave Thirteen pounds six shillings and eight pence; the interest of it to the poor of Stonebeck Up. The house at Martingall in Middlesmoor built with the above money. Christopher Pailey of Stean gave Ten pounds; the interest to be paid to the poor of Stonebeck Down: the Minister and Chapelwardens of that Township trustees: the principal is in George Downes hands. Mr Roger Bayne of Woodale gave Thirteen pounds six shillings and eight pence; the interest of it to the poor of the Chapelry of Middlesmoor; the Minister and Churchwardens to distribute the same on St. Thomas day yearly, for ever: Christopher Raynor's house at Low Lofthouse purchased with the above money.   William Craven of Colthouse in his will dated A. D. 1680, relates that Richard Browne then of Gisburne his father in law, gave the yearly sum of Twenty shillings payable out of lands at Low Lofthouse, called the Holme and Twistyeate to the poor of Ramsgill and Hearefield; that his son William Craven late of Dublin in Ireland, gave also the yearly sum of twenty shillings payable out of

K

162
NIDDERDALE.

lands at Low Lofthouse, called Collyer Holmes to the poor in the Chapelry of Middlesmoor; all which, he, in the said will, confirms; appointing his Heirs for ever to distribute the two doles yearly on the 25th of March; and for their trouble, he gives the further sum of six shillings yearly, out of the said Collyer Holmes. He also provides in case of failure heirs in his family that the Minister of the Chapel, the Churchwardens, and Overseers of the poor, distribute the two doles of twenty shillings each, together with a like allowance of six shillings for their trouble."*

The Registers are not in a good state of preservation; they commence in 1662, but have occasional deficiencies afterwards. We make a few extracts having reference to the general affairs of the Chapelry—

"I was informed by letter on X^tmas day of the bounty being got by lot, to this Chapel, the Michaelmas term before O. S. Anno. 1751."

"I was informed March the 12th one thousand seven hundred and seventy five, of the Queen's bounty being got by lot to this Chapel, the Michaelmas term before, 1774."

"I was informed Feb. 24th 1786, of the Queen's bounty being got a fourth time by lot to this Chapel, the Michaelmas term, before the two first lots were appropriated to this Chapel in 1751, and a purchase in lands made thereof in 1763, for the use of the Chapel, by me William Frith. May the fourth, 1787. O: S:"

"Thos. Lodge, Clerk, Master of Arts, was licensed to the Cure of Middlesmoor on July 15th, in the year 1792. Revd William Frith died July 4th 1791."

"I was informed in March 1793, of the Queen Anne's bounty being obtained by lot to this Chapel for the fitfh time. The inhabitants of the Chapelry have likewise subscribed £200, toward getting of it a sixth

---

* The compilers of this table have been very negligent in giving dates of the times when the benefactions were left. Lawton in his Collecto rerum Ecclesiasticarum, &c., adds, *The Rev. Dr. William Craven's Charity,* by deed 24th August 1812. Dividends on £200 five per cents. to be distributed by the Minister and Churchwardens—and *W. Swithenbank's gift.* Rent charge of £1 6s. 8d. per annum.

STONEBECK UP. 163

time. A purchase was made at Staveley, by the Revd T. Lodge, of £1,025."

" Gathered & collected by the Sexton. A briefe ffor loss by ffire at Newport w'thin the county of Salop, in the Chapell at Middlesmoor 5s 7^d Sept. 1668."

" Twentie pounds given by William Craven of Dublin in Ireland, to William & Richard Craven, that they should put the same out for the use of the poore within the Constablary of Stonebeck Down. And on the 8th day of June, 1672, they, the said William & Richard Craven did bye for the sum of £20, one meadow, House and barne, called Collyer Holme gate........for the use of the poore of Stonebeck Down."

" The honourable John Yorke Esq. made a present or Gift to this Chapel on Easter Sunday morning which was April the third, one thousand seven hundred and seventy four, of two Silver Flagons, and a Large Silver Patten."

" John Faris and Agnes his wife's Absolution was read publickly in a full Church, on Sunday the 11th of July, 1784, and the next two Sundays following by me William Frith, Minister."

" Christopher Horsman and his wife Ann's Absolution for Adultery. —Christopher with Agnes Joy, and Ann with John, Agnes's husband, was read and published in this Church, on Sunday the fourteenth day of June, 1789, by me William Frith, Minister."

" John Bell and ———— Knowles his wife did penance in this Chapel for Antimatrimonial Fornications and Adultery on July 21st 1794."

In the church yard are many memorials of the departed fathers of the hamlet, some of whom have attained to a great age before their departure hence. One stone, near the base of the tower bears the names of four persons whose ages amount to 355 years—

" Abraham Metcalfe of Low Riggs, who died March 14th, 1791, aged 88 years."
" Mary, his wife, who died Sept. 3rd, 1791, aged 85."
" John Spence, who died June 17th, 1771, aged 92 "
" Isabella, his wife who died Feb. 11th, 1837, aged 90."

On other stones will be found the names of

" John Bayne of Limley, who died Nov. the 17th 1802, in the 98th year of his age."

" John Eglin of Hazel Close, who died March 16th 1815, aged 81; and Mary, his wife who died Oct. 27th 1822, aged 94 years."

"John Loftas of Ramsgill, who died Sept. 17th 1829, aged 95 years."*

Against the outside of the chancel wall is a stone to the memory of Simon Hanley, of Middlesmoor, who died Jan. 11th, 1687 ; Mary, his wife, who died Jan. 2nd, 1719 ; Sarah Horner, their daughter, who died Feb. 2nd, 1736 ; John, son of John and Sarah Horner, who died Feb. 23rd, 1768 ; Mary, daughter of George and Isabel Horner, of Woodale, first wife of Richard Craven of Colthouse, who died 15th Aug., 1686, and left one daughter, married to Francis Taylor, of Knaresbrough.

The view from the chapel yard is one of considerable extent and surpassing beauty, embracing the whole of the valley downwards, as far as Guy's-cliffe below Bewerley. The river winding down the centre, the strip of land on each side, extending to the base of the hills, as level as the bed of a lake ; the slopes of the hills with their green meadows, divided from each other by crooked fences, variegated with frequent patches of woodland, and studded with numberless small buildings ; above which rise on each side the lofty, brown, heathy moors, enclosing the whole.

The Living is an Augmented Perpetual Curacy in the gift

---

* The situation of a Physician in Nidderdale would be similar to that of one mentioned in Clark's survey of the English Lakes, whose reply to the query was—" My situation is a very eligible one as a gentleman, I can enjoy every species of country amusement in the greatest perfection ; I can hunt, shoot, and fish among a profusion of game of every kind—but as a physician I cannot say that it is quite so alluring to me, for the natives have got the art of preserving their health, without boluses or electuaries ; by a plaister taken inwardly, called Thick Pottage. This preserves them from the diseases which shake the human fabric, and makes them slide into the grave without pain, by the gradual decay of nature."

STONEBECK UP. 165

of the Vicar of Kirkby Malzeard; the particulars of which will be best seen from the following copy of—

"A true and perfect Terrier of the Glebe lands, and other appurtenances belonging to the parochial Chapel of Middlesmoor, to be presented at the primary visitation of his Grace the Archbishop of York, to be holden at Ripon on the 20-sixth day of June 1809. A Messuage house and tenement with the Lands and appurtenances thereto belonging, situate at Low Lofthouse, within the Chapelry of Middlesmoor.— Dimensions of the house—The front on the outside is five yards and one foot; the breadth eight yards and one foot; the height, to the square, two yards and two feet; the walls, old and built of stone; the roof lately covered with slate and ling:—the rooms are, one little kitchen in front, a little Bedroom and Milkhouse backwards:—the floors of stone: the partition between the Kitchen and other rooms is studded and laithed and plastered with Lime. The peat house is in length five yards, in breadth five yards, and in height two yards to the square, and covered with ling. A little swine hull, in length three yards, and breadth one yard and half, covered with slate. One barn, in length eleven yards, breadth six yards, and height, to the square two yards and two feet. One other building in length four yards, in breadth five yards and two feet, and in height to the square two yards; both the said buildings are covered with ling. (The whole of these buildings have been unroofed and repaired by the present Incumbent, at a very great expense.) The closes and lands belonging to the same, are Lawen or Backenhole, by estimation five acres; Backenhole hill, the Throstlenest, and Farbank, by estimation five acres; the Stackgarth-plain, by estimation three acres and a half; the Westbank, seven acres, and the Calf-close, one acre. There are one Oak, and two small Ash Trees growing thereon. The above lands are in a ring fence, and the abuttals are, on the south, the High-road leading to Pateley Bridge; on the east, by Mr. Reuben Craven's estate; on the north and west, by an estate belonging to Hornby Church. The commons are extensive, but of bad quality; the privileges are unlimited. One other estate situate at Staveley, in the county of York, in the diocese of Chester. One good dwelling-house, consisting of three rooms in front, one of them has a boarded floor, the other two are flagged with brick; the chambers above the same with boarded floors. One dairy, floor brick, the whole built of brick and covered with slate and tile. One Barn, ten yards in length, five in breadth, built of brick, and covered with tile. One three-stalled stable, built of brick, covered with slate. One Hogg Coat. One other building, now used as a Blacksmith's Shop, built of brick and covered with slate and tile. One Garth, adjoining the house, with one garden and one orchard, containing one acre and half, more or less, with one close adjoining the garth, called Ings Close, being one acre one rood, more or less; lands called Carr's, with one close adjoining them called Town Close, being in the whole Thirty Acres, more or less; lying in a ring fence, bounded on the west by a fence belonging to John Hembring; on the north by Fleet Beck; on the east by a fence belonging to the said estate, and on the south by the highway leading from Staveley to Boroughbridge. This last mentioned estate was purchased with the Queen Ann's Bounty, for the sum of one thousand and twenty-five pounds; Twenty-five pounds of the said purchase money was paid by John and Simon Horner, Esquires, of Kingston-upon-Hull, as an equivalent for two annuities, amounting to twenty shillings paid by their ancestors to the officiating minister of Middlesmoor Chapel. The Chapel furniture,—One Bell, Two folio and octavo Common Prayer Books. One folio Old and one folio New Testaments. One Book of Homilies, and one Book of Offices. Two Surplices. A Patten. Two Chalices. Two Flaggons. All of silver :— weighing about nine pounds twelve ounces, Troy weight. And one Font-baron of Stone. One Table Cloth, and Two Towels. A velvet cushion. And a Hearse and Harness. The Chapel yard wall is repaired on the west by the Chapel wardens, on the south by Simon Horner, Sen., Esq. ; on the east by John Dovenor ; and on the north by John Dovenor and Richard Ryder, Senr.

There is likewise one Sheep-gate upon Middlesmoor Peat ground, allotted at the late enclosure. The Chapel is repaired by the Chapel wardens. The Clerk is appointed by the minister ; his wages are one pound three shillings per annum ; and paid by the Chapel wardens. The Sexton is appointed by the Chapel wardens, and his wages are one pound one shilling, and paid by the Chapel wardens."

The present annual value of the living is about £127.

John Yorke, Esq., of Bewerley, is Lord of the Manor, with all mineral rights and royalties. At this place, if we are to credit a very vague tradition, was an early residence of the family of Yorke, before they built Gowthwaite Hall ; if so, it must have been for a very short period ; as no great length of time elapsed between their purchase of the estate, and the erection of Gowthwaite. This tradition received the counten-

168 NIDDERDALE.

ance of Dr. Whitaker, who says—"An increasing fondness for warmth and shelter, and latterly for picturesque beauty, has uniformly operated upon this family in the successive changes of their habitations. Tradition records, that their first residence was considerably above Middlesmore, and almost at the head of the valley; thence their first migration was to Middlemore, whence the names of Hall Garth and the Park still denote the site and ornament of their mansion. Here too, for several generations was their burial place, indeed long after they had abandoned the place as a residence."*

"Midlesmore 8m. W. Ys. part belonged to ye Mowbrays, & at ye E. end of ye ch. is a hill with closes, called ye Hall Garths, & a park on ye N. side ye ch.',†

At present tradition points to a locality on the west side of the village, opposite the school as the place where the Manor house formerly stood; the Park, which was probably never enclosed as such, was that stretch of hilly ground extending to Foulshaw, or Fogshaw Lodge and beyond. None of the early topographers appear to have visited Nidderdale, doubtless deterred by the badness of the roads, and its distance from any of the centres of population, hence the meagreness and inaccuracy of their accounts.‡

* Richmondshire, Vol. II. p. 112.

† Drs. Burton and Johnson's MSS, 1669.

‡ Leland writing of Nidderdale merely says— " Nid ryver risethe by west 5 miles above Pateley-Bridge of wood; a little a this side a chapell cawllyd Medlemore, and as I could learne it is in the paroche of Kirkeby Malesart." This is sufficient to prove that he never saw the rise of " Nid ryver," or "Midlemore." Dr. Whitaker can never have seen it, or he would not have written the following account—"This is Nedderdale, corruptly pronounced Netherdale, which, rising at the foot of Wherniside, after merging for a considerable distance, re-appears near Middleham, and continues its course through this parish to Brereley, and afterwards to Hartwith. This tract was the toto Nedderdale of Mowbray's comprehensive charter, which in few words assigned a little

STONEBECK UP. 169

Besides the Lord of the Manor the principal land owner is Mr. William Harker, who has recently purchased an extensive estate from George Reynard, Esq., of Sunderlandwick. Part of this estate belonged to Simon Horner, Esq., already mentioned; his nephew, Horner Reynard, made considerable purchases in the dale, including the farms called Northside Head, Thrope, Far Pasture, and lands at Lofthouse; his son, George Reynard, sold the whole estate comprising 2,612 acres, in September, 1862, to Mr. William Harker, the present owner.* The lands in Fountains Earth are freehold, those

province to the Monks of Fountains. From them it past after the dissolution to Sir Thomas Gresham; and by purchase from him or his immediate descendants, to the Yorkes, a wealthy family, and merchants of the staple, whose descendent, John Yorke Esq is the present possessor."

The different places in Nidderdale are thus enumerated in an account (previous to 1296,) of the extent of the jurisdiction of the prebend of Masham—

"Angram, Westhouse, Loge, Skyrhouse, Hackenker, Woldall, Newhouse, Lyme, Trop, Middlesmore, Sterme, Stodfold, Lofthouse, Morehouse, De Stene, Brathwaite, Ramsgill, Ragel-house, Calf-hull-house, Goldethwayte, Sixford, Irfeld, Effald, and one part of Hewith, Wynnesley, Brimsle, all in Nidderdale."

* The advertisement by which the sale of this estate was announced to the public is a most singular piece of composition, we give it as a curiosity.

"The Picturesque, Pastoral, and Sporting Estate of MIDDLESMOOR, containing about 2,612 scres situate in the townships of Stonebeck Up and Fountain's Earth, in the parish of Kirkby Malzeard, in the West Riding, and forming conspicuous features of one of the most romantic of the Yorkshire Dales—Netherdale or Niddsdale. And familiar to the naturalist and antiquary, who has ventured into the grand cavern of 'Goydon-Pot-Hole,' to explore the mysteries of the river Nidd, in its subterraneous course beneath this Arcadian domain; eight miles by carriage road from Pateley Bridge—a market town—galvanized by a station of the 'Nidd Valley' Railway, that must push its civilizing influences still further up the fertile dale, and give to agriculture the benefits of such inexhaustable beds of limestone as enrich the Middlesmoor Estate.

MR. DONKIN, in the exercise of a trust so liberally committed to his charge, now advertises the Estate of Middlesmoor for Public sale,

NIDDERDALE.

in Stonebeck Up are leasehold, for the remainder of a term of 8,000 years, granted by Sir John Yorke and Dame Julian, his wife, about the year 1609. The lord of the manor still retaining all the royalties of hunting, hawking, fishing, and fowling, with free liberty for his deer to feed and depasture at will; and all mines of lead, copper, iron, coal, slate, freestone, and all metals and minerals whatsoever; and also all woods and underwoods, with liberty to cut and carry the same away, which last reservation is highly prejudicial to the improvement of the dale, as the plantation of trees would add much to the beauty as well as value of the lands.

An annual fair is held at this village for the sale of lambs, cattle, &c., on the 17th September.

The mineral productions of Stonebeck Up are numerous and valuable, but as yet undeveloped to their full extent, consisting of lead ore, ironstone, limestone, gritstone, slates, flags, and coal. The following geological description and section, chiefly applicable to this township, are by Professor Phillips.*

within the George Hotel, Pateley Bridge, on *Wednesday, the Twenty-fourth of September*, at one o'clock punctually. The estate is almost wholly pastoral, and contains 2,612 acres, of which 133 are of freehold inheritance, the remainder leasehold for a term of 2,000 years, subdivided into small farms, with commodious farm houses, hay barns, and other offices, in the yearly occupation of respectable and industrious tenants, together with several dwelling-houses, cottages, gardens, and allotments, in the village of Middlesmoor and Lofthouse. The quality of the pasturage is diversified between the richest old sward and the mountain heath, affording sound and healthy grazing for sheep and cattle, sheltered by thriving ornamental plantations, copses, and hedgerows. Game is plentiful, and having a SHOOTING BOX, *a beau ideal* of its kind, where the heather bell and hyblean honeycombs can be enjoyed in their solitudes. It is nothing strange that the grouse shooting upon Middlesmoor has long been viewed on the 12th August, as the *summum bonum* of the Sportsman's earthly aspirations.

Bywell, Felton, August 28th, 1862."

Mr. Donkin must be a professor of elocution as well as an auctioneer."

* Geology of Yorkshire, Vol. II. p. 26, 28, 29.

In this valley the limestone series is seen in Stean Beck, and, with two interruptions, in the river Nidd, and its banks from Angram to Lofthouse, where it is thrown down by faults. This gritstone corresponds to the lower grits of Greenhow, and the "bearing grits" of Grassington; and is a rock of much geological interest, as affording a term of reference where one was much needed.

Taking our station at Lofthouse, we find the lower scar limestone mass, cut into both by the Nidd, and a branch of nearly equal importance, called Stean Beck. Passing up the Nidd, the limestone is seen covered by four feet six inches of shale, with thin argillaceous limestone in the upper part; then six feet of unevenly bedded blue limestone, then a bed of plate fourteen inches, on which is a "famp bed" (indurated wavy calcareous shale), and above all five feet of black compact laminated limestone. Some plate comes on, and then, for half a mile further, the river runs in a solid coarse pebbly grit rock—and above this for a vast height is a succession of thick sandstones, and shales, with coal. Further up the valley the great limestone rises to some height; and after it is thrown down by a fault, pebbly grits appear in the river again. Higher, the Nidd is found flowing on the same black cherty limestones and plates as those which cover the great limestone at Lofthouse; about ten feet of limestone resting on twenty feet of plate. Above, on each side towards Middlesmoor, and towards Little Whernside, are enormously thick shales, (plates) surmounted by flagstones and shale, with coal and a coarse grit rock above. Still higher, are more shales and grits for a great height. In Ramsgill, below Lofthouse, the lower limestone is covered by alternating plates, cherts,

172 · NIDDERDALE.

and limestones, above five fathoms, and on these lies a grit rock eight fathoms thick with coal.

SECTION IN THE UPPER PART OF NIDDERDALE.

Upper grits......of Brimham, &c., only partially seen.

		feet.
Upper plate and flagstone group.	Consisting of grits and plates, the former mostly laminated, and yielding flagstones at several points	200
Middle grit.	Strong square blocked grit rocks of coarse texture	30
Lower plate group.	Plate .... Coal bed of Trope scar, Wogill, &c. .... Plate, thick .... Thin rough gritstone .... Plates, thick..................... Coal bed in Ramsgill	300
Lower millstone grit.	Flaggy grit .... Pebbly grit .... Lower coal seam in Ramsgill	90 or 120

Chert, plate, and Limestone.

		ft.	in.
Black Limestone group.	Plate	5	0
	Black, compact limestone	1	6
	Famp bed (platy)	1	2
	Plate	1	2
	Blue Limestone	6	0
	Plate	4	6
Lower Limestone series.	Coral bed (Cyathophyllum)	2	0
	Shale and crinoidea ...	0	0
	Grey Limestone	15	0

The coal of Colsterdale, Trope, and Wogill, is identical with that of Scrafton.   That of Parkhead corresponds to the lower Nidderdale, or Ramsgill and Greenhow coal.

The state of cultivation will be seen from the following statistics taken in 1854 :—

TILLAGE.	a.	r.	p.	GRASS, &c.	a.	r.	p.	CATTLE.	No.
Wheat	8	8	0	Pasture........	2846	0	0	Horses..........	64
Barley	2	0	0	Meadow	1209	0	0	Colts	7
Oats	58	2	0	Sheep Walks ..	6805	0	0	Milk Cows	247
Turnips	20	8	0	Houses, Gardens, Roads, &c. ..	61	1	0	Calves..........	288
Mangold	0	2	0					Other Cattle	259
Potatoes	10	8	0	Waste attached to Farms ..	245	2	0	Tups	58
Fallow	0	2	0					Ewes	4425
				Woods	15	0	0	Lambs	8465
				Commons......	8876	2	0	Other Sheep	175
Total Tillage..	96	8	0	In holdings less than 2 acres.	5	0	0	Swine	62
Grass	14068	1	0						
Total 14160		0	0	Total Grass, &c.14068		1	0	Total Cattle ..	9040

The quantity of arable land is surprisingly small, and confined to little patches on the sides of the valleys; the bottoms and lower slopes are chiefly devoted to meadow; the pastures and sheep walks come next in the ascending scale, and the commons are wide heathy wastes extending to the mountain tops, the favourite abodes of the red grouse, which are numerous, and afford excellent sport in the season. The moors yield peat, which is in common use as fuel; the damp places or *whams*, abundance of rushes; and the drier parts near the edges of the valley, fern or breckons. Such is the steepness of the hills, that the sledge is in common use instead of the cart; the peat from the hills, the hay from the meadows, and even the manure to the fields are carried on, or in sledges.

The annual value of the township as assessed by the overseers in 1857, was £2,955; as rated to Income tax in 1858, £3,750; and assessed to the county rate in 1859, £3,430.

174 NIDDERDALE.

The population at the different decennial periods was in 1801, 304 ; 1811, 341 ; 1821, 361 ; 1831, 333 ; 1841,   ; 1851, 419 ; and 1861, 374.   The decrease in population during the last ten years is quite unaccountable, for not only is the number less, but the excess of births over deaths should be reckoned, which will be considerable, as the dalesmen are generally a longlived race.

FOUNTAINS EARTH.

This township extends along the north-eastern side of the valley, being bounded on one side by the river Nidd from a short distance above Beggarmote Scar, to where Doubergill falls into the same river, near the hamlet of Wath; on the south Doubergill divides it from Bishopside, on the east and north-east it abuts on the townships of Laverton and Grewelthorpe, in the parish of Kirkby Malzeard, and to the northward on that of Masham; from which it is divided by imaginary lines, generally passing along the ridges of hills, the summit of drainage; the township of Stonebeck Up forms the boundary on the west. No part of Fountain's Earth is mentioned in Domesday, and the first recorded owner is Roger de Mowbray, who, 9th of Edward I, was summoned by writ of Quo Warrrnto to shew by what authority he claimed to have free chace in Kirkby Malzeard and Niderhal;—Replied, that free chace in Kirkby Malzeard and the forest of Nidderdale had been held by all his ancestors from the time of the conquest.

By Inquisition post mortem 26th Edward I, Roger de Mowbray held " Nidordale chacea, Baggworth boscus, Glomescalle boscus," which were within the Manor of Kirkby Malzeard.*

---

* These names are difficult of identification. *Baggworth* is probably *Bagwith*, a place in the township of Kirkby Malzeard, while *Boufale* is likely to be *Bouthwaite* in Fountains Earth, and within the manor of Kirkby Malzeard, of *Glomescale* we know nothing.

176   NIDDERDALE.

Notwithstanding the free chace and woods reserved, the
lands had been given to the Abbey of Fountains, extending
along the river Nidd from Iwedon to *Beckermote*.* From this
gift the township doubtless received its name.†

In the year 1485, it was agreed between the abbot and convent of Fountains and John de Mountfort A.M. vicar of Masham and Kirkby Malzeard, that the former should pay
annually to the latter £5, in lieu of tithe hay in Thwayt-houses,
Thrope, Lofthouse, Borethwaite, Calf-house, Holme-house,
Senford, Butterstane, Daylagh, and Bramley; which was
confirmed by Thomas Pearson prebendary of Masham and
Kirkby Malzeard.

All these places are in Fountains Earth, with the exception
of Butterstanes, (Lunterstone) and Daylagh (Dallowgill) which
are in Laverton, and Bramley, which is in Grewelthope.

The monks held their possessions here until the dissolution
of their house, when they came to the crown; whence they
were soon sold or granted out, and are now held by many
different owners. The royalties were obtained by the lords of

---

* This old word appears to mean the *meeting of the waters*, and might
with propriety be applied to the junction of the Nidd, How Steam beck,
and Blayshaw gill, below Lofthouse; though from the similarity of name
and situation it is more likely to be the place yet known by the name of
Beggermote scar, near the place where the waters of the Nidd dive
underground, at the north-western extremity of the township. The
name occurs again in early times, in an agreement made by the Monks
of Byland and Fountains, concerning certain lands, lying between *Bas-
tonber* and *Begarmot*. The former of these appears to mean the *low
stone water*, and is probably the brook now called *Backstongill*, which
flows from the moors to the Nidd, a short distance east of Middlesmoor
parsonage.

† The name of this township has frequently misled topographers,
those who make their books without ever seeing the objects they attempt
to describe; who have placed here the ruins of Fountains Abbey, from
which it is distant more than a dozen miles.

Studley Royal; Earl de Grey and Ripon being the present lord of the manor.

During the monastic period the whole township was divided into a number of farms or granges, known as Thwaite-house, Lofthouse, Sikes, Burthwaite, Calfal House, West Holme House, East Holme House, and Syxfurth or Sikesworth; all of which yet retain their original names, but slightly altered by the use of 300 years; the buildings have all been renewed, some of them two or three times over.

Of these old Granges, the most westerly is THWAITE HOUSE, situate above Beggarmote Scar, between the river Nidd and the rock strewn eminence called Thrope Edge; the lands around generally consist of steep slopes, rugged and uneven, with large breadths of stunted underwood, in many places thickly studded with grey crags. Below the house is a steep cliff of mountain limestone, above rises a lofty range of gritstone rocks, in which a seam of coal was worked about thirty years ago. It the *Valor* at the time of the dissolution this place is styled a manor, " Manui: de Thawithouse" and said to be worth £4 per annum. It has now been for many generations in possession of the family of Stoney. Blueburnings is a steep hill, up which the road winds from Nidderdale to Masham.

LOFTHOUSE was the site of another Grange, and is now the only place in the township that can be styled a village. In early times it was held by a family of the name of Hebden, of whom Simon, son of Simon de Hebedene gave to God and the Church of St. Mary of Fountains, two tofts in Lofthus,

L

178 NIDDERDALE.

with all royalties which Pam de Lofthus* held, with free common of turbary and fernary† which belonged to one carucate of land.

William, son of Simon de Hebbedene, confirmed to the same monks, a rent of three shillings arising out of that half carucate of land in Lofthouse, which Thomas, son of Alexander the Dean held of him.

Henry de Treskfeld confirmed the gift of the above rent.

---

* We have grave suspicions that the family of Lofthouse or Loftus, Marquises of Ely, derived both their name and origin from this place, and that this Pam de Lofthus, is an earlier ancestor of the family than any who have yet found their way into the pedigree. He probably obtained his name from living in a house of two stories—the *house* with the *loft*, such erections being rare at that time. We suppose their first migration was to Swineshead in Coverdale, about half-a-dozen miles to the north of this place, where, an unsupported tradition says, they flourished from the times of King Alfred, though the names of none are mentioned of so early a period as this Pam. Christopher Lofthouse was Prior of Helangh in 1460. Thomas Lofthouse was settled at " Swineshedde," in 1557. Edward Loftus, of Swineshead, was father of Robert Loftus, (whose son Sir Adam Loftus, was Lord Chancellor of Ireland in 1619 ;) and also of another son named Adam, who was Archbishop of Dublin in 1567, and Lord Chancellor of Ireland in 1578, from whom the present Marquis of Ely is directly descended.

† Turbary and Fernary were two valuable privileges, as turves and peat, which are both included in the first term, were than, as well as now the principal fuel of the inhabitants ; the latter makes an excellent fire, and when thoroughly dry does not emit large quantites of smoke ; it was used in the hall of the noble, as well as in the kitchen of the monastery, and the right to dig it was by especial grant. In 35, Edward I. Minister et fratres de Knaresbrough petunt quod ipse, et eorum tenentes fodiant *turbas & Vletas* in foresta de Knaresbrough." Rot. Par. 35, Ed. I. Fern is obtained from the dry hill sides for winter bedding for cattle, and forms an excellent manure. Until a very recent period it was collected and burned for the sake of the ashes, which were used in the manufactory of soap and glass ; the places where it was burnt are yet to be seen in many places in the dale ; near the Helks they are piled round with stones like a fire place, the stones yet bear evidence of the fierce heat to which they have been subjected ; near Brimham rocks they appear in the form of shallow pits in the ground.

FOUNTAINS EARTH.

At the dissolution, this Grange was valued at £6 18s. 4d. per annum. It is now divided among many proprietors.

The Village consists of a small collection of houses placed in the same manner with regard to each other, as those already noticed at Ramsgill and Middlesmoor; amongst which is an Inn, and two Chapels, one belonging to the Wesleyan, the other to the Primitive Methodists; one of the oldest houses bears on the door head the date 1655. The School is situate a short distance out of the village; an account of its foundation and history is contained in the following memorial—

" On the second day of April in the year of our Lord 1743, John Lazenby of Ramsgill[*] made his last will and testament, bequeathing thereby a small estate near Lofthouse, to three friends, their heirs and assigns for ever, in trust nevertheless for the endowment and establishment of a free school on the premises, wherein ten poor boys were to be instructed in reading, writing, and arithmetic; and also in the principles and duties of the Christian religion. The boys are eligible from the townships of Steanbeck Up, Steanbeck Down, and Fountains Earth. On the above friends as trustees he conferred the appointment of the Master, and Superintendence of the affairs of the School; ordering upon their demise that the heirs of the last survivor of them should always act in conjunction with the Churchwardens and Overseers of the Poor for the Chapelry of Middlesmoor. The school had been carryed on without interruption upwards of a century, when the late heir, ill-advisedly preferred his claim

[*] He appears to have died in the same year in which he made his will; his burial is thus entered in the Middlesmoor Registers:—
" Ramsgill. John Lazenby buried Jan. 25th 1743."

180

NIDDERDALE.

to the property of the School, intending to apply it to his own use, under the alleged ground that the devise was void under the Statute of Mortmain. The Rev[d] H. M. Hutchinson, B.A. Incumbent of Middlesmoor, assisted by Mr. William Beckwith of Stean, Churchwarden, interfered in the matter and put the case into Chancery, where it was decided by the Master of the Rolls in favour of the School; now legally and permanently established under the management of new Trustees, who are invested with power of election to vacancies, sanctioned by the Court. The case of the above Charity was tried on the 15th day of February, 1855, and enrolled on the 18th of the same month, in the same year.

Counsel for the Plaintiff—J. Murray, Esq. Lincoln's Inn.

Solicitors. T. Murray, Esq. } Whitehall Place,
C. P. Froome Esq. } London*

Trustees. { The Rev[d] Henry M. Hutchinson, B.A.
William Beckwith.
Thomas Harrison.
Richard King.
Robert Smith."

The endowment consists of lands which usually let for £23 per annum, which the master receives as his salary.

The Parsonage belonging to the Middlesmoor Chapelry is situate less than half a mile from this village, immediately above the place where the waters of the Nidd emerge after their subterraneous journey from the mouth of Goydon-pot. It is

---

* The above gentlemen, on account of the small endowment of the Charity, very benevolently and honourably gave their time and labour, refusing all compensation, and received only what they actually expended out of their own pockets in conducting the suit.

FOUNTAINS EARTH.

181

a substantial building of stone erected by subscription in the year 1831.*

SIKES GRANGE, another of the monastic establishments, valued at the dissolution at 66s 8d per annum, is situate a short distance east of the Parsonage. None of the buildings are old ; a door head in the present house, evidently an insertion from an older one bears I. S. 1602. The name is evidently derived from *Sikes* watercourses, which are very abundant, nearly every enclosure having one, with its stream gurgling down its sides.

LONGSIDE is the name of a long stretch of meadow and plantation on the slope of a hill, on which two or three farm houses are pleasantly situated.

ELKS or HELKS is another farm house situate a short distance eastward, towards the moor, commanding a fine prospect over the valley, and looking directly into the rugged and picturesque glen known as Helks Gill. This gill is deepest as it cuts through what may be called the shoulder of the hill in its downward course from the moorlands to the valley ; near the middle on the southern side, is a lofty, rugged cliff

---

* Copied from a memorial preserved at the Parsonage—" This Parsonage House, belonging to the Perpetual Curacy of Middlesmoor, situate on the Glebe Land, near Lofthouse, was erected in the year of our Lord 1831; and the income of the Living was augmented by Queen Anne's Bounty, obtained by the benevolent and pious contributions of the following friends of the Church—Simon Horner, Esq., Hull, £100, John Yorke. Esq., Bewerley Hall, £100, Revd. James Charnock, Bishopton Close, £20, Revd. W. Reynard, Ripon, £10, John Coates, Esq., Ripon, £5, Rev. Charlton Staunton, Sedgebrook, Notts., £10, Richard Croft, Esq., £2, Mrs. Laurence, Studley Royal, £200. The Master and Fellows of Trinity College, Cambridge, £15, William Danby, Esq. Swinton Park, £50, Revd. Webb Edge, £10, Reuben Craven, Esq., Hull, £10, Mrs. Whitaker, Hull, £5 5s., Horner Reynard, Esq., Sunderlandwick Lodge, £30.

182 NIDDERDALE.

of gritstone, shale, and plate, from which slates and flags have been quarried. A brisk mountain torrent runs at the bottom.

> " Child of the mountain glen, he comes
>   With music on his way;
> Now sings aloud, now gently hums,
>   A merry roundalay.
> Now down many a pebbly fall
>   Making gushing music,
> Then moping in a lonely hole,
>   Like a booby love sick.
> Soon again he dashes wild,
>   Among the roots and rocks,
> While echo, idly babbling child
>   His surly moaning mocks.
> Beauty dwells in every look,
> Of the merry mountain brook."

Above the house the slopes approaching the crest of the hill, are strewn with broken fragments of rock in huge irregular patches and masses. In one place, on a hollow piece of broken ground is a barrow of a square form, about twelve yards in length by four in breadth, and three feet in height. It is of a different form to those generally found in the neighbourhood, and does not appear to have even been opened or disturbed; the land about it consists of broken slopes, covered by grey rocks, and generally clothed with fern. No probable conjecture can be formed as to the time of its construction.

> " Who sleeps below? who sleeps below?
>   It is a question idle all!
> Ask of the breezes as they blow,
>   Say do they heed or hear they call?
> They murmur in the trees around,
> And mock thy voice, an empty sound!
>
> A thousand summer suns have showered
>   Their fostering warmth and radiance bright;
> A thousand winter storms have lower'd
>   With piercing floods, and hues of night,
> Since first this remnant of his race,
> Did tenant this lone dwelling place."

FOUNTAINS EARTH.

The Common called Fountains Earth moor, consisting of 3,377a. 2r. 21p. was enclosed in the year 1856, Mr. George Henry Strafford, Valuer. Three turbary grounds were left for the use of the inhabitants, two of twenty acres each and one of ten acres. On this moor is a large group of naked rocks, some of them of enormous bulk called Sypeland Crags; they are of the coarse millstone grit, like those of Brimham; the grotesque grandeur of which they imitate, though on a smaller scale, two of them a short distance from the main group are tall upright pillars, and at a distance have the appearance of giantesses in broad bonnets, from which resemblance they have received the names of "Jenny Twigg, and her daughter Tibb." When the enclosure was being made an ancient road was found, upwards of four feet in breadth, paved with stones, which for some length were taken up and used in the construction of fence walls. It appeared to have passed across the moor from Bouthwaite to an old road called *Potter Lane* in Dallowgill. If not a work of the monastic brethren of Fountains, it must have been of a much earlier age. Some of the hills on the eastward of this township, adjoining the Laverton boundary attain a considerable elevation, Jordon Moss being 1,200 feet, Kettlestang Cross 1,250, Harry Cross Edge 1,292, and Hambleton Hill 1,330.

BOUTHWAITE* is a small hamlet situate close to the road leading from Ramsgill to Kirkby Malzeard; at the back of it runs the Helks Gill Beck. This was another of the monastic granges, and worth at the dissolution £10 per annum. After that period it appears to have come into possession of a family of

---

* Written at different periods *Burthwaite*, *Brathwaite*, *Birthwaite*, and finally *Bouthwaite*, nearly every one of these terms admitting a different etymology.

184 **NIDDERDALE.**

the name of Inman, who held it for many generations ; their names are abundant for a long time in the Middlesmoor registers. One of the best and oldest houses, bears on the door head R. I. 1673. The Wesleyan Methodists have a small Chapel here.

CALVAL HOUSES* are situate lower down the valley, near the junction of a brook called Calval-house-gill with the river Nidd. Here was another of the farms of the monks, worth at the dissolution £6 18s. 4d. per annum. No remnants of the old buildings are visible—they might be of timber, and so have perished completely. At present here are two farm houses with barns, and out offices clustered around them. The buildings are all modern. On a stone over the door of the more westerly house is F. 1685. A walnut tree of considerable age and bulk appears to be the only connecting link of the monastic age with the present. This is one of the shallowest and least picturesque of the lateral gills which intersect the valley. Many plantations, chiefly of larches, have been made here ; and adjoining the moor are large patches of native wood.

WEST HOLME HOUSE, and EAST HOLME HOUSE, situate lower down the valley, near the river, were both monastic establishments, and valued at 66s. 8d. each at the dissolution. The present buildings are all modern. Opposite these places the course of the Nidd is remarkably crooked and flexuous, and has evidently changed its course more than once—hence the name of these houses,—*Holme* being a term mostly ap-

---

* The name of this place is evidently derived from the place where the calves were housed, that is from Calf-and-*hull* a low building; written at different times *Calfal House*, *Calf-house*, *Calf-hull-house*, and finally *Calvall*, or *Covill House*.

FOUNTAINS EARTH.   185

plied to a piece of low land adjacent to a running stream, which has been deposited or formed from alluvial matter washed from higher grounds.

SIGSWORTH GRANGE* is the last of the monastic farms, and was valued at the dissolution at 100s. per annum. It is situate on a ridge of land overlooking the rugged, wild wood clad gen of Doubergill, also commanding a fine view of the valley towards Bewerley and Guy's-cliffe. The present house and buildings are all modern ; in an enclosure a short distance to the westward are traces of the foundation of a building which appears to have been composed of large stones ; a great part of which has been removed for the purpose of forming fence walls. A field adjoining, full of native rocks, bears the name of "Robin Hood's Park." A spring of pure water in the wood below, is called " Robin Hood's Well." How singular to find the renowned outlaw's name associated with places so remote from his general haunts ; but as he loved to chase the deer of the monks as well as those of the king, he certainly might enjoy that sport in Nidderdale, where deer were plentiful at a much later period than that in which he lived. It is also pleasing to contemplate the outlaw quenching his thirst at this rock-born fountain.

> " Beside this crystal fount of old,·
> Cool'd his flush'd brow—an outlaw bold ;
> His bow was slackened while he drank,
> His quiver rested on the bank,
> Giving brief pause of doubt and fear,
> To feudal lords and forest deer :—
> Long since the date, but village sires,
> Still sing his feats by Christmas fires ;
> And still old England's free born mood,
> Stirs at the name of Robin Hood."

* Written at different times *Sixford, Syxfurth, Sexforth,* and now *Sigsworth,* the derivation is evidently from *Sike,* a water course, and *ford* or *furth* a crossing.

186

NIDDERDALE.

The sides of Doubergill are steep and clad with native wood, among which the hazel is very abundant. The Badger, now a rare animal in the dale is occasionally found here: Owls are abundant both here and generally in the valley. Iron has been smelted in this gill, as is evident from the heaps of slag or cinders yet remaining. At the junction of this brook with the Nidd is a small hamlet called Wath, where was some time ago a small cotton spinning factory, now converted into a corn mill.

The mineral productions of this township are not so various and valuable as in those on the opposite side of the valley. Gritstone is abundant, in many places forming large groups of crags, in others presenting bold edges; flags and slates are also found. At the upper part, at Thwaite House, coal is found, and near Lofthouse the mountain limestone appears, though not at present applied to any useful purpose.

The following statistics will show the state of cultivation, and number of cattle in 1854.

TILLAGE.	a.	r.	p.	GRASS, &c.	a.	r.	p.	CATTLE.	No.
Wheat	20	0	0	Clover	11	1	0	Horses	55
Barley	7	0	0	Pasture........	1448	3	0	Colts	18
Oats	130	3	0	Meadow	718	0	0	Milk Cows	190
Turnips	45	0	0	Sheep Walks ..	1445	0	0	Calves...............	191
Potatoes	19	1	0	Houses, Roads, &c.	161	0	0	Other Cattle	188
Fallow	0	2	0					Tups	99
				Waste attached to Farms ..	244	0	0	Ewes	1747
								Lambs	1157
				Woods	27	0	0	Other Sheep	504
				Commons......	2333	0	0	Swine	71
Total Tillage..	222	2	0	Occupiers of less than 2 acres.	6	0	0		
Grass	6389	0	0						
Total	6611	2	0	Total Grass, &c.	6389	0	0	Total Cattle ..	4110

The annual value of the township as assesed to the poor rate in 1857, was £1791 ; as rated to Property and Income

FOUNTAINS EARTH. 187

tax in 1859, £2972; and as assessed to the county rate in 1859, £2770.

The population at the different decennial periods has been, in 1801, 329; 1811, 381; 1821, 441; 1831, 413; 1841, ; 1851, 389; and in 1861, 415.

GREENHOW HILL.

After a thorough examination of the lower and upper parts of the dale, the tourist cannot do better than devote a day to an excursion to the mining grounds of Greenhow hill, and an exploration of the Stump Cross Caverns. To the geologist this will be interesting above all other things, as he will have an opportunity of surveying this metalliferous region externally as well as internally should he think proper to do so. From Pateley Bridge, the best route for a pedestrian is to pass up the west side of the river Nidd, until he reaches Foster beck, which near its junction with the former stream gives motive power to a mill for the rolling of sheet lead, and also to a bobbin turning manufactory. This brook, which is the boundary between the townships of Bewerley and Stonebeck Down, derives its water from the mining grounds, and no inconsiderable quantity of it from the mines themselves; it has generally a dirty appearance from being employed in washing the ore. On the northern side are the lead smelting works of John Yorke, Esq., of Bewerley, where all the ore raised within his royalties is smelted. These works were rebuilt in 1855, on the most modern and improved principle; by which means the noxious fumes of the lead that used to escape with the smoke, are not merely prevented from spreading their deleterious influence around, but converted into a source of profit. The external appearance is that of a long, low building of stone one storey in height, within which are two roasting furnaces, and four smelting hearths ; after being calcined in the first, the ore is smelted at the last, and run into pigs of 8 stones, or 112 lbs weight each. The blast at the smelting hearths is derived from a fan, driven by a large wheel worked by water power. After leaving the furnaces and hearths, the smoke is conducted by a series of underground flues to the condenser, where by means of another fan, also driven by a powerful water-wheel, it is forced to pass sixteen times through water before it enters the long flue or chimney ; which last is carried underground for upwards of a mile and a quarter, and the little vapour that remains after passing this tube finally escapes from an upright shaft erected on the top of Heathfield Rigg. This flue winds up the slope of the hill, and is so formed that it can be entered at different places for the purpose of clearing out the condensed smoke, or leaden soot. There is a tank provided for receiving the matter which may be washed out of this flue, by water getting into the interior. This smoke or soot has the appearance of painter's priming colour, in fact it is the same material, only wanting the oil. The quantity of lead obtained immediately from the ore, is the same as by the old process, while that which formerly escaped, but is now retained, is of considerable value ; one cleansing of the flue, which is done annually, yielding about 900 pigs of lead, worth about £800 ; the most valuable matter being obtained near the top of the flue. Previous to the erection of the present works, which immediately adjoin the old site, not a blade of grass grew on the hill for a con-

190   NIDDERDALE.

siderable distance around; the trees were blasted and withered, and even cattle grazing in the fields below were *belloned* by the pestiferous vapours :—now, a coat of vegetation is beginning to creep over the formerly naked hill, the trees in the neighoourhood retain their foliage, and cattle graze unharmed in the pastures around. The ores smelted here are those obtained from the mines of the Appletreewick Company, those of Burhill, Craven Moor and Merryfield. The lead is generally poor in silver, yielding only about $2\frac{1}{4}$ ounces to the ton, and consequently not worth the cost of extraction. The pigs at present are cast in iron moulds or pans, with the name of the mine from which the ore was won at the bottom. In early times they appear to have been cast in stone pans; one of which, yet preserved, was found inverted under the foundation when the old smelting mill was pulled down; the cavity in which the pig has been cast is about 2 feet 6 inches in length by six inches in breadth, narrowing suddenly at each end to something like a handle.

A short distance above this place, Mosscar beck, and Merry-field beck form a junction; from the latter stream is derived the water which turns the wheels and fans at the smelting works.

The valleys down which these brooks flow, and the lateral glens from which they are supplied, are the most singular, rugged, irregular, broken, disjointed pieces of ground it is possible to conceive; and if the term " riddlings of creation" can with propriety be applied to any place, it is applicable here. Their whole appearance seem to indicate that the force acting from beneath, which upheaved the limestone, that forms the mounts of Coldstones and Greenhow, has cast the super-incumbent beds of gritstone topsy-turvy in huge irregular masses, and that these masses have afterwards been subjected to the action of water in rapid motion. Seldom has it been our lot to witness such a series of

> " Crags, knolls, and mounds, confus'dly hurl'd,
> Hurl'd by primeval earthquake shock,
> And here in random ruin piled."

On the northern side the rock is gritstone, alternating with beds of shale, on the southern rises the great mass of mountain limestone, to a height of 1,400 feet above the sea level, which Professor Phillips thus describes*—" The Greenhow hill ridge rises into two eminences, called Greenhow hill and Coldstones; from both of them the beds dip rapidly to the north and south, (the dip diminishing as the distance from the axis augments) 40° 30° 20° 10°. Many metalliferous veins cross the ridge, ranging E. or E. S. E. and are traversed by north and south lines of irregular cavities called *gulphs*, which are full of broken portions of the bordering rock, and are said to ' ruin the veins.' Shales and grits of great thickness, inclosing a thin limestone, envelope on all sides the oval mass of Greenhow limestone, which is more than one hundred fathoms thick, the bottom having never been reached."

In these valleys are the levels, or openings of the principal mines now worked; and here also a great part of the mining population is located.

> Here many a hamlet-peopled well
> With hard-faced workmen smokes from the dell,
> Cunning to work with axe and hammer;
>   Cunning to shear the fleecy flock;
>   Cunning with blast and nitrous clamour,
>   To split the useful rock."

Many of the houses and clusters of houses are placed in

*Geology of Yorkshire, Vol. II. p. 245.

192 NIDDERDALE.

such holes and corners, that they can scarcely be seen till you are close upon them. At Hole-bottom, a very appropriate name, for the hills overtop it all around, is a house of a superior class, resembling the style of those erected during the reign of the second Charles. The hamlets of Hardcastle, Near and Far, the Barracks, and other thickly populated spots are located here, and the lead mine named "Prosperous," where is another smelting mill; at which the ore won from the Prosperous, Perseverance, Stony Grove, and Providence Mines is smelted. All the ground bears evidence of workings old or new, and the surface is spread with heaps of stony matter which have come from the bowels of the earth, among which are immense quantities of fine white spar.

The works of the "Sunside Mining Company" are the easiest of access, being situate about half a mile north of Greenhow hill village, at a place called Cock Hill, in a hollow between the conical mounts of limestone and the congeries of hillocks already mentioned. This Company's mines have been worked upwards of eighty years; they have workings at North Coldstones, Cockhill, East Galloway, West Galloway, and Blue Rigg. Their smelting works are at Cockhill, where is also the entrance to their principal mine. The have between eight and nine miles of "horse level," or underground tramway, which is travelled by horses in bringing out the ore; they have also, in one place a "man level" nearly two miles in length, and in another, one a mile and a half in length. The workings generally extend southward under the limestone hill, at a depth, to the horse level of one hundred and twenty yards; below which they have a shaft forty yards in depth, where a steam engine is employed. A strong current of water flows from the main level, which is turned to good account afterwards in washing the ore. Sometimes the metal is found embedded in clay, when it is easily won by the pick and shovel, but most frequently in the limestone when the operation of blasting the hard substance with gunpowder is resorted to, a more costly and tedious process, not unattended with risk, for should a shot explode by accident the life of the workman is in great danger. The horse levels, as the name implies, are of sufficient capacity to admit a moderate sized horse, and are arched overhead, where the rock is not solid enough to stand by itself; the horses walk between the rails of a tramway, drawing the low trucks or waggons, which are placed on four wheels, with a trap door at the bottom, for the more ready discharge of the load ; when brought to the *teemings*, which is an elevated wooden platform, the pin fastening the bottom is removed, the door opens, and the load at once falls through the opening. A great deal of clay, and other earthy matter is sometimes mixed with the ore, to remove which, a strong current of water, (directed at will to any point, by means of wooden troughs and spouts), is poured upon it, from a height of seven or eight feet ; while the mass below is stirred with rakes, by which means the loose earth is at once washed away. In order to remove the stony matter with which the ore is generally encrusted, sometimes limestone, spar, cawk or barytes, which last is most difficult of removal on account of its weight, the whole is broken to pieces, with a broad-faced iron mallet called a *bucker* ; after which it is again subjected to another washing in the *hotching tub*, a moveable box worked by means of a frame and long handle in water, in which it is shaken by a slight jerking mo-

194 NIDDERDALE.

tion. After this washing, it is passed through the roasting furnace, then crushed between iron rollers; thence removed to the smelting hearth, where it is purified by fire, resolved into a liquid mass, and cast into pigs, each of twelve stones weight. The mill for crushing the ore, and the bellows which produce the smelting blast are all worked by water power. The number of workmen employed by this company is about eighty. The following geological section was supplied by the late Mr. Nathan Newbould to Professor Phillips, and inserted in Geology of Yorkshire, under the title of

SECTION OF THE ROCKS AT GREENHOW HILL, IN COCK HILL LEVEL.

		feet.
Upper grit group 100 to 360.	of Brimham, Guiscliff, Poxtones, and the Wharfdale crags	
Upper plate group 186.*	Flaggy grit, called top grit...	86
	Ellenscar plate, with laminar chert, coal, and flagstone	150
Middle grit	Sandgill grit (coarse grit) ...	48
Lower plate group 345.	Grits and plates, alternating	42
	Fine grit	18
	Grits and plate alternating...	120
	Plate	144
	Top limestone	13
	Plate	8
Lower millstone grit 177.	Grit	93
	Plate	12
	Grit	48
	Plate	2
	Coal	1
	Grit	21
	Limestone and plate ...	12
	Great mass of lime stone ... and more.	600

The village of Greenhow Hill is situate on the sides of the turnpike road leading from Skipton to Pateley Bridge, at a distance of three miles from the latter place, and at an elevation of more than 1000 feet above it. The situation is high and bleak, exposed to the wind from all quarters, and possessing from its elevation a naturally cold climate. The houses are substantially built of stone, among which is an inn, "The Miner's Arms," and a Wesleyan Methodist Chapel, the latter erected in 1775. The Church, dedicated to St. Mary the Virgin, is believed to stand on the highest ground of any church in England, being upwards of 1800 feet above the level of the sea. It is a small unpretending fabric, consisting of nave and chancel under one roof, and will accommodate about 200 hearers. In style it resembles the churches of the 18th century; the east window has three cusped openings under one hood mould, and is filled with stained glass, representing our Saviour, St. John the Evangelist, and St. Peter. In the west gable are two single lights, those on the south side are double, on the north single; the intention being to have as little window space as possible, compatible with the due admission of light, on account of the stormy situation. The porch forms the first story of a small low tower, containing one bell and a clock. The pulpit and font are of stone, carved in pannels. The corner stone * was laid by Dr. Bickersteth, Bishop of Ripon, on the 3rd of June, 1857, being the first ceremony of the kind performed by him after his appointment as bishop. It was consecrated by him on the 26th of May in the following year. W. R. Corson, Esq., of

* On which is cut "This stone, laid by Robert, Bishop of Ripon, in the name of the adorable Trinity, June 3rd, 1857."

196   NIDDERDALE.

Leeds and Manchester, was the architect. The funds were raised by public subscription;* the site for church, burial ground, parsonage, and garden, was given by T. F. A. Burnaby, Esq., of Newark-on-Trent. The parsonage, erected in 1862, is an elegant and substantial building, close adjoining, and in a style corresponding to that of the church. The living (said to be only worth £80 a year) is in the gift of the Dean and Chapter of Ripon.

The district attached to this church is thus described in the *London Gazette* of August 3rd, 1860, from which time Greenhow Hill became a separate parish.

" All that part of the township of Bewerley in the parish of Ripon, in the county of York, which is situate to the west of an imaginary line, commencing on the boundary between such township, and the township of Stonebeck Down, in the middle of Ashfold Side Beck, at a point marked **A** on the plan hereunto annexed, which is opposite to a boundary stone placed on the southern bank of such Beck, and marked with the letters **G. H. C. C.** and extending thence southward in a straight line to the boundary stone on the Skipton and Pateley Bridge turnpike road, which is marked with the letters **B. M.** 1123. 2, and extending thence eastward in a straight line to the point of junction of two streams, respectively known as Sand Gill and Raven's Gill, and extending thence southward up the

---

* One circumstance connected with this subscription is deserving of mention ; the defaulter Leopold Redpath, at that time in the height of his credit, gave £20 towards the building of the church, which on the discovery of his defalcations, was returned by the Incumbent of Greenhow Hill, to the estate of Redpath then bankrupt and a prisoner, which act was noticed in terms of commendation by the Bankruptcy Commissioners.

middle of the last named stream, to the boundary between the said township of Bewerley and the township of Dacre.

And also all that part of the township of Thornthwaite, with Padside in the parish of Hampsthwaite, in the said county and diocese, which is situate to the west and north of an imaginary line, commencing on the boundary between such last named township, and the township of Dacre aforesaid, at the boundary stone marked with the letters and figures **B. M.** 1112. 8, near the south-west end of a path known as Plumpton Way, and extending thence westward in a straight line to a point in the middle of the river Washburn, which is marked **B.** on the said plan, and which is opposite to a boundary stone placed on the eastern bank of such river, and marked with the letters **G.H.C.C.** ; and extending thence up the middle of such last named river to the point where such river joins a stream called Tarn Gill, and extending thence up the middle of such last named stream to Blow Tarn, and extending thence along the north-eastern bank of such Tarn, to the boundary between the said township of Thornthwaite-with-Padside, and the township of Appletreewick, in the parish of Burnsall, in the hereinbefore mentioned county and diocese.

And also all that part of the said township of Appletree-wick, which is situate to the east of an imaginary line, commencing on the northern bank of Blow Tarn aforesaid, on the boundary between the said township of Appletreewick, and the said township of Thornthwaite-with-Padside, and extending thence north-westward in a straight line to the boundary stone, near Stubb Cross, which is marked with the letters and figures **B.M.** 1086.4, and extending thence north-eastward in a straight line to a point near Jack Hull, on the boundary between the said townships of Appletreewick and Bewerley, which is marked **C,** on the said map hereunto annexed, and which is indicated by a boundary stone marked with the letters **G. H.C.C.** ; from thence to the point first above named in the middle of Ashfold Side Beck, marked **A.** on the plan aforesaid."

The whole of this district is high ground, hardly any part of it being less than 1000 feet above the level of the sea, and the village itself 1300 ; nearly the whole of the male population is employed in, or about the mines. Many of the cottages have small farms or parcels of grass land attached ; agriculture is out of the question, the climate being too cold for corn to ripen. The fences of some of the enclosures are curiosities in their way, the stones of which they are built being of all sizes and forms, their sides presenting all kinds of lines but straight ones, and all kinds of angles but *right* ones. It is surprising that they stand, considering the tempests to which they are exposed.

Coldstones and Greenhow are the highest points of land, both of equal altitude, 1400 feet above the level of the sea,— both of a conical form, but the former is the greater mass; Greenhow being less in bulk, appears the higher from the steeper slope of its sides. Limestone is quarried and burnt on its southern side not far from the summit. Both are covered with short grass, which is invariably the case where the limestone comes to the surface; which, when manured with lime burned from the stone beneath, is remarkably rich and sweet, and when devoted to pasturage is eagerly eaten by cattle; the hay grown upon it is also of excellent quality. Trees do not thrive here, owing to the exposed situation; a few thorns and sycamores are alone to be seen near the houses, even the hardy holly and the gorse refuse to grow.

The Common, called Bewerley Moor, of which Coldstones is a part, was enclosed in the year 1858, and contained 2,804a. 1r. 25p.; Mr. James Powell, of Harrogate, valuer. One piece of ground was set apart for exercise and recreation for the use of the inhabitants of Greenhow hill, containing 8a. 3r. 20p, situate at Greenhow hill, on the north side of the road leading from Pateley Bridge to Skipton. Two Turbary Grounds and one Quarry were allotted to the Churchwardens and Overseers in trust for the use of the inhabitants.

The whole of this district for miles around is strewed with refuse from old lead mines; shafts, and openings, where the veins have been worked from the surface abound, accompanied with the remains of reservoirs which have contained water for the purpose of washing the ore. In some places the *old man* is yet worked over with profit.

Craven Keld is the name of an insignificant water course, over which the road passes near the upper end of the village; it forms the boundary between the manors of Appletreewick and Bewerley, between Craven and Nidderdale, so that insignificant as it appears, it was formerly of considerable importance. A short distance to the northward formerly stood Craven Cross, the point where the royal chase of Knaresborough forest, and the fees of the potent families of Mowbray and Clifford touched each other. At what time it was erected we know not, but the original cross was demolished before the year 1577, as is stated in an account of a perambulation of Knaresborough forest made in that year, which describes the boundary as passing "over Monga gill, to a place where

Craven Crosse *stood*, which is over against the end of Monga gill." A tall building erected for an engine house in more recent times bore the name of Craven Cross, as standing near its site. The top of this building commanded a most extensive prospect of hill and valley; it could also be seen from a great distance on all sides, but more especially from the east and west. This landmark was destroyed a few years ago. The Craven Moor Mining Company have some works immediately adjoining.

On the morning of Thursday, December 15th, 1859, the whole of the mountain limestone district, of which this place may be considered as the centre, was violently shaken by an earthquake, which took place about two o'clock in the morning, when the atmosphere was bright and clear. The surface of the ground heaved with very sensible vibrations for about six seconds, this motion was accompanied by a rumbling noise like the sound of heavy carriages passing over a hard pavement. The shock was felt in the deepest mines as well as on the surface; the miners quitted their work and fled with precipitation, thinking the roof of the mine was falling upon them; the residents in a cottage near one of the smelting mills, thought that the whole of the buildings were falling to the ground. This vibration reached as far eastward as Masham and Dallowgill, where the houses were shaken in a similar manner; and the like noise was heard also down the valley of the Nidd, as far as Dacre Banks; in a southerly direction to Blubberhouses, and up the vale of the Washburn, to the source of that river; and also along the valley of the Wharfe to its head. At Grassington the doors were thrown open, and beds heaved beneath their astonished inmates as if shaken

GREENHOW HILL.

by a strong man; many arose and searched their houses thinking to find some unwelcome intruder within; and ludicrous stories were related of others during their terror and alarm. Some miners, who were at work on Grassington Moor, sixty fathoms below the surface, felt the shock and heard the attendant noise, and thought it was the falling in of the mine. At Middlesmoor, the houses were sensibly shaken, and the windows clattered, and the upheaving of the beds were so much felt that many persons arose, thinking the houses were falling. This vibration of the earth and noise took place precisely at the same moment all over the district we have specified, nor was it felt much beyond it, being confined to the carboniferous region, extending but slightly into that of the millstone grit.

Our account of Greenhow would be incomplete were we to omit mention of its native poet, Thomas Blackah, a working miner, who has produced many pieces of poetry, which taking into consideration his situation in life are alike creditable to his talents and industry. The following verses will serve as specimens of the productions of this " mountain bard."

WINTER.

The icicle hangs on the cottage eaves,
  Not a flower adorns the green,
The trees are bereft of their beautiful leaves,
  And the robin alone is seen.

Barriers of ice obstruct the stream,
  Through the air the snow flakes fly,
And, driven along by the northern blast,
  Are drifted 'till mountains high.

The children slide on the frozen pool,
  Pursuing each other in fun;
The silent gloom of the forest departs
  At the sound of the sportsman's gun.

The upland heights where the heather grows,
   And the wild grouse rears her young,
Are coated o'er with the driven snows,
   Like a glacier all along.

The sun is veiled with the fleecy clouds,
   And refuses all day to shine;
The meadows are wrapped in their wintry shrouds,
   And the farmer has housed his kine.

No bird of the wood pours forth his song,
   Not a flower adorns the green;
Of all the hosts of the woodland throng
   The robin alone is seen.

Old Christmas comes with his hoary locks,
   With the misletoe and the holly;
The yule log in the kitchen cracks,
   And scares away melancholy.

Then the Christmas loaf and the wassail bowl
   Are passed around with joy:
Though the roaring storm without may howl
   The pleasure it cannot destroy.

When the winter of death in gloom shall come,
   With its breath so chill and keen,
May our spirits soar to that happy home,
   With Jesus for ever to reign!

This is not the production of a man who has read other poets, and reproduced their imagery and descriptions, but of one who copies from nature, and describes the scenery of his own bleak hills. We give another specimen from a poem entitled

TO THE RIVER NIDD.

Flow lovely Nidd along thy winding bed,
By towering firs, and stately oaks o'erspread!
Vale of my fathers—still to memory dear;
Thy rose-plumed bowers, though distant, I revere.
In memory's glass reflected oft I see,
The joyous scenes which graced my infancy;
The rural thicket, and the barkless pile;
The winding pathway to the well known stile;
The o'erhanging rock above the rippling rill;
The blooming heather on the adjoining hill;
The arching branches o'er the pathway spread;
The modest violet on its humble bed;

GREENHOW HILL.

The robin perching on his favourite thorn ;
The fragrance on the genial breezes borne ;
The well-known crag with prickly brambles crown'd ;
The conies sporting on the grassy mound.
When pictured deep in memory's mellowing glass,
Those lovely scenes before my memory pass,
Some secret place to muse alone I seek,
The tear drop stealing down my burning cheek.

STUMP CROSS CAVERNS.

These caverns are situate about a mile from Greenhow hill, on the left of the turnpike road leading from Pateley Bridge to Skipton and Grassington, about four miles from the first mentioned town. They were discovered in January, 1860, by William and Mark Newbould, two miners in the employ of the Craven Moor Mining Company, who were in search of lead ore, and at a depth of nine fathoms happened to cut into these subterranean caves. For easier access, a flight of steps has since been formed, and doors placed at the entrance to prevent the unauthorized ingress of the public, and also to protect it from spoliation. These curious freaks of nature are now shown as a curiosity.

After a descent of about fifty steps the entrance is reached, a natural opening in the rock, varying considerably both in height and breadth, being in some places so lofty that the roof is hardly to be seen, in others so low, that the visitor is obliged to stoop, almost to creep; sometimes the breadth is that of a large room, in other places it is only that of a narrow passage, barely admitting one person. The roof and sides are adorned with stalactites in every variety of size and form, from the smallest points, to those many feet in length which extend from the roof to the floor of the cave; these continue all along the sides and roof from beginning to end, though in some places more abundant and beautiful than in others. Frequently the snow-white stony icicles descending from above have corresponding ones rising from below to meet them, the same drops of water which lengthen the upper, falling upon and also adding to the altitude of the lower ; which, as the homely verse of Cotton says

> " doth still increase
> In height and bulk by a continual drop,
> Which upon each distilleth from the top,
> And falling still exactly on the crown
> There break themselves to mists, which trickle down,
> Crust into stone, and (but with leisure) swell
> The sides and still advance the miracle."

. Such is the process continually going on, and countless ages must have elapsed since it began, and even yet some of the petrefactions are of very diminutive size.*

The smaller stalactites are invariably hollow for some space at the lower extremity, and all of them when slightly struck have a metallic ring, and emit musical sounds, varying according to their bulk and length, like the notes of an *Harmonica*. Some of them assume the shape of curtains or depending

---

* Professor Phillips gives the following calculation as to the time occupied in the formation of stalagmite.—"The time consumed in the formation of even one stalagmitical boss is not easily determined. One of these in Ingleborough Cave, of a remarkable form, called the Jockey Cap, is fed by one line of drops. It measures about 10 feet in circumference at the base. The height is about 2 feet. It appears to contain about 8 cubic feet, or 9,450,000 grains of carbonate of lime. The drops were collected by Mr. Farrer, on the 9th of October, 1851, after a rather wet period, and it required 14½ minutes to fill one pint;-say 100 pints in a day. In this pint was found only one grain of calcareous earth, or 100 grains a day. If the water were supposed to yield up all its contained salt of lime, the number of pints of water consumed in producing this boss of stalagmite=9,450,000; and the years which elapsed in its formation=$\frac{9,450,000}{100 \text{ by } 365}$=259. In drier seasons the water is probably richer in carbonate of lime."—Mountains, Rivers, and Sea Coasts of Yorkshire, p. 84.

drapery, even to the folds, with borders of divers colours, varying from light brown to a delicate pink hue.

> " Yet all the art the chisel could supply,
> Ne'er wrought such curious folds of drapery ;
> And yet the pleats so soft and and flowing are,
> As finest folds from finest looms they were."

Frequently the details display such exquisite nicety of workmanship, that all the efforts of man's artistic skill are insignificant in comparison.

Leaving the entrance, the visitor is conducted along a succession of curves and bends,

> " like the Cretan labyrinth of old
> With wand'ring ways and many a winding fold."

No stranger should enter it without a guide, for should he happen to lose the proper direction, and nothing is more likely, and his light become extinct, he might wander for hours without being able to find his way out.

The floor is covered with a crust of stalagmite, which shines like ice ; indeed, the whole cavern, top, sides, and bottom, present nothing so prominently to the mind as an idea of frost work ; the stalactites resemble nothing so much as icicles, the floor nothing so much as a coat of ice, and the sides, where the darker native rock appears, sparkle with innumerable small stars, each flashing its tiny ray against the intruding lights of the visitor. In some places the passage has been deepened to give more easy access into the interior, when the thin coat of crystalized matter has been broken through, and a bed of sand two or three feet in thickness is found in thin beds or layers, evidently deposited from water flowing through intermittingly, intermixed with which are numerous fragments of broken stalactites. No water at present flows through, nor can any have done, so loaded with sand, since

STUMP CROSS CAVERNS.

the formation of the crust of stalagmite commenced: hence arises the question, by what means has this flow of water been cut off? or whence has come this bed of sand? Other parts of the floor bear evidence of greater abundance of water than is found at present, in the shape of small partially dried up pools, the crooked sides or ruins formed of stalagmite; and there is often a bright sheet of thin sparry deposit spreading widely from the side over the surface of the water, like a sheet of snowy ice, or the leaf of a crystal plant, narrowing the area of these fairy lakes. The explanation of this is simple. The waters charged with calcareous matter, and trickling down the stalagmitic sides of the cave, is sufficiently freed from carbonic acid when it reaches the level of the water to deposit the earth, and thus by continual accretion the edge spreads out into a surface, and the sheet of spar appears to float on the water."* Many of these small pools having become completely dry, have left the thin film of stone lying like scales at the bottom.

Many parts of the cavern have received names, generally from some peculiarity of appearance, one is called *The Pillars*, from columns of snowy whiteness rising from the floor to the roof, about 6½ feet in height, with swelling bases, curled and wrinkled all over. Some of the stalactites have the shape of the ear of a large pig or an elephant; and when a light is held within them have a most beautiful appearance, being transparent, and of different shades of colour. Though comparatively dry for its situation, it is not without its living spring, for "by the side of the path as the traveller goes" is *The*

* Phillips's Mountains, &c., p. 80

Fairy Fountain, a small well of the clearest water, supplied by a single drop from the roof, which keeps the cup filled to its brim, more curious still the water forms the cup in which it stands.

> " Deep in the heart of this stony mountain,
> Liveth a tiny fairy fountain ;
> From the marble dome it drippeth,
> Faster than the swart gnome sippeth,
> And from itself the cup it mouldeth,
> That its crystal treasure holdeth ;
> Dripping, dripping on for ever,
> Stopping, ceasing, failing never."

The Snow Drift is a congealed mass of dazzled whiteness on one side of the cavern ; *The Crystal Column* is an upright cylindrical shaft rising from floor to roof, and dividing the passage into two. Frequently from the ice-like floor rise pillars of the same substance, of the most curious and fantastic shapes imaginable, sometimes assuming those of animated natural objects ; one has the form of a gigantic pigeon, the head, neck, bill, eyes, and wings, all distinct ; two others in the place called *The Church*, have the appearance of swans; others resemble in appearance large snow white fowls, covering their chickens with their wings. Beyond the *Crystal Column* the cave is of considerable height, and the floor is composed of crystalizations resembling the head of the cauliflower. A lofty part, about four yards in height and ten in breadth, is styled *The Church*, in which a series of stalactites close together against one side may be called the *The Organ;* to make the comparison yet closer, when slightly struck in rapid succession, they emit musical sounds, like a set of bells. Here is one stalactite of uncommon beauty and singularity of form, about eighteen inches in length, hollow, and depending from a point about an inch in diameter, and gradually widening until at the orifice it is about three inches; on a light being held within the whole becomes transparent and displays a rich variety of colouring, which would do credit to the magic lamp of a fairy palace. Occasionally scenes of great beauty are produced by the guides retiring with their lights to distant parts, or behind columns, when the transparency of some of the stalactites, the snow-white hue of others, and the flashing stars which gem the roof and sides are seen to great advantage; yet, under whatever aspect we view it, the idea of the " beauteous work of frost " intrudes itself on the mind.

The *New Cavern*, which has been the most recently opened, is principally a long, narrow, flexuous passage, not very convenient to pass along. At the farthest extremity which has been yet explored, is a lofty, irregular cave, or hall, divided into aisles or avenues by rows of stalactites of many different shapes; some of them have the forms of large leaves, the edges finely cut; others are like ruffles, and seem as though they had been embroidered with variegated colours, which hues have probably been produced by the " mother water", containing a small quantity of iron in solution, along with the carbonate of lime, but then, to produce the different lines of colour it must have been intermittant; this is called *The Parlour*; the floor resembles the waves of a miniature sea petrified, curled, and wrinkled with fringes of stony foam. When lights are arranged at a distance from each other in this place, they have a remarkably fine effect; and the noise made by the guides in passing along the avenues is much augmented, and their voices sound much louder than ordinary; hence it is probable that a horn or musical instrument played here would produce some singular combinations of sound.

210 NIDDERDALE.

This is the end of the discoveries yet made, though it is almost certain that other caverns lead from these; indeed, on the sides appear openings into deeper and darker dens than any yet explored, and new wonders may be added in time to those already known.＊ The length of the parts already explored, is about 1,100 yards.

After having examined these caverns, should the tourist think proper to extend his researches further in this direction, the mountains, rocks, and caves of Craven are before him, the ruins of Barden Tower, Bolton Abbey, and the beauties of Wharfdale are on his left hand, to visit which, he may pass from the lonely "Moor Cock Inn," down the seldom visited, but highly romantic "Trowler's Gill," until he reaches the valley of the Wharfe, near Barden Tower.

＊ This is not the only cavern which has been opened at Greenhow and the neighbourhood. Professor Phillips says—"One of the most interesting caves I ever saw was opened in the course of lead-mining at Greenhow Hill. In 1825, when I reached it, by a miner's climbing shaft, it had much the appearance of a Franconian bear cave,—dust on the floor, stalactites of great size and brilliant beauty everywhere depending from the roof. It was, however, soon robbed of its sparry ornaments by tasteless visitors and greedy miners, and must now be mentioned as one of the lost wonders of Yorkshire."—Rivers, Mountains, &c,, p. 72.

SEASON FOR VISITING THE VALLEY.

The time when the scenery of this valley is seen to the greatest advantage is, from the middle of August till about the middle of October; at that season of the year there is a fine proportion of natural harmony in colour through the whole scale of objects;—in the tender green of the aftergrass upon the meadows; in the masses of grey or mossy rock, crowned by shrubs and trees; in the small irregular patches of standing corn, or stubble fields; in the hill sides glowing with fern of divers hues; in the calm and bright reaches of the river; and in the foliage of the trees, through all the tints of autumn— from the pale and brilliant yellow of the birch and ash, to the deep green of the unfaded oak and alder, and the ivy upon the trees and rocks.

The next best time is probably in the latter part of May and the month of June, as then the days are long and the weather generally fine; and there is a novelty in seeing the country put on its summer dress. The native trees are scarcely in full leaf, but the want of depth of shade is compensated by the diversity of foliage,—in the blossoms of the fruit and berry bearing trees, which abound in the woods; in the golden flowers of the broom, which is found in many of the copses and gills. In the woods also, such as Ravensgill, Guy's-cliffe, and others, with a northern aspect, and in the deep dells, many of the spring flowers still linger, while the more open and sunny places are stocked with the flowers of approaching summer. And over all, there is the pleasure of listening to the music of the thrushes and linnets, chanting their songs in the copses, woods, and hedgerows; and the larks thrilling theirs in the bright blue air above,

> " O'er fell and fountain sheen,
> O'er moor and mountain green,
> O'er the red streamer that heralds the day,
> Over the cloudlet dim,
> Over the rainbow's rim
> Musical cherub, soar, singing away."

The voice of the cuckoo has also a sound of more than ordinary interest when heard in the depths of a lonely glen; then there are the flocks of lambs, with their confident black and white faces, bounding in glee along the slopes of the hills; then also comes the shadowy cloud, the gleam of sunshine, and the rainbow.

Wet weather is certainly the least propitious time to visit a mountainous country, but even that is not without its advantages, for the brooks which flow down every gill, during dry weather trickle in slender streams, or creep unseen along their rocky beds, after a rainy day, or a sudden thunder shower, come bounding down like cascades of bubbles and foam; and the waterfalls, though not numerous or of large proportions, then put on their grandeur and are well worthy of a visit.

Even in winter on a fine day, there is a beauty left, after the splendour of autumn has passed away; the oak coppices on the sides of the hills retain their russet leaves, the birch stands conspicuous with its silver stem, the hollies, with green leaves and scarlet berries, have come forth to view from among

SEASON FOR VISITING THE VALLEY.

the deciduous trees, whose summer foliage had concealed them; the ivy is now plentifully apparent upon the stems and boughs of the trees, and upon the steep rocks. In place of the deep summer green of the herbage and fern, many rich colours play into each other over the surface of the hills; turf, beds of withered fern, and grey rocks being harmoniously blended together. The mosses and lichens, are never so fresh and flourishing as in winter, if it be not a season of frost, and their minute beauties prodigally adorn the foreground. Wherever we turn we find these productions of nature scattered over the walls, banks of earth, rock and stones, and upon the trunks of trees, with the intermixture of several species of small ferns, now green and fresh; and to the observing passenger, their forms and colours are a source of inexhaustible admiration.*

DWELLINGS IN THE DALE.—These are scattered over the valley, with the exception of the one town, and three or four small villages, seated under the hill sides, and generally at the intersection of some of the lateral gills; to particularize which would be useless, as the traveller cannot fail to see it at once from Pateley Bridge upward to the head of the valley. They are frequently single, though sometimes in clusters of two or three,

> " Clustered like stars some few, but single most,
> And lurking dimly in their shy retreats,
> Or gleaming on each other cheerful looks,
> Like separated stars with clouds between."

The dwelling-houses and out-buildings are the colour of the native rock of which they are built, and generally covered with

---

*For some of these observations we are indebted to a small work by the late W. Wordsworth, entitled *Lake Scenery*.

214   NIDDERDALE.

thick grey slates, also obtained in the valley; the yellow
tinge of the stone, in a few years becomes weather-stained,
and partly over-grown with lichens, so as in a short time to
mingle in the landscape without any violent contrast of colour.
Many of them have porches at the front entrance, and a few
yet remain thatched with ling from the neighbouring moors,
but these are .rapidly on the decrease, a great number of
houses in the valley having been built within the last sixty
years, the custom being to build on a new site near the old,
which is left standing to do service as a stable or cowhouse.
In the front is commonly a small garden, with potherbs
and borders for flowers, for the dalesman likes to have a
flower in the button hole on a Sunday: sometimes a small
shed for bees, a plum, cherry, or other fruit tree is occasionally trained on the front, which generally faces the south;
orchards are rare; a spout conveying water from some
spring into a stone trough near the door, may be said to complete the external appearance of the generality of dwellings in
the dale. Near some of them we find a clump of sycamores,
which form a broad and grateful shade in summer.

The height of the country, coldness, and wetness of the
climate, make it necessary that the cattle should be housed in
winter; for this purpose numbers of buildings are scattered
about amongst the enclosures, for holding the cattle and the
hay on which they are fed.

ROADS.—Until within the last fifty years, the roads in the
valley were of the most miserable kind, and wheel-carriages
were rarely used, the sledge performing the farm work, articles
to and from a distance were carried on horses backs. Now
there is a good road from Pateley Bridge to Lofthouse, and no

ROADS. 215

further, for though it passes by way of Middlesmoor and the Lodge into Coverdale, it is seldom in good repair. Owing to the population not being collected in villages, but scattered as it were at random all over the dale, the whole district is intersected by lanes and pathways, leading from house to house and from field to field; these are never in straight lines, but form curves and zigzags of every imaginable kind, and where fenced with stone walls, in the lower parts of the valley, are often bordered with a fringe of ashes, hazels, and wild roses, with lines of tall fern at their base, while the walls themselves, if faced with a bank of earth, are overspread with mosses, small ferns, (Polypody), wild strawberries, geraniums and lichens. Along these roads and tracks are numerous bridges and stiles often of the rudest and most primitive kind, some of them in wild picturesque spots are appropriate subjects for the artist's pencil.

INHABITANTS, MANNERS, CUSTOMS, LANGUAGE, &c.

The genuine Nidderdale dalesman is a tall, athletic personage, with considerable length of limb, plenty of bone and muscle, but not much inclined to corpulency; somewhat of the Watt Tinlinn type, described by Sir Walter Scott, as

> " of stature passing tall,
> But sparely formed and lean withal."

or, as his brother dalesmen of Wensley were more familiarly described in the old ballad of Flodden Field, as

> " Lusty lads and large of length,
> Who dwelt on Seimer-water side."*

* The men of Nidderdale are also mentioned in this old ballad as taking part in the battle:—

> "With many a gentleman and squire,
> From Rippon, Ripley, and Rydale,
> With them marched forth all Massamshire,
> With Nosterfield and Netherdale."

The men of the Craven dales, to whom those of Nidderdale have a close affinity are thus described:—

> "From Pennigent to Pendlehill,
> From Linton to Long Addingham,
> And they that Craven coasts did tell,
> All with the lofty Clifford came.
> All Staincliff Hundred went with him,
> With striplings strong from Worledale,
> And all that Haughton hills did climb,
> With Langstroth too, and Littondale.
> Whose milk-fed fellows, fleshly bred,
> Were fit the strongest bows to bend
> All such as Horton Fells had fed,
> On Clifford's banner did attend."

INHABITANTS, LANGUAGE, ETC. 217

His countenance is fair, generally florid, the freshness of the colour being retained, even to old age ; with great strength and agility, and a physical conformation altogether that wou not have disgraced an old Viking, or Scandinavian sea-king. Though not so quick witted and wide-awake as the inhabitants of large towns, they are shrewn and intelligent, kind and sociable, and almost every one with characteristic peculiarities of his own, distinct from those of his neighbours ; not drilled into a dull uniformity by the influences of an useless civilization, speaking more freely their genuine thoughts and feelings with little of duplicity or crooked cunning in their composition ; their general uprightness of conduct is beyond question ;* but like the northern people, Danes and Norwegians, from whom they are descended, they have no objections to join in " the feast of shells," as one Scottish bard would style it, or in the words of another :

> " To sit bousing at the nappy,
> Getting fou and unco happy."

On these occasions when provoked they are somewhat quarrelsome, but seldom have recourse to the law to settle their differences. In short, they are a community of farmers and shepherds, for the tradesmen are not exclusively so, but occupy a few acres of land in the valley, and have also a right to dig

---

* This freedom from crime is not only remarkable at present, but appears always to have been so. Among the list of applicants for admission into the sanctuaries of Durham and Beverley we only find the name of one man from Nidderdale. John Wilkinson of Bewerley, and he was only a debtor, owing money to divers persons in London and York, which he was unable to pay, and fled to Durham fearing he should be imprisoned for nonpayment thereof, Aug. 19th, 1521. No traditions of murder exist save that which gave name to "Deadman's Hill." A solitary instance of sheep stealing is nearly all that the memory of the oldest inhabitant can supply; there certainly are a few poachers, but this is not regarded as a very heinous offence, the inhabitants generally having a liking for the sports of the field.

218 NIDDERDALE.

peat on the moors; with no superior among them, they mingle on equal terms, masters and servants all sitting and eating at one table. They are not skilful as agriculturalists for which their steep hill sides are not adapted; but they have considerable knowledge of cattle and sheep; indeed, the getting of their hay and the care of their cattle and sheep are their chief employments; very rarely do you meet a farmer in the upper part of the dale without his attendant dog or dogs. The tenor of their lives is sober and uniform; with occasional exceptions, as at a wedding, when all the friends of the parties muster in strength, and ride to church on horseback, and return at anything but a sober, steady pace. A general display of hospitality is also made at funerals by the more wealthy class, numbers are invited, and all must have dinner; a Methodist Love Feast, or Camp Meeting is also a great day with the more youthful part of the population; but above all and over all, the annual feast (sometimes called rather profanely, we think, " Nidderdale Rant,") is the grand rejoicing time; the whole population then appears to abandon itself to festivity and pleasure; hospitality is practised with a liberal hand; to enter a house at that time and not partake of the good things provided for the occasion is considered in the light of an insult. In rambling over the dale collecting materials for this volume, in every house we entered, we found a frank and kindly welcome, and never to our numerous inquiries did we receive a rude answer, or a curt reply. The inhabitants of the dale are also distinguished for their love of music, and their general skill as performers, both vocal and instrumental. The Yorkshire dales have long been noted for their excellent singers, and Nidderdale is not behind them in this respect. The editor of the *Musical Times*,* in writing of one of Jackson's oratorios being performed in the church of Pateley Bridge, thus mentions the musical talent of the neighbourhood :— " by far the larger proportion of the players and singers were of the Dale, and judging from the few houses and many performers, every roof appeared to render its tribute, and the excellent method of their reading shewed that the fame this part of the country enjoyed, even in Handel's time, is still well-deserved." Many of them are also skilled in meteorology ; dwelling in lonely places, they observe the positions of the clouds and mists on the hills, the direction of the winds, and the sounds of the waters in the valley, and prognosticate the weather with almost unerring certainty.

The inhabitants of the upper part of the dale generally intermarry with their neighbours, and a large amount of relationship consequently exists among them. Some families are very numerous, reckoning their various subdivisions, amongst which that of the BAYNE'S was at one time conspicuous, at the beginning of the eighteenth century they were occupiers of land in nine different places in the chapelry of Middlesmoor alone. The HORNERS were another numerous family, who at the same period were occupiers of land in seven places ; both these families appear to have declined in number in more recent times. VERITY is now a very common surname, especially in the upper townships. RAYNER, is also a name of frequent occurrence. SMITHS, though not wanting, are not numerous as in some places. GRANGE is a common name in the lower part of the valley, which may be partly accounted for by the many granges of the monastic houses

* Vol. III, p. 51.

220 NIDDERDALE.

formerly located here, of which some of their progenitors might be occupiers, and thence derive their surname. NEW-BOULDS are abundant in the mining districts; and the SCAIFES' are numerous in Hartwith and Dacre.

Of LANGUAGE.—The most enduring parts are those terms which have been conferred on natural objects, as mountains and rivers. A few British words may be found in Nidderdale, as in

Douber-gill—the black water—applied to a stream which rises on the eastern side of the dale, and running in a south-westerly direction, divides the townships of Bishopside and Fountains Earth; the syllable *gill* is superfluous, and added afterwards by another people.

Nidd, the name of the principal river, is also probably British.

Castlestead from *castellum*, a fort, is due to the Roman occupation; and also those other places where *castle* occurs, as *Hardcastle*, &c.

Of Saxon nominatives we have not many, none of their *tons* or towns appear to have been located here; of their *hams* or homes, we have not many, *Brimham* being the most prominent; of their *halls*, from its Domesday spelling *Wiveshale*, we can readily believe that one stood where *Wilsill* now stands; of their *lea*, or *ley*, a field, we have instances in *Winsley*, *Pateley*, *Bewerley*, and *Limley*; of *field* itself, we have *Heathfield*, *Merryfield*, *Blaesfield*; of *ing*, a meadow by a river side, we have no instance except perhaps in *Angram*—the home in the watery meadow—which would serve to prove that however thinly their dwellings were scattered, the Saxons had settlements along the whole length of the dale.

INHABITANTS, LANGUAGE, ETC. 221

Whernside or *Quernside*, the millstone hill, or the place whence the *querns* were obtained is also referred to a Teutonic origin. This term is now applied to two of the highest mountains in the dale. *Hambleton*, or *Hambledon*, the name of another hill of a conical form, is from the *Alemmanic himmel*, a covering, from the supposed resemblance of the shape of the hill to the *heavenly vault;* this term occurs in many different languages, and in widely distant places, as in the *Himalaya* mountains in India.

Of Danish and Norwegian occupation and nomenclature we have more numerous instances—

Dale, a valley, is from the Scandinavian.

Thwaite, an isolated piece of land, "severed from a wood, grubbed up and made arable," of which within our limits are *Gowthwaite*, *Bouthwaite*, *Armathwaite*, *High Thwaite*, and *Thwaite House*.

Force or *Foss*, a water fall, of frequent application, as *Padkin Foss, Park Foss, Cliff Foss*, &c.

Fell, a mountain, occurs in *Meuphar Fell*, and is also a general term. *How* and *Haugh*, applied to a round hill, are not uncommon, as in *Greenhow hill*, the *hill* superfluous, and added afterwards by those who did not know that *how* signified the same thing, *How-Stean-beck, How-gill*, &c.

Holme, is also a common term for a piece of low land by a river side, we have *Holme House*, &c.

Rigg, is frequently applied to the back of a hill, and also to nearly everything else that has a back, we have *Heathfield Rigg, High Riggs, Low Riggs*, &c.

Of *Thorpe*, Danish, a village, we have no instance, except perhaps *Trope* may have been originally such. We select a few more terms of common occurrence applied to natural objects.

Tarn, a Norse term, applied to a small mountain lake is also common, as *Brimham Tarn*, *Guy's-cliffe Tarn*, *Blow Tarn*, *Priest's Tarn*, *Poxtones Tarn*, *Woodale Tarn*, *Coverdale Tarn*, &c. *Beck*, Danish, a brook, as applied to a considerable stream of water is almost universal, instances will occur to every one.

Croft and *Garth*, as applied to small enclosures near houses, are common.

Jordan, occurs at least three times, applied to elevated mosses, or pieces of watery ground, and is also from the Norse *earth*.

Don, a hill, occurs sparingly, *Yeadon* being the only instance, and it is sometimes written *den*.

Knott, a small rocky protuberance on the side of a mountain, is found two or three times, once as applied to a rather high hill near the Stump Cross Caverns—*Nursa Knott*, 1274 feet in height.

Scar, an escarpment, or range of rocks, as *Beggarmote Scar*, *Scar-house*.

Slack, is a hollow, or shallow valley. *Wham* is much the same, but marshy, and always accompanied with water.

Grange, notwithstanding the almost universal and long continued Monkish occupation of the valley, this term for a monastic farm, with its homestead and appurtenant buildings is not common—*Bollershaw Grange*, *Sigsworth Grange*, and *Sikes Grange*, being the only instances.

Shaw, an open space between woods, occurs in *Hayshaw*, *Blayshaw*, *Bollershaw*, *Fogshaw* and other places.

INHABITANTS, LANGUAGE, ETC. 228

Keld, applied to a spring head or well of water, is of frequant occurrence.

Sike, a natural water-course, is very common.

Dike, is most frequently applied to an artificial water-course, but not always, we have sometimes even heard this term applied to a large river.

Laverock is twice found in the valley of the Nidd, once affixed to *House* and once to *Hall*, and is probably from the Scottish *Laverock*—a skylark.

Stang, occurs twice within our district, applied to hills of a considerable height.—Kettlestang on the east, 1250 feet, and Rainstang, near the top of the dale, 1488 feet high.

Many more terms of this kind might be given, but the above will be sufficient for the general reader, and the philologist if not already aware of their existence, knows where to find them.

Much of the bread used in the upper part of the dale is made of oatmeal, baked into thin cakes called *clapcakes* ; this household institution is claimed by Professor Worsade as essentially Danish ;" in order to make the oaten-bread commonly used in these parts, for *clap-bread*, (Dan *Klappe-bröd*) or thin cakes beaten out with the hand, the dough is laid on the *clap-board*." The learned Professor is quite correct as to the name, and also to the use of oaten bread in both countries, but not so as to the method of making the *cakes*.

There are some peculiarities in the dialect of Nidderdale seldom heard elsewhere, one is the use of the pronoun *ye ;* in all cases where *thou* or *you* is used by others, the dalesman puts in his emphatic *ye*. Another is the use of the open vowels, especially *a*, which he nearly always pronounces as

224   NIDDERDALE.

aa; for instance, dale becomes *daal*, sale—*saal*, ale—*yaal*, and so of others. Another is their frequent and excessive use of *rr*, while some affectedly strive to avoid its utterance at all, the dalesman gives it full force, and frequently doubles it, for instance, near is *narr*, there—*tharr*, hair—*harr*, and even these is *thirr*. These remarks only apply to the upper part of the valley; near Pateley Bridge and lower down frequent intercourse with strangers has smoothed the language. At Greenhow hill the dialect of Craven may be heard, slightly modified by that of Nidderdale, the chief difference being in the pronunciation of of some of the words. There are not many popular rhymes or songs in the dialect, we only remember one piece, of which the following is a specimen, and it does not contain any of their peculiar idiomatic expressions—

      "Dear Lockwood,— Hevin a lile bit o' time,
An knawin ye werr fond ov a lile bit o' rhyme,
I thowt I wad write e that queer composition,
An tell ye our Journa an' present condition,
On the day that we parted beside Bardin mill,
We paddled on slowly towards Greenha hill,
But lile did we think when we left ye at Bardin,
That our journa to Greenha wad hae been sike a hardin;
Why it rain'd, an it reekt, barn, ye nivver saw sike weather,
'T wad hae wet a coaat throu 'at warr maad 'o bend leather.
An th' sky aboot Girstan warr as black as a raaven,
You mud really hae thowt it warr boune to drownd Craaven.
This lasted a lang time, an then it grew finer,
An an last we gat saaf to th' Arms o' the Miner;
Whaar Sunter the landlord, ten barns an a wife,
Whaar tuggin awa at the trials o' life."•

Short proverbial expressions or rather similies are abundant, and frequently applied ;† many persons have peculiar phrases

• We have been told that this piece was written by Mr. Benson Bailey, once a schoolmaster at Lofthouse.   •

† These are short pointed expressions, as—"White as snow," "Green as grass," "Blue as a whetstone," "Grey as a Badger," "As big as a house end," "as dark as *pick* (pitch)" "As wet as sap," "As dry as a fish out of water," &c., &c.

INHABITANTS, LANGUAGE, ETC. 225

of their own, which they introduce whether they will suit the subject of conversation or not. This subject might be extended to any length, and a dictionary compiled of the dialect; but we shall content ourselves with noting a few peculiar words, omitted by Johnson, Walker, and the other fashionable lexicographers.

Arr, the mark of a healed wound. *Arran*, a spider. *Aáske*, a water newt. *Agworm*, an adder. *Anters*, or *Ananters*, in case of, as *Ananters* he come, in case he should come. *Addle*, to earn. *Anenst*, over against, opposite.

Bain, near; the *Bainest way* is the shortest way. *Badger*, a travelling grocer and butter merchant, also a buyer and seller of corn on a small scale. The former of these is a well-known character in the dales, going round from house to house collecting butter, eggs, poultry, &c., and supplying the inhabitants with groceries and other light goods. *Baarn*, a child, but not unfrequently in familiar language applied to a grown person. *Beild*, a shelter. *Barguest*, a terrific being, an imaginary hobgoblin, sometimes applied to a worthless, ragged, ill-mannered fellow. *Brant*, the steep slope of a hill. *Brownleeming* or *leemer*, a ripe hazel nut. *Blea*, lead colour, spoken of the face or hands of any one discoloured with cold. *Blake*, a deep yellow colour. The housewives of Nidderdale like to see their butter *blake*. *Busk*, a bush, *Brea*, the broken bank of a river. *Bunch*, a kick with the foot.

Cadger, in many places understood to be a beggar, but not so here,—he is a miller's man who goes from house to house collecting corn to grind, and returning it in meal. *Cletch*, a brood of chickens, goslings, &c. *Cowl*, to scrape together. *Creel*, a kind of basket made of thin slips of the hazel or willow.

o

226 **NIDDERDALE.**

Cheslop-skin, the stomach of a calf salted and dried, which is used in the making of cheese to coagulate the milk, rennet.

Dowly, lonely, dull. *Dree*, tedious, wearisome. *Dwine*, to pine away.

Easings, the eaves of a house. *Eldin*, fuel, chiefly applied to peat and turf.

Fash, labour, hardship. *Feal*, to hide. *Fettle*, to clean, to improve, to be in good condition is to be in *good fettle*. *Flay*, to frighten. *Fluzz*, to make blunt, to bruise. *Fore-elders*, forefathers, ancestors.

Gate, way, a road, a *fooit-gaate*, a foot-path. *Gain*, near, synonymous with *bain*. *Gimmer*, an ewe lamb. *Grip*, a narrow open drain. *Gob*, the mouth.

Helm or *Hellam*, a shed for cattle, carts, &c. *Hippins* stepping stones across a brook or river. *Hullot*, an owl, often called a *Jinny Hullut*.

Kelk, to kick. *Kite*, the belly. *Lake*, to play. *Lait*, to seek. *Lea*, a scythe. *Laith* or *Lair*, a barn. *Lile*, little. *Loffer*, lower. *Lite*, to expect, to wait for. *Lick*, to beat, a good *licking, benselling, walloping, hideing, drubbing, paiking, hezeling*, are synonymous, and equivalent to a thorough *beating;* the language of the dale is rich in words of this class, we have not given them all. *Lowe*, a flame. *Lown*, calm. *Limmers*, the shafts of a cart.

Mad, angry. *Maddled*, confused. *Masalgin*, a mixture of rye and wheat. *Moudy-warp*, a mole.

Neaf, the fist. *Neb*, the bill of a bird. *Nope*, a blow. *Neuk*, a corner.

Reaan, the piece of land by the side of a fence in a ploughed field. *Reasted*, applied to a horse that gibs, and

INHABITANTS, LANGUAGE, ETC.

will not work, restive ; also *rusty* bacon. *Reek*, smoke. *Roaak*, small, hazy rain. *Ruckle* or *Rockle*, a small heap or pile of anything ; peat on the moors is piled to dry in *ruckles ;* and an upright pile of stones, placed as a boundary, is a *stone-ruckle.*

Scaddle, unsteady, easily frightened. Is this the·original of the Americanism *Scedaddle!* *Scroggs*, low, rough bushes. *Scumfish*, to stifle. *Shive*, a slice. *Swelted*, overdone with heat. *Sleck*, to quench. *Sipe*, to drop slowly, to ooze. *Stirken*, to congeal, to stiffen. *Swap* or *Cowp*, to exchange.

Tharf, slow, unwilling, afraid ; this word appears to be synonymous with *Arf*. *Threave*, a measure of number containing twelve sheaves of straw, and twenty-four of ling. *Torfle* or *Turfle*, to die a natural death, chiefly applied to animals, especially sheep. *Uncuth*, strange. *Urchin*, a hedgehog.

Walsh, insipid, tasteless. *Wankle*, weak, uncertain. *Weng*, a thong. *Whemmel*, to turn a vessel upside down. *Whelk*, a great lump. *Wizzand*, shrivelled, withered.

Many fragments of old superstitions and customs yet linger among the lonely dwellers in the valley of the Nidd. The "night-tripping fairies" have hardly·yet passed out of real existence ; some of the older inhabitants yet see, "or think they see" them gambol on the hills and dance in the meadow, forming the dark green circles in the grass "whereof the ewe bites not." A belief in witchcraft, or something resembling it, called the evil wish, even now exists, though far from general. The dreaded *Barguest* used to pace his midnight rounds, striking the hearts of the belated villagers with fear ; and which said barguest was often a most ugly beast, some-

228   NIDDERDALE.

times like a bear, sometimes like a dog, with eyes of large dimensions, and often dragging a chain along with him. The ghost or spirit yet haunts the place where murder was most foully done ages ago. There is rather a dark superstition connected with the badger, an animal formerly very numerous in the dale—that they are the *pigs of the "evil one;"* and stories are told of their capture alive by poachers, and of their attempting to carry their prizes home in sacks, until the demonaic swine became so heavy that they were obliged to be abandoned from inability to carry them further. The croaking of the raven yet bodes death ; but the raven has now become a rare bird in the valley. The magpie crossing the traveller's path yet indicates ill-luck. To kill the robin or the swallow, is certain to be followed by misfortune to their destroyer ; a harmless superstition which often protects those homely and beautiful birds.

The old Christmastide festivities derived from Danish and Saxon ancestors, yet linger in the dale as loathe to leave. The *yule-clog* is yet lighted with due solemnity on Christmas eve ; in some cases a fragment of that of the previous year has been preserved, and is used to ignite the new one, which after burning a certain length of time is preserved in its turn to light that of the following year.* This blaze of logs at *Yule-*

---

* Among the words in the popular language that still remind one, of ancient Scandinavian customs, those of *yuletide,* *yuling,* (Christmas), *yule-candles,* (Dan. Julelys), and *yule-cakes,* (Dan. Julekager), deserve particular notice. Christmas was certainly kept as a solemn feast among the Anglo-Saxons, but it does not appear to have had that importance with them which it had with the Scandinavians ; of which this is a proof, that the old name of Christmas (*Yule*) is preserved only in those districts of the north that were more especially colonized by the Northmen. Yule, or the mid-winter feast, was, in the olden times, as it still partly is, the greatest festival in the countries of Scandinavia.

tide is doubtless derived from the Danes, who settled extensively in the kingdom of Northumbria, and who celebrated the festival of their great idol *Iol*, (*Yule*), at mid-winter, with holiday, drinking, feasting, and dancing, which festivities they did not forget to celebrate when they became Christians, changing the object of their worship, while the rites remained the same.

> " Each age has deem'd the new born year
> Fit time for festival and cheer.
> Even heathen yet the savage Dane
> At Iol the more deep the mead did drain ;
> High on the beach his galleys drew,
> And feasted all his pirate crew—
> Then in his low and pine-built hall,
> Where shields and axes deck'd the wall,
> They gorged upon the half-dressed steer,
> Caroused in seas of sable beer :
> Or listened all in grim delight,
> While scalds yell'd forth the joys of fight.
> Then forth in frenzy would they hie,
> And wildly loose their red locks fly ;
> And dancing round the blazing pile,
> They make such barbarous mirth the while,
> As best might to the mind recall,
> The boisterous joys of Odin's hall."
>
> Sir Walter Scott—*Marmion.*

The festival yet remains among the descendants of this people, though far removed from their native home— the feast of

Yule bonfires were kindled round about as festival-fires, to scare witches and wizards ; offerings were made to the gods—the boar, dedicated to *Freyr*, was placed on the table, and over it the warriors vowed to perform great deeds. Pork, mead, and ale abounded, and yuletide passed merrily away with games, gymnastics, and mirth of all kinds. It is singular enough that even to the present day, it is not only the custom in several parts of England to bring a garnished boar's head to table at Christmas, but that the descendants of Northmen, in Yorkshire, and the ancient Northumberland, do not even now neglect to place a large piece of wood on the fire on Christmas Eve, which is by some called the *yule-block*, by others *yule-clog*, or *yule-log*, (perhaps from the old Scandinalian *låg*, *log*, a felled tree; (Norwegian, *laag*. Superstitious persons do not, however, allow the whole log to be consumed, but take it out of the fire again, in order to preserve it until the following year. Exactly similar observances of Christmas customs still exist in the Scandinavian North,"—Worsaae's Danes and Norwegians in England, p. 83—4.

firmity, *(frumity,)* cheese, and the loaves of spiced bread, with the nut-brown ale foaming over the rim of the old family tankard ; the tall mould candle, (the annual gift of the family grocer), proudly rising above the well-furnished board, with decorations of evergreen boughs. Bands of singers gather together on the eve, and sally forth at midnight to serenade the villagers and dwellers in the lonely farm houses with a perfect storm of music. The churches and windows of the houses are decorated with twigs of the laurel and holly. Crowds of children on the morning of Christmas and New Year's day pass from house to house with loud clamourous greetings, asking for Christmas boxes and New Year's gifts. *He* who enters his neighbour's house first on the morning of Christmas day is styled *the lucky bird,* should a female enter first it is regarded as an evil omen. As part of the cheer provided in every household for Christmas is a cheese, the guest is often pressed to taste it with the current expression, " *come yer'r like to taaste it, for ye kna tharr's a month's happiness for ivvery different cheese ye taaste.*" This appeal is generally final, as who can resist such a temptation ? The graceful and martial sword dance is yet practised at Christmastide by the young men of the dale ; their dresses for this purpose are of many colours, and their persons are adorned with a profusion of ribbons and other ornaments. In spite of all the changes of modern times which have swept old customs away life chaff, we are happy to know that

> " Still linger in our northern clime,
> Some remnants of the good old time."

Much might be written on these subjects ; the language spoken in the valley of the Nidd offers a fruitful field of inquiry to

INHABITANTS, LANGUAGE, ETC. 281

the philologist, and would yield much curious and interesting matter for dissertation in the hands of a person well skilled in the ancient northern languages of Europe, as a great part of it is of Scandinavian and Saxon origin, and even yet possesses a close affinity to those tongues. The language of old Chaucer, " that well of English undefiled," and that of our earliest English writers, might be elucidated from the current speech of Nidderdale. Though not an usual custom in works of this kind to particularly notice the manners, customs, and language of the inhabitants, we could not quit our subject without giving a hasty glance at each of them, as we believe, if properly elucidated, they form a chapter in the history of human nature, both useful and interesting, not merely to the antiquary and local historian, but to the man of thought and the philosopher, whose study is humanity under all its shades and forms.

THE END.

THOMAS THORPE, PRINTER, PATELEY BRIDGE.

APPENDIX.

———o———

LOCAL COINAGE.

In the latter part of the 17th century, in order to remedy the great deficiency of small change, many of the tradesmen in the towns of England issued small coins, half-penny and penny tokens; generally bearing the name of the issuer, the date, and the value; the last of which was little more than nominal, as they were often very thin, and less than a farthing in size, and of very inferior design and workmanship. One of these was issued at Pateley Bridge, which bore the following legend—

Obverse. ROBERT x DOWNS x IN x   A sugar loaf between 16-69.

Reverse. PAITLAY x BRIDGE x

In the field. HIS HALF PENY x

This species of coinage continued in circulation from the year 1648 till 1672, when it was ordered to be discontinued by royal proclamation.

FOSSILS FOUND IN NIDDERDALE.

POLYPARIA.

Ratepora nodulosa	....	....	....	Greenhow Hill.
.... pluma	...	....	....	....	do.

MILLEPORA.

Millepora interporosa	....	....	....	Pateley Bridge.
Calamapora tumida	....	....	....	Greenhow Hill.
Cyathophyllum regium	....	....	....	Lofthouse.

APPENDIX.

CRINOIDEA.

Cyathocrinus quinquangularis		....	....	Greenhow Hill.
Producta comoides	....	....	....	do.
.... fimbriata	....	....	....	do.
Sperifera octoplicata	....	....	....	Pateley Bridge.
.... humerosa	....	....	....	Greenhow Hill.
.... resupinata	....	....	....	do
Terebratula sacculus	....	....	....	do.
Orbicula nitida	....	....	....	Pateley Bridge.

Phillips' *Geology of Yorkshire, Vol. II.*

The following CHARITY, of which the account was omitted in its proper place appears now to be completely lost to the poor of Lofthouse to whom it rightfully belongs :—

Peter Kilvington, of Ripon, gentleman, by his will bearing date September 8th, 1753, amongst other bequests, makes the following :—" I give, devise, and bequeath unto my grand-nephew, Francis Parker, son of my nephew, Francis Parker, all my messuages, lands, tenements, and hereditaments, situate and being at Lofthouse, in the said County of York, to hold to him and his heirs for ever; but my will and mind is that the same shall be charged and chargeable, nevertheless, with the payment of one pound per annum to the poor of Lofthouse, at Christmas, in every year for ever."—The said Peter Kilvington was buried at Pickhill, June 27th, 1755. The estate has since passed into other hands and the humane intentions of its owner have become a dead letter.

Since the pedigree of the family of Skaife, of Braisty Woods, at page 111, was printed, additional information has made the following alterations and corrections necessary :—

Robert Skayf had charge of the Abbots' sheep at Brimham, in 1456-7, and in 1458-9 was keeper of the cattle at Braithwaite Grange in Nidderdale. His son

Robert Skayffe, was keeper of the cattle at Braisty Woods, for the Monastery of Fountains in 1480, and also in 1484; his son

William Skayff was also keeper of cattle at the same place in 1493. He had issue, two sons—Robert, who died in 1569, and* William Skafe of Braisty Woods, in 1540. He had, with other issue—a son

* In a survey, &c.

APPENDIX.

John Skaife, of Low Laithe, in Braisty Woods, who was twice married. By his first wife he had five sons, John, (from whom the Skaifes of Low Laithe), William, Richard, Francis, and Robert. By his second wife Margaret Hardcastle, (m. 12th April, 1562.) he had, with other issue, a son,

Thomas Skaife, born in 1563, who, in 1601, purchased a lease of an estate at Braisty Woods, for the term of 999 years, from Sir William Ingilby, Knight, of Ripley, which is yet held by his descendants, and what is most singular the owner for nine generations in succession has borne the name of Thomas.

Thomas Skaife, son of the above, by his wife Alice, had, with other issue, a son

Thomas Skaife, born in 1616-7; he built the present house in 1656, and died about 1662. By his wife Ann, he left, with other issue, a son

Thomas Skaife, born in 1651-2, who married in 1677, Jane, daughter of John Lupton, of Braisty Woods, and died in 1703, being succeeded in the estate by his only son

Thomas Skaife, of Braisty Woods, gentleman, born in 1688, married in 1715, Ann, daughter of Lawrence Allanson, of Littlethorpe, near Ripon.

On page 112, at line 14 from the top—for " Manchester " read " Littlethorpe."

BEWERLEY v. DACRE.

Of the somewhat remarkable and protracted law suit between the townships of Bewerley and Dacre, mentioned at page 76, we were in expectation of giving a full and particular account, and also the substance of some of the documents produced on that occasion, which have special reference to the history of the latter township, but in this we have been disappointed. Suffice it for the present to say, that the townships of Bewerley and Dacre, from about the year 1666, maintained their poor in a kind of union with each other, using a common poor house, but at the same time each paying proportionally to the number and cost of their respective poor. This arrangement led to an impression in some quarters that the two places were one township. On the formation of the Pateley Bridge Union, the Poor Law Commissioners, (properly, as

APPENDIX.

was afterwards proved,) entered them as two townships, each entitled to bear its respective proportion of parochial burthens and assessments, without reference to the other. This was not acquiesced in by the authorities at Bewerley, who took proceedings at law to compel the overseers of Dacre to make payments towards the union fund, by summoning them to attend the petty sessions at Knaresborough, in February, 1849, when the magistrates present decided that the overseers of Bewerley were right ; and those of Dacre refusing to pay, warrants of distress were issued, and the goods of the Dacre overseers sold by public auction to satisfy the demand. This proceeding produced much irritation in the minds of the inhabitants of the township, who promptly came forward to the assistance of their overseers to secure them against loss. Legal proceedings were at once commenced against the magistrates who had issued the distress warrants, and the cause was tried before the judges of assize at York, first in July, 1849, again in March, 1850, the final decision was expected to have been given in July, 1851, when the judges found the number of witnesses so great that there was no possibility of getting through with the case within the limited time ; the hearing in consequence was postponed until October in the same year, when an immense mass of documentary evidence was adduced on both sides—for the defendants, indentures, bastardy orders, indemnities, removals, appointment of constables, &c. The prosecutors produced extracts from Domesday book, the valor ecclesiasticus, ministers' accounts, ancient accounts of the possessions of the Monks, subsidy rolls, appointment of constables for the township of Dacre, land tax assessments, and a great many miscellaneous documents, in each of which either the township of Dacre, or the township of Bewerley was separately named. After a protracted hearing of six days' duration, and the examination of a great number of witnesses, it was finally decided that Dacre and Bewerley were separate townships, and the damages to be paid by Bewerley were £1,115 17s. 1d.

Page 155, for " *Elgin's Hole*" read *Eglin's Hole*.

Page 194, it is stated that the lead ore " is passed through the roasting furnace, then crushed between iron rollers," this is erroneous, it is crushed *before* it is roasted.

Page 204, line 14, for " the entrance," read " the cavern."

J. METCALFE & SON'S
UNRIVALLED
PALE ALES
AND
PORTER.

THE CROWN HOTEL,
PATELEY BRIDGE,
ESTABLISHED 1767.
WILLIAM NEWBOULD,
PROPRIETOR.

THIS OLD-ESTABLISHED AND FIRST-CLASS
FAMILY AND COMMERCIAL HOTEL
Has every accommodation for Parties Visiting

PATELEY BRIDGE, STUMP CROSS CAVERNS,
BRIMHAM ROCKS, &c.

WINES AND SPIRITS
OF THE FINEST QUALITY.

DAY PARTIES
Will find every attention paid to their comfort.

WELL-AIRED BEDS.

INLAND REVENUE OFFICE.

TO TOURISTS

AND OTHERS,

VISITING PATELEY BRIDGE

AND THE NEIGHBOURHOOD.

THE

FISHPOND, RAVENSGILL, AND GUY'S-CLIFFE WOODS,

Belonging to JOHN YORKE, ESQ., BEWERLEY HALL,

WILL BE

OPEN

ON TUESDAYS AND THURSDAYS

ONLY,

Between 9 a.m., and 6 p.m., on Payment of

SIXPENCE EACH.

Tickets and Guide to be had of Mr. DAVID PARKINSON, Bewerley.

SCHOOLS WILL BE

ADMITTED AT REDUCED RATES,

ON APPLICATION BEING MADE TO

MR. WARWICK,

AGENT TO JOHN YORKE, ESQ.

☞ *TO COMMENCE 5TH OF MAY.*

For a description of Ravensgill, Guy's-cliffe, Stump Cross Caverns, Stean Beck, Goydon Pot Hole, &c., see " History of Nidderdale," published by T. Thorpe, Pateley Bridge.

J. SHUTTLEWORTH,

BOOKSELLER, &C.,

ILKLEY,

Is now Publishing an entirely new series of

STEREOSCOPIC VIEWS,

By a first-class Artist, embracing nearly all the Picturesque

SCENERY OF WHARFEDALE,

Price One Shilling, post free ;

LISTS SENT ON APPLICATION.

J. S. has just ready a New

GUIDE BOOK TO ILKLEY AND VICINITY,

By a Person thoroughly acquainted with the locality ;

It contains 100 pages of Letterpress, three page Engraving, and Map, Price ONE Shilling. London Agents, Messrs. Hamilton, Adams, & Co.

THE BAY HORSE

PATELEY BRIDGE,

FAMILY AND COMMERCIAL HOTEL, AND POSTING HOUSE,

Mrs. Dougill, Proprietress.

———

Gentlemen and Parties visiting this beautiful neighbourhood will find every comfort and accommodation at this Hotel, at moderate charges.

CABS, DOG CARTS, POST HORSES, &C., &C.

BRITISH AND FOREIGN SPIRITS, PALE ALES, &c.

THE GEORGE HOTEL,
PATELEY BRIDGE.

COMMERCIAL GENTLEMEN, FAMILIES AND TOURISTS

VISITING

THIS ROMANTIC NEIGHBOURHOOD,

Will find superior accommodation, with moderate Charges,
at the above Hotel.

DINNERS ON THE SHORTEST NOTICE.

FINE OLD WINES, BRITISH AND FOREIGN SPIRITS,
LONDON AND DUBLIN PORTER,
FINE OLD ALES, &c.

WELL-AIRED BEDS.

GOOD STABLING, COACH HOUSES, &c.
GEORGE WATSON, Proprietor.

NIDDERDALE.

PATELEY BRIDGE.

THE KING'S ARMS,

FAMILY AND COMMERCIAL HOTEL,

NEAR THE STATION.

PARTIES VISITING

BRIMHAM ROCKS, RAVENSGILL, GUY'S-CLIFFE, STUMP CROSS CAVERNS, &C.,

Will find every accommodation in this old established
and first-class Hotel.

**A Waggonette, for Pic-Nic Parties, &c.; Dog Carts,
Cab, &c., &c.**

THOMAS THORPE,

Publisher, Printer, Book & Music Seller

STATIONER, & NEWS AGENT, PATELEY BRIDGE,

Calls attention to his varied Stock of

BOOKS, PLAIN AND FANCY STATIONERY,
ACCOUNT BOOKS, LEDGERS, DAY BOOKS, &c.

*Views of Bewerley Hall and Grounds, Ravensgill, Castle-stead,
Pateley Bridge, Ramsgill, (the birth-place of Eugene Aram,) &c., &c.*

These are kept in large sized Photographs, and in Lithographs, by
Messrs. Day & Sons, London.

NIDDERDALE PRINTING WORKS.

LETTER-PRESS PRINTING in all its Branches;

BOOK-WORK, &c. Estimates given to AUTHORS and others,
if required.

Guide to BRIMHAM ROCKS, price 4d.

UNICORN HOTEL,

AND

POSTING HOUSE.

COLLINSON'S UNICORN
FAMILY AND COMMERCIAL HOTEL AND
POSTING HOUSE.

PARTIES VISITING

RIPON, STUDLEY, FOUNTAIN'S ABBEY, and NEIGHBOURHOOD, will find every accommodation in this old-established and first-class Hotel.

Omnibuses, Broughams. Open Carriages, Cabs, Gigs, Phæton, and Conveyances of every description.

N.B.—Wedding Carriages, Hearse & Mourning Coaches.

PROPRIETOR—R. E. COLLINSON, Wine and Spirit Merchant.

ELIGIBLE FREEHOLD LAND,
AT PATELEY BRIDGE,
FOR SALE, OR LEASE, IN BUILDING LOTS.

TO BE SOLD BY PRIVATE CONTRACT,

OR LET ON BUILDING LEASES IN CONVENIENT LOTS,

A small FREEHOLD ESTATE, located at the outskirts of the Town of Pateley Bridge, and having an extensive Frontage to the Ripon and Pateley Bridge Turnpike Road.

The Property occupies rising ground, well sheltered from the North and East, with an unobstructed South and West aspect, abounds in Stone suitable for Building purposes, and from its elevated position commands extensive and varied views of the beautiful Valley of the Nidd, Bewerley Hall and Park, Castle-stead, Guy's-cliffe, Ravensgill, and other surrounding Mountain Scenery, offering advantages rarely combined, for either Villa, Semi-Detached, or Cottage Residences.

The Lots will either be Sold, or Let on Building Leases, for a Term of 500 Years, at moderate Ground Rents, with the option of purchasing the Freehold, within a fixed period, if required.

To suit the convenience of Purchasers, the purchase money may be paid by Instalments; or, if desired, a portion may remain at Interest on Security of the Plot Purchased.

A Plan of the Estate, shewing the projected Roads and the respective Lots, may be inspected, and every information obtained, on application at the Offices of **MR. THOS. SYKES,**

SOLICITOR, PATELEY BRIDGE.

TOURISTS AND TRAVELLERS, **VISITORS TO THE SEA SIDE, AND OTHERS,**

PERSONAL ELEGANT REQUISITES UNDER THE PATRONAGE OF ROYALTY, AND THE ARISTOCRACY OF EUROPE.

Exposed to the scorching rays of the Sun, and heated particles of Dust, will find

ROWLANDS' KAYLDOR

A most Refreshing Preparation for the Complexion, dispelling the Cloud of Languor and Relaxation, allaying all Heat and Irritability, and immediately affording the pleasing sensation attending restored elasticity and healthful state of the Skin.

Freckles, Tan, Spots, Pimples, Flushes, and Discolorations are eradicated by its application, and give place to a healthy clearness and transparency of complexion. In cases of sunburn, and stings of insects, its virtues have long been acknowledged. Price 4s 6d & 8s 6d per bottle.

ROWLANDS' MACASSAR OIL,

A delightfully fragrant, and transparent preparation, and as an invigorator and beautifier of the Hair beyond all precedent.

Price 3s 6d and 7s; 10s 6d (equal to four small), and 21s per Bottle.

Rowlands' Odonto, or Pearl Dentifrice,

A White Powder, compounded of the rarest and most fragrant exotics. It bestows on the Teeth a Pearl-like Whiteness, frees them from Tartar, and imparts to the Gums a healthy firmness, and to the Breath a grateful purity and fragrance. Price 2s 9d per Box.

Sold at 20, HATTON GARDEN, LONDON, and by CHEMISTS and PERFUMERS.

☞ Ask for "ROWLANDS'" Articles.

BRIMHAM ROCKS.

NOTICE.

The Public are respectfully informed that no parties will be allowed to visit BRIMHAM on Sundays; or at any time without a Guide.

VISITORS TO PAY SIXPENCE EACH.

RICHARD WEATHERHEAD,

BRIMHAM HOUSE,

Accommodates Parties with Tea, Coffee, Lemonade, Ginger Beer, Soda Water &c., on the Shortest Notice.

TO VISITORS BY RAIL.—As the railway is now open to Dacre Banks Station, the nearest point to Brimham Rocks, R. W. respectfully informs the numerous visitiors that they can have Plates, Dishes, and Crockery of all kinds provided on reasonable terms, for those who bring their own refreshments.

☞ *The Roads have been recently improved.*

Lightning Source UK Ltd.
Milton Keynes UK
UKOW022035141212

203707UK00006B/196/P

EASY DESIGN
ON YOUR COMPUTER

using *only* Microsoft® Word 97
or Microsoft® Office 97

Anna Claybourne

Designed by Isaac Quaye
Cover design by Russell Punter

Edited by Jane Chisholm and Philippa Wingate
Design manager: Russell Punter
Illustrated by Isaac Quaye
Photographs by Howard Allman

Technical consultant: Janette Bailey
Design consultant: Biggles

This is a product of Usborne Publishing Ltd., and is not sponsored by
or produced in association with Microsoft Corporation.

What does easy design mean?

Contents

2 What does easy design mean?

GETTING STARTED
4 What do I need?
6 All about good design
8 Using Microsoft® Word 97
10 The Word 97 screen

WORKING WITH WORD
12 Start simple
14 Creating pictures
16 Adding pictures
18 Fonts
20 Colours
22 Sizes and shapes
24 Folding documents
26 Sticker sheets
28 Text effects
30 Make a newsletter
32 Four-page booklets
34 Lots of pages
36 Design a logo
38 Fashion design
40 Magazines

GOING FURTHER
42 What is DTP?

44 Saving, printing and scanning
46 Glossary
47 Web sites
48 Index

This book is all about how you can design and produce your own publications ~ from cards and books to T-shirts, stickers and stationery ~ using only a computer and Microsoft® Word 97.

It's easy because you don't need to be a design genius or brilliant at art to put words and pictures together to make effective, eyecatching designs.

Why design?

Design influences everything. Whether you're trying to create a birthday card, poster, magazine, newsletter or school project, the way it looks can make all the difference. The design you choose decides whether something comes across as funny, exciting, serious or sophisticated. If a design doesn't work, it can end up looking dull, old-fashioned ~ or just silly.

This book is about graphic design ~ the kind of design that deals with words and pictures. Today, most graphic designers work on computers. Doing graphic design on a computer is sometimes called desktop design or desktop publishing (DTP for short).

Computers make designing easier, because you can rearrange things as much as you like on the screen. Then, when you've finished, you can print out as many copies as you want.

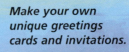
Make your own unique greetings cards and invitations.

Design software

Most professional graphic designers use special DTP software. However, this is usually very expensive, and as a beginner you probably won't need it. This book shows you how to get great results using a less expensive word-processing program, Microsoft® Word 97.

You can publish books and newsletters for friends and family.

Find out how to create interesting lettering styles.

How this book works

This book has been divided into three sections to make it easy to use.

• The **Getting Started** section deals with all the equipment and software you need to get going, and explains the basics of good design.

• The main section, **Working with Word**, shows you all the different ways you can use Word 97 as a design tool. Each double page introduces a new skill, such as adding pictures, choosing lettering styles or arranging text and pictures on the page. With each new skill, there's a new project to try. This will help you build up your design skills step-by-step. But you don't need to work through every project, especially if you've used Word before.

• The **Going Further** section, at the end of the book, is about DTP software. It gives you a brief introduction to the way professional designers work and the programs they use.

 Design tips

Look out for "design tips" boxes like this throughout the book. They'll give you extra ideas and suggestions to help with particular projects.

You could put your designs onto clothes, wrapping paper, stickers and badges.

You can print out personalized stationery featuring your own logo.

GETTING STARTED

What do I need?

Here are the basic things you need to become a desktop designer. You may have all of them already, especially if your computer is quite new.

Your computer

This book has been written to be used with a PC (personal computer) which is using the Microsoft® Windows® 95 or 98 operating system. It could be a desktop PC, like the one in the picture, or a smaller laptop or notebook PC.

If you have a different type of computer, such as an Apple Mac, you can still use the design tips and project ideas, and adapt them for your own system. You probably won't be able to follow all our word-processing instructions exactly, but most word-processing programs are quite similar. You should be able to use the 'Help' function in your word-processor to work out how to do the same things.

This computer has an inkjet printer. Inkjets are the cheapest and most common printers available, and are recommended for all the projects in this book.

Word-processing software

The projects in the main part of this book use Microsoft® Word 97. This is a general word-processing program which many people have on their computers. If you don't have Word, you should still be able to do some of the projects using a simpler word-processor such as Microsoft® WordPad, which is included with Windows® 95 and 98.

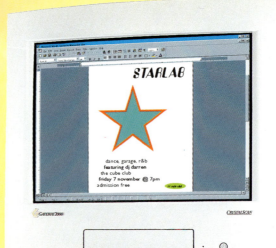

This is a desktop PC. Your PC may look slightly different, but it should have a main processing unit, a monitor, a keyboard and a mouse.

— Monitor

Processing unit

Mouse mat

Mouse

Keyboard

4

Other software

If you want to create your own pictures, you'll need an art program such as Paint. Paint comes free with Windows® 95 and 98, and most computers come with some type of art software.

You can also use software packages containing pictures and fonts (lettering styles). There's more about these on pages 17 and 18.

Printing

You'll need a printer (an inkjet is best) to turn your finished designs into paper publications. Most printers today can print in colour, but you can get good results using just black and white. If you don't have a printer, you might be able to get your work printed out at a copy shop or a library, at school or at a friend's house.

Some of the projects also require special types of computer printing paper and card. There's more about printers and printing materials on pages 44-45.

You can buy special printer papers, also known as special media, at computer stores.

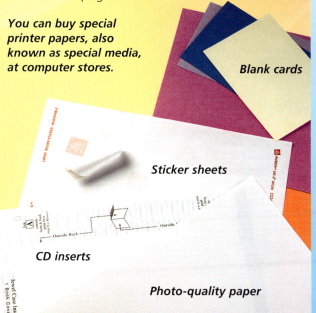

Blank cards

Sticker sheets

CD inserts

Photo-quality paper

Extra stuff

These things will be useful when it comes to finding pictures for your publications...

A scanner
This lets you copy photos, artwork and other pictures into your computer to use in your designs. If you don't have your own, you can pay to use a scanner at a copy shop or library. There is more about scanners on page 45.

An Internet connection
If your computer is connected to the Internet, you'll be able to find lots of extra pictures and fonts (styles of type or lettering) on the World Wide Web. You can often download them and use them for free in your desktop design publications.

To get connected to the Internet, you need a telephone line, a modem, Internet software and an account with an ISP (Internet Service Provider). Your computer shop should be able to help you with this.

A CD-ROM drive
is also very useful, because software, pictures and fonts often come on CDs. Most PCs come with a built-in CD-ROM drive, but you can also buy them separately.

GETTING STARTED

All about good design

A really good piece of design makes people interested, so they'll want to have a closer look. It also makes information easy to understand, and creates the right "feel" or mood, using a combination of different elements.

Design elements

Design elements are the different things that make a design work. These are the main design elements:

Lettering Also known as the **font** or **typeface**. By changing the size and style of the lettering, you can change the impact of the text, and make important bits, such as titles, stand out.

Layout Layout is the way the text and pictures are positioned or "laid out" on the paper. Good layout makes the page look balanced, and helps the reader to see everything in the right order.

Colour Designers choose colours that look good together and send the right message. For example, bright, simple colours such as blue, red and yellow are often used in comics and cartoons.

Illustration A big part of a designer's job is choosing the right illustrations, or pictures. The style of the pictures should match the whole design.

Decoration Extra bits of decoration, such as rules, borders, boxes, bars, icons and patterned backgrounds, can add to the mood and make your designs look more professional.

Keep it simple

One of the most important rules of good design is to keep all the elements quite simple. Too many different fonts, colours and pictures can be ugly and confusing. A cluttered, complicated layout could make your publication hard to read.

These two posters show how a designer could present the same information in two different ways.

On this poster, the title is too small - it would be hard to see from a distance.

The colours clash, making the picture hard to see and the text hard to read.

The important details about when the play is on are lost among the decorations at the bottom.

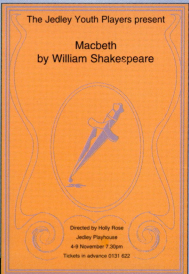

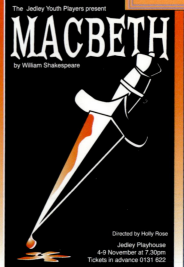

This title here is in a large font, which makes it stand out better. It has a spooky, old-fashioned feel, suited to the subject.

A simple picture, using just two contrasting colours, helps reinforce the horror theme.

The design process

It takes time to plan a design, try different styles and make decisions about all the elements. So don't worry if it doesn't look right at first. It's best to work through a "design process", like this:

Research Look at the designs used in magazines, TV shows and books to work out how to get the feel you want. In the pages below, from a science fiction magazine, blue colours and computer-style fonts are used to give a space-age feel.

Planning It can help to make small, rough design sketches, called thumbnails, on a piece of paper, to test out different ideas before using your computer.

Setting the style Next, choose the fonts, colours and other elements you're going to use. This is known as "setting the style".

Layout Once you've collected all the elements, you can start arranging them. Designers usually experiment with several different layouts and choose the one they like best.

GETTING STARTED

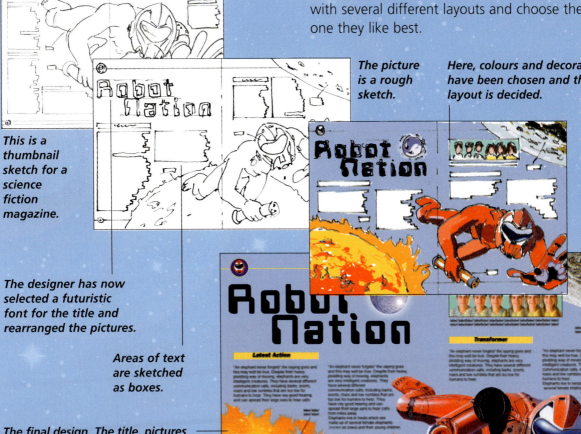

This is a thumbnail sketch for a science fiction magazine.

The picture is a rough sketch.

Here, colours and decoration have been chosen and the layout is decided.

The designer has now selected a futuristic font for the title and rearranged the pictures.

Areas of text are sketched as boxes.

The final design. The title, pictures and logos give a science fiction feel, but the main text is in a more normal font to make it easy to read.

Using Microsoft® Word 97

GETTING STARTED

The next four pages explain the basics of Microsoft® Word 97, for those who haven't used it before. You can turn back to these pages if you get stuck while you're doing the projects later on in the book.

What is Word?

Microsoft® Word 97 is a word-processing program, which means it's usually used for writing letters, essays and other documents. However, it also lets you add pictures and decorations, and do interesting things with text, so it's ideal for desktop publishing projects as well.

Finding and opening Word

Once your PC is switched on, you can open Word. Click on *Start* in the bottom left-hand corner of the screen, then move your mouse pointer over *Programs*. You should see a list of the programs on your computer. If you have Word, it should be there. Click on it to start the program.

(If you have bought Word, but it isn't on your computer yet, follow the instructions that come with it to find out how to load it onto your PC.)

The "paper" you see on the screen corresponds to the shape of the paper you'll print your work out on.

What you see

When you start Word, it automatically opens a new document for you to work in. The document looks like a page of white paper on the screen. If you click on *View* in the menu bar at the top of the screen, you can choose from several different ways of looking at your document. The easiest is probably *Page Layout*, as it shows you exactly how your finished page will appear.

This is what the screen will look like when you've chosen the Page Layout viewing option.

Paper

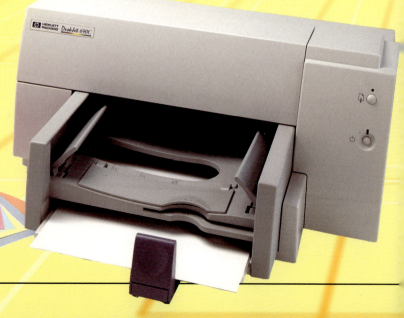

Setting up your page

First you need to tell Word what size of paper you want to use, and whether you want it to be upright (portrait) or on its side (landscape).

To do this, click on *File* in the menu bar, then click on *Page Setup...* from the drop-down menu. When the *Page Setup* dialog box appears, click on the *Paper Size* tab at the top. You can now choose the paper size. Start with the type of paper you normally use, such as A4 or letter paper. You can also choose whether to make it portrait or landscape.

You choose the paper size here. Click the arrow to see a menu, then click on the paper you want.

You can use these boxes to enter a "custom" paper size ~ one that isn't in the menu.

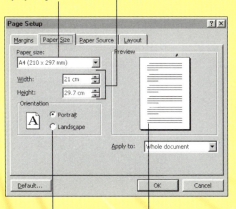

Choose either portrait or landscape here.

This box shows you what your chosen page setup will look like.

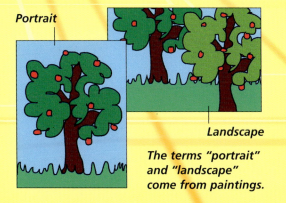

Portrait

Landscape

The terms "portrait" and "landscape" come from paintings.

Setting margins

You may want to change the margins (the gaps around the edge of the paper), especially if your printer leaves large margins when it prints. To do this, click on the *Margins* tab in the *Page Setup* dialog box. It allows you to type in the size of the top, bottom, left and right margins.

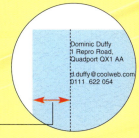

Margin measurement

You fill in the margin sizes you want in these boxes.

The preview box shows how the margins will look.

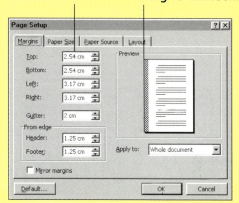

Don't worry about the other options in the Page Setup dialog box ~ just leave them as they are.

Ready to write

When you've set your paper size and margins, click on *OK*. The *Page Setup* dialog box will disappear, and you're ready to write. The flashing cursor, which looks like a small vertical line, shows where the text will appear when you start typing. Once you've written some text, you can move the cursor to anywhere in the text to make changes or corrections. To do this, just click on the text with your mouse.

GETTING STARTED

The Word 97 screen

Word tools

Word's main screen may look complicated, but it makes sense once you know which symbols represent which tools, and what they can do. If you let your cursor rest over a symbol for a moment, a label will appear telling you the name of the tool. If you first select *What's This?* in the *Help* menu, then click on a symbol, a label will appear describing what that tool does.

Is Word correcting you?

Your Word software may have been set up to make changes to things you type. This is called **AutoCorrect**. For example, if you start a sentence with a small letter, it might change to a capital automatically. To change this kind of setting, click on *Tools* in the menu bar and select *AutoCorrect...* The dialog box that appears will let you switch off AutoCorrect functions you don't want.

When you're using Word, if something doesn't work, it may help just to try it again. If your computer "crashes" (freezes up), you may need to switch it off and start again.

When you first start up Word, the screen will probably look similar to this. If you can't see all these symbols on your screen, click on View *and select* Toolbars. *Then select* Formatting, Standard *and* Drawing *from the list.*

New – opens up a new document

Open – opens up an existing document

Print – prints out your document

Spelling and grammar – checks text for mistakes, and suggests corrections

Save – saves the document you are working on

Copy – copies text or an image, which you can then paste somewhere else

Print preview – shows you how your printed document will look

AutoShapes menu – lets you draw different shapes (see page 17)

Cut – removes text or an image you have selected, so that you can paste it somewhere else

Paste – inserts text or an image which you have cut or copied

10

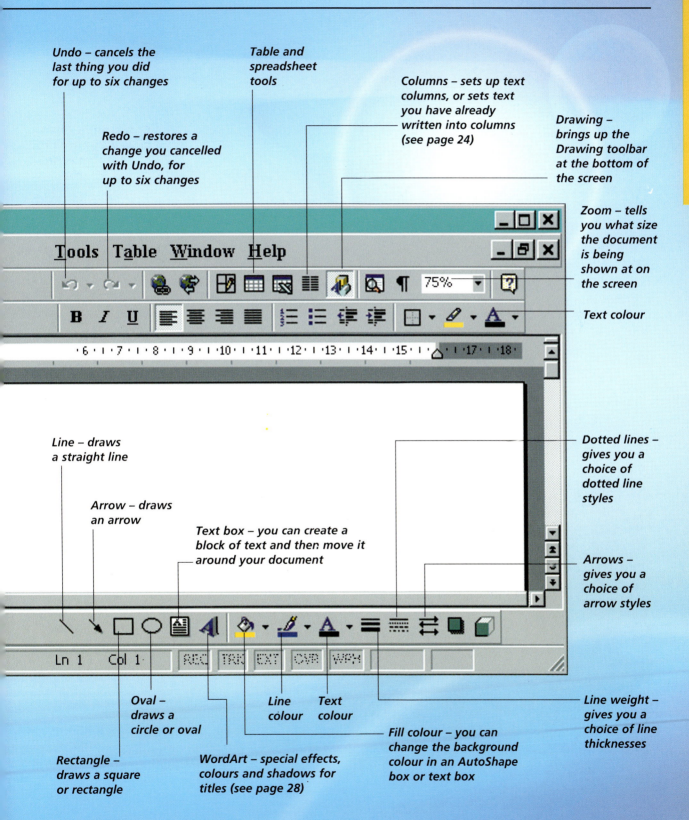

Start simple

For your first design project, try something simple, such as a letterhead to make all your letters look smart and professional. This project lets you experiment with lettering and layout.

Getting started

Start your Word program and choose the paper size you normally use for letters (probably A4 or letter paper). For a reminder of how to do this, see page 8.

Then type in all the details you want to include, like your name, address, phone number and e-mail address.

Word adds these red and green squiggles to words and sentences it doesn't recognize. You can ignore them for now ~ they won't show on your printout.

d.duffy@coolweb.com

*Press the **Return** key to make a line break for each new line.*

Here are some style and layout ideas for your letterhead:

Change the style

To change the style of text, you have to highlight it. Move your mouse pointer to where the text starts, hold down the main (left) mouse button and move the pointer to the end of the text. When the words are highlighted, release the mouse button.

Font list — **Font size list** — **Style buttons** — **Highlighted text**

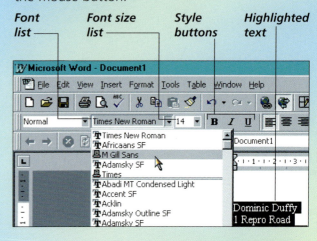

A rule under the text makes the letterhead look neat.

Try using italic for the details.

Try using small letters or capitals for all the words. What kind of effect does this have?

Dominic Duffy
1 Repro Road · Quadport QX1 AA · d.duffy@coolweb.com

Dominic Duffy
1 Repro Road,
Quadport QX1 AA
d.duffy@coolweb.com

dominic duffy
1 repro road
quadport
qx1 aa

d.duffy@coolweb.com

12

WORKING WITH WORD

- To change the lettering, or font, click on the arrow in the font list, which is a small box near the top left of the screen (shown in the picture opposite). A list of fonts will appear. Select one of them, and your highlighted text will change to that font. (You may not have many fonts just yet, but you can find out how to get more on pages 18-19).

- To change the size, click on the font size list next to the font list. Font size is measured in points (one point is 1/72inch or 0.035mm). 12 or 14 points is a good size to start with.

- To make text **bold**, *italic* or underlined, highlight it and click on one of the style buttons. To undo a style, click again on the same button. When you've finished, click somewhere else in the document to undo the highlighting.

Change the layout

There are lots of ways to change the layout of your letterhead to make it more interesting. Here are just a few.

- Use the *Return* key to insert extra spaces between lines.

Return *key*

- You could put all your details onto one long line. Use the *Delete* key to undo any line breaks and line spaces you've put in.

Delete *key*

- To add a rule right across the page under your details, type three minus signs, then press *Return*. Use three equals signs in the same way for a double rule.

Minus *key*   **Equals** *key*

- To change the alignment (the way the text lines up), highlight the text and click on one of these buttons, which appear in the toolbar at the top of the screen.

This button aligns text along the left of the page, like this.   *This button centres text in the middle, like this.*   *This button aligns text along the right of the page, like this.*

Print it

When you're happy with your letterhead, save it and print it out. For extra help with printing, see page 44.

You can either type out your letter, or print out the letterhead and then write your message by hand.

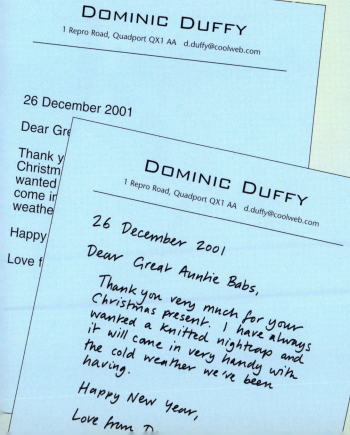

13

Creating pictures

Most of the projects in the book include pictures as well as words. The next four pages show you how to create and collect pictures that can be used on a computer, and how to put them into your desktop designs.

Digital pictures

The simplest way to add pictures to your designs is to draw or paint them onto the paper after printing out the words. This works well if you're good at drawing. However, using digital (computerized) pictures in your designs gives you much more choice and control. You can move pictures around on the screen, and try different effects and layouts before printing out your final design.

If you want to add artwork by hand, leave a space in your document before printing it out.

Creating pictures with Paint

Microsoft® Paint is a painting and drawing program that comes with Windows® 95 and 98. You'll find it under *Accessories* in the *Programs* menu. You can use it to make digital pictures, which you can then save and use in your Word designs (see the next page for how to do this).

The Paint screen has a drawing area and a selection of tools and colours which you select with the mouse. Some of the things you can do with Paint tools are shown on the opposite page.

 Design tips

When you're using Paint, you don't have to try to make your pictures look like real-life painted pictures. Instead, experiment with the Paint tools to make bright, bold images.

Printing your document on coloured paper makes it more eye-catching.

14

WORKING WITH WORD

This is the Paint screen. The fish has been drawn using the Brush, Circle, Fill and Spray tools.

Use the Help option from the menu bar to find out all the things you can do with Paint.

The white area is the "paper".

You can draw perfect circles and ovals with the circle tool.

Toolbar

The body and fins were drawn freehand, using the mouse like a brush. You can choose from several different line thicknesses.

A yellow spray paint effect has been used on this fish.

Colours

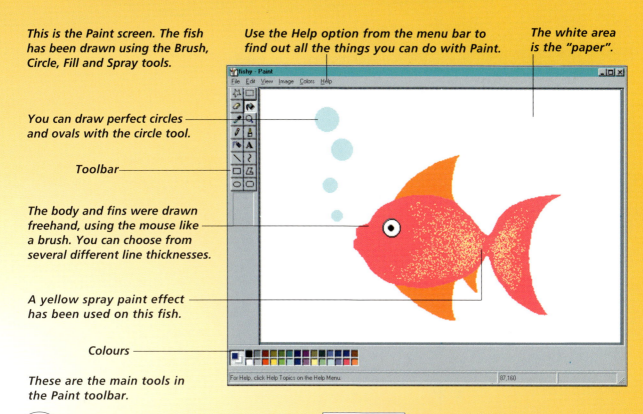

These are the main tools in the Paint toolbar.

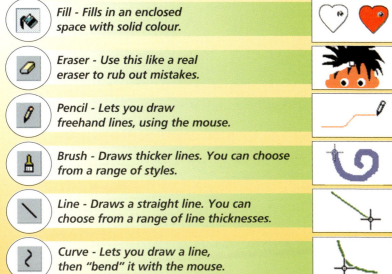

Fill - Fills in an enclosed space with solid colour.

Eraser - Use this like a real eraser to rub out mistakes.

Pencil - Lets you draw freehand lines, using the mouse.

Brush - Draws thicker lines. You can choose from a range of styles.

Line - Draws a straight line. You can choose from a range of line thicknesses.

Curve - Lets you draw a line, then "bend" it with the mouse.

Rectangle - Draws rectangle shapes, or (if you hold down the Shift key) perfect squares.

Ellipse - Draws perfect ovals. Hold down the Shift key to make perfect circles.

Saving picture files

When your picture is finished, click on *File* and *Save*. Paint will let you name the file and will automatically save it with the ending .bmp, short for "bitmap". For example, the picture above is called "fishy.bmp". A bitmap is a type of picture file which can be used in Word documents.

It's a good idea to make a special folder on your computer to store all your pictures in. Then, when you want to use them in your design documents, they'll be easy to find.

15

Adding pictures

This page explains how to put a .bmp picture file, such as a Paint file, into a Word document. The opposite page shows you some other ways of finding and creating pictures to use in your designs.

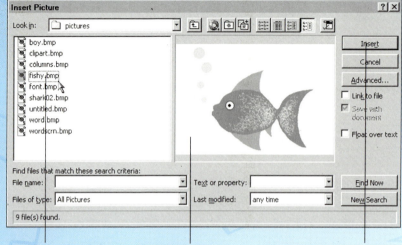

Highlight the right picture file here.

The picture is shown in this box.

Click on Insert to put the picture into your Word document.

Adding a picture

To add a Paint picture to a Word document:

• Click on *Insert* in the menu bar. Click on *Picture*, and then select *From File...* from the menu that appears.

• A directory of the folders on your computer will appear. Find the folder where you stored your picture, and highlight the file.

• Click on *Insert*. The picture will appear in your Word document. If you click on it, you'll see that it is in a box. You can drag the picture with your mouse to move it around, or make it bigger or smaller by clicking and dragging the box's corners.

If you move the box's edges, you can stretch the picture.

Cropping the picture box

Once you've inserted a picture, the picture toolbar shown here should appear somewhere on your screen. (If it doesn't, click on *View* and select *Toolbars*, then *Picture*.) If you click on the *Crop* tool, moving the corners of the picture box makes the box smaller, without changing the size of picture.

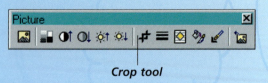

Crop tool

This way, you can make sure the picture box doesn't take up too much space on the page.

Add text

If you click away from the picture, you'll be able to write text as normal. For example, you could make a letterhead like the ones on page 12, and decorate it with a picture.

AutoShapes

Word can draw a selection of shapes for you. To do this, click on *View* in the menu bar. Select *Toolbars*, then *Drawing*. The drawing toolbar will appear near the bottom of the screen. Click on *AutoShapes*.

You can now choose from several groups of shapes. Try *Basic Shapes* to start with, and click on a shape you like.

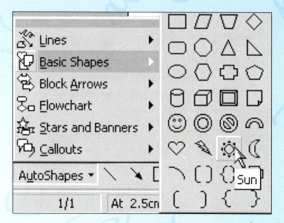

Now click and drag with the mouse to draw the shape on your page. If you hold down the *Shift* key, it will stay the same shape. If you don't press the *Shift* key, you can stretch the shape. You can also move the shape by clicking on it and dragging it with your mouse.

You can still change the shape after you've drawn it, by moving the corners.

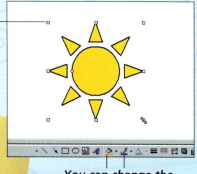

You can change the fill and outline colours with these tools.

Clip Art

Clip Art is a name for picture files that anyone can use in their designs. There are several ways to get Clip Art pictures:

Microsoft® Clip Gallery
Word has its own selection of Clip Art pictures for you to use. Click on *Insert* in the menu bar, select *Picture*, and select *Clip Art...* You'll see the "Microsoft Clip Gallery" box, which contains Clip Art pictures organized into groups. Click on one you like, and select *Insert*. The picture will appear in your document.

A Clip Art picture of a tortoise from the Microsoft Clip Gallery

On the Web
Lots of Web sites provide free Clip Art (see page 47). To copy a picture from the Web, click on it with the right mouse button. Select *Save Picture As...* from the menu that appears, name the picture and choose the option that lets you save it as a bitmap (.bmp) file. You can then store it on your computer and copy it into Word.

A picture of cherries from the www.clipartconnection.com Web site

CD-ROMs
You can buy CD-ROMs full of Clip Art pictures on all kinds of subjects, such as sports or science. Look out for them at your computer store.

Fonts

A font is a set of letters, numbers and other characters in a particular style. Choosing the best fonts for your designs helps you create the right mood and get your message across.

Types of fonts

There are thousands of fonts, divided into several main groups. Each font has its own name.

• **Serif fonts** have small tabs or serifs on each letter. They make good body fonts, because the serifs help your eye move along lines of text.

serif

This traditional-looking serif font is called Garamond.

• **Sanserif or "sans" fonts** don't have serifs. They look clean and modern.

This popular sanserif font is called Gill Sans.

• **Body fonts** are easy to read and usually have serifs. They are used for long passages of text.

This body font is called Times.

 *GhoulyCaps*

 WantedPoster

 *OldEnglish*

• **Display fonts** are eyecatching with a strong "mood". They're ideal for large poster titles, or for stickers or badges.

• **Dingbats** are fonts made up of little pictures instead of letters.

Webdings

Changing fonts in Word

When you're using Word, you can change any character, word or chunk of text into a different font. Just click and drag the mouse to highlight the bit of text you want to change, then choose a font from the font list near the top left of the screen. You can also change the size of the font, using the font size list.

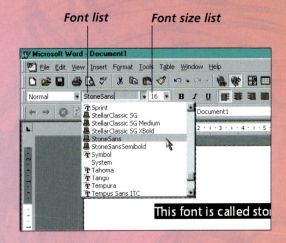

Get new fonts

Word comes with a few fonts, but what if you need more? Just like Clip Art pictures, you can buy large collections of fonts quite cheaply on CD-ROMs at your computer store. You can also download free fonts from the Web. Some good free font Web sites are listed on page 47.

Start designing

You only need a few fonts to create eyecatching posters, flyers and leaflets. The example opposite shows some of the design tricks you could try.

Poster planning

First, work out what your poster needs to say and try out a few small sketches. Start a new Word file, select A4 or letter paper (see page 9), and type in all the text. Then you can start to experiment with different fonts and layouts.

The image on a poster should be bold and simple. You can use a Clip Art picture (see page 17), but posters can also look effective if you use a shape from Word's *AutoShapes* menu, or even a picture from a picture font.

Design tips

Don't use lots of fonts in the same design ~ it will look confusing. Stick to just one or two.

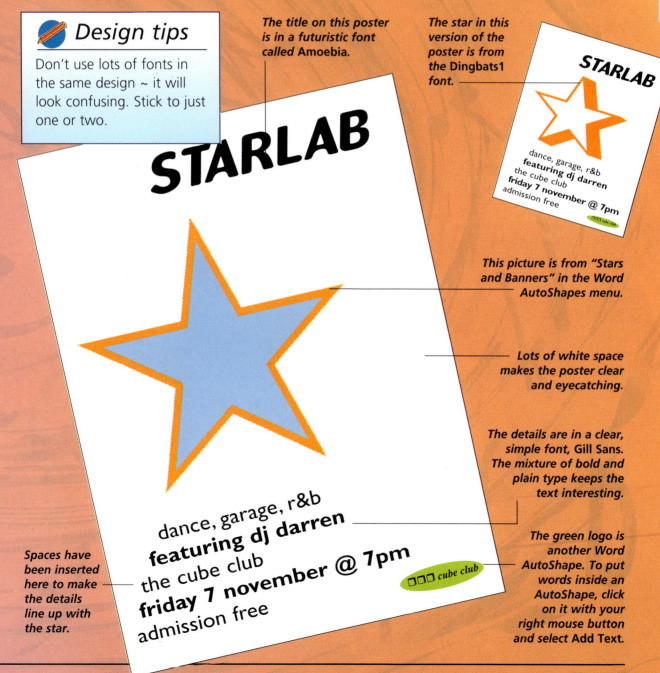

The title on this poster is in a futuristic font called **Amoebia**.

The star in this version of the poster is from the **Dingbats1** font.

This picture is from "Stars and Banners" in the Word AutoShapes menu.

Lots of white space makes the poster clear and eyecatching.

The details are in a clear, simple font, Gill Sans. The mixture of bold and plain type keeps the text interesting.

The green logo is another Word AutoShape. To put words inside an AutoShape, click on it with your right mouse button and select **Add Text**.

Spaces have been inserted here to make the details line up with the star.

WORKING WITH WORD

19

Colours

Like fonts, colours can have all kinds of different effects. This page explains how to use colour in your designs.

Colour combinations

It's a good idea not to use too many colours at once. The best book covers, logos and posters are often made up of just two or three colours which go together really well. You'll need to experiment with different colour combinations for each project, but here are some suggestions:

Orange/blue, red/green and purple/yellow are contrasting combinations. They have a bright, jumpy effect.

Lime green with another bright colour has a very modern, funky feel.

Black and red together look bold and dramatic.

You can also get a striking effect by mixing black with another bright colour such as orange or yellow.

If you combine lively colours such as red, bright pink and orange, you'll get a vibrant, dizzying effect ~ the colours will seem to vibrate when you look at them.

Two similar colours such as blue and green, or two shades of the same colour, have a calming, slightly old-fashioned feel.

It's a wrap...

When designers need some wrapping paper, they just make their own on the computer.

To do this, start a new A4 or letter-paper size Word document, and simply arrange coloured AutoShapes, Paint pictures or picture font pictures (see pages 14-17) all over it.

You can repeat the same picture or AutoShape by duplicating it. Move your mouse pointer over the shape until you see a four-way arrow, then click to select the shape. Then hold down the *Control* key and press D (for "duplicate"). A copy of the shape will appear, and you can move it to where you want it using the mouse.

When it's ready, print out a few sheets of your wrapping paper in colour, and tape them together until you have a piece big enough to wrap your present.

The moons and stars, circles, rockets and diamonds on these designs are made up of different Word AutoShapes.

Personal paper

If you're making wrapping paper for a particular person, why not put their name on it? The easiest way is to draw a large AutoShape, then click on it with your right mouse button and select *Add Text*. You can then write the person's name or a birthday message inside the shape.

The flower design below was drawn in Paint, then inserted into a Word document.

Computer colours

Paint and Word have a wide choice of colours. Paint also lets you create new ones:

• **Paint** Paint has a palette of colours at the bottom of the screen. To make a new one, click on *Colors* in the menu bar (in some versions, you'll find *Colors* under *Options*). Select *Edit Colors...* In the box that appears, click on *Define Custom Colors*. Choose a new colour and add it to the palette by clicking on *Add to Custom Colors*.

Use the mouse to select a colour here.

The colour you've picked will show here.

Move this marker to select the right shade.

• **Word 97** To change the text colour, highlight the text and click on the arrow by the *Font Color* button at the bottom of the screen. You'll see a choice of colours ~ click on one and the text will change. If you click on *More Colors...*, you'll see an even wider range of colours.

For AutoShapes, move the pointer over the shape until you see a four-way arrow. Click to select the shape, then click on the arrows next to the *Fill Color* and *Line Color* buttons to see a choice of colours.

Font Color *Button*

Fill Color *Button*

Line Color *Button*

WORKING WITH WORD

21

Sizes and shapes

You don't have to stick to A4 or letter paper for your desktop designs. Word can create documents in many other sizes, from postcards to bookmarks.

Special media

Things like postcards and invitations work best if you print them on special "media", such as card or stiff paper. You'll have to adjust your printer for special media ~ check with the printer manual. You'll also have to move the printer's guides to keep smaller media in place. (For some useful printing tips, see page 44.)

You can buy plain blank postcards from stationery stores.

Art stores often sell individual sheets of card in different colours and textures, which you can cut to any size and shape.

If you use dark card, dark or bright colours will look best on the printout.

These pictures were done in Paint and inserted into Word (see page 16). For the words, add a text box on top (see page 29).

Make a postcard

If your card is an unusual size, measure it along both edges and write down the measurements. Then start a new Word document (see page 8), and in the *Page Setup* box, type the size of your card into the *Width* and *Height* boxes.

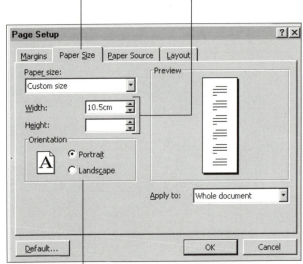

Paper Size tab — **Type the measurements in here.**

Choose Portrait or Landscape here.

Set the margins as small as you can (Word will correct them if you make them too small.) Now you're ready to design and print your postcard. Like posters, postcards look best with a simple picture and message.

Invitations

Postcard-sized cards make good invitations. Or, if you want to make a lot, you can do several invitations on one bigger piece of card, and cut them up afterwards.

To do this, start a new Word document and set the paper size to the same size as your card (such as A4).

Next, draw a table. To do this:

• Click on *Table* in the menu bar. Select *Insert Table...* This dialog box will appear:

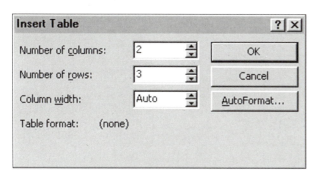

• Fill in the boxes as shown above. (It's best to have just a few columns and rows so your invitations aren't too small.) Click on *OK*.
• You'll now see a table on your page.

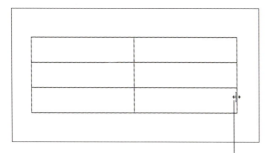

You can make the table wider by clicking and dragging the lines with your mouse.

Multiple copies

Type the text of your invitation into the first box ~ the box will get bigger as you write. Now design the layout. Try using different fonts, adding pictures, or putting text in AutoShapes. Press the *Return* key if you need to add space.

When it's done, copy it into the other boxes. To copy text, highlight it and press the *Control* key and the *C* key. Then move the cursor to the next box and press *Control* and *V*. To copy an AutoShape or picture, move your mouse over it until you see a four-way arrow, then click to select it. Then copy it using *Control* + *C* and *Control* + *V* again.

This is an AutoShape with text inside (see page 19).

When you've printed out the page, cut out each invitation along the lines with a craft knife or scissors.

WORKING WITH WORD

Folding documents

When you're making a folding card or leaflet, you have to know where to put the design on the page so that it looks right after it's printed out and folded.

Plan the layout

For a simple greetings card, you'll need a piece of thin or medium card. Make a new Word document the same size as your whole piece of card, using the *Page Setup* box (see page 22). To make a portrait-shaped card like the ones here, select "Landscape" in the *Paper Size* menu. Set the margins as small as you can. Your Word document will look like this:

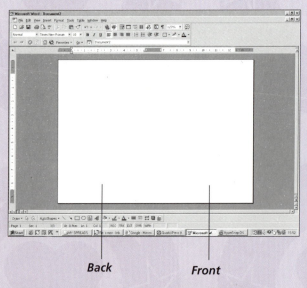

Back   **Front**

The right-hand half of the page will become the front of the card, and the left-hand half will become the back, as shown in the picture above. To divide it in half, click on *Format* in the menu bar, select *Columns...* from the drop-down menu, then choose *Two*.

Press the *Return* key to insert spaces in your document until the cursor appears at the top of the right-hand side. You're now ready to design the front of your card.

Adding words

If you want to add a message, such as "Merry Christmas" or "Congratulations!", make a text box by clicking on *Insert* in the menu bar and selecting *Text Box*, then type the text in the box. You can then move the text around to position it where you want it.

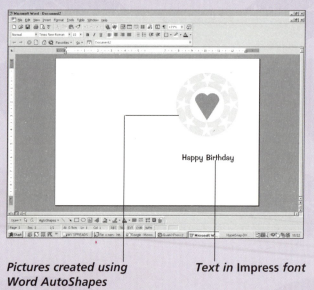

Pictures created using Word AutoShapes   **Text in Impress font**

Remember that when you print, your printer will leave a margin around the edge of the card.

You could also print a design onto paper, cut it out and stick it onto card.

WORKING WITH WORD

Print it out

When you print out your card, remember to set your printer to the right size and thickness for the paper or card you are using (see page 44). Then gently score a line down the middle using a ruler and a blunt knife or a pen that has run out of ink. You can then fold the card neatly.

A message inside

You can just write inside your card with a pen. But if you want to use Word to add more text or pictures to the inside of the card, simply make another Word file just like the first one. Again, write the main message on the right-hand side. Then print this document out on the other side of your card before you fold it in half.

More folding

You can make three-way folding cards and leaflets by choosing three columns instead of two. This diagram shows one way to fold them.

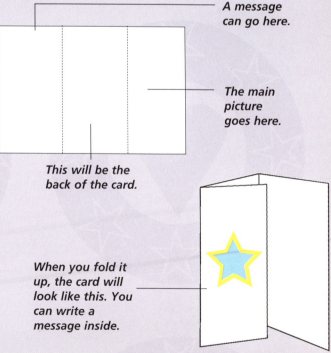

A message can go here.

The main picture goes here.

This will be the back of the card.

When you fold it up, the card will look like this. You can write a message inside.

25

Sticker sheets

Want to make your own cool stickers? You can buy sticker sheets in computer stores and stationers, full of blank stickers waiting for your designs.

Measure your sheets

First of all, measure your sticker sheet. Write down how big the stickers are and how far each one is from the top and left-hand side of the sheet.

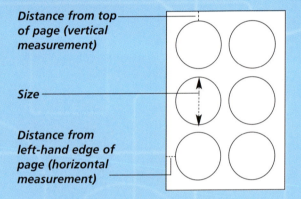

Distance from top of page (vertical measurement)

Size

Distance from left-hand edge of page (horizontal measurement)

Create a sticker document

In Word, start a new document. Set the paper size to the same size as the sticker sheet. Then use Word AutoShapes to draw each sticker in roughly the right place on the page. For example, if your sheet has six round stickers, draw six round AutoShapes as guide shapes.

Now click on the first shape with your right mouse button, and select *Format AutoShapes* from the menu that appears. You'll see a box like the one shown on the right. Under the *Size* tab, enter the size of your sticker. Under the *Position* tab, enter the distance of the first sticker from the top and left-hand side of the page. When you click on *OK*, the guide shape will be exactly the right size and in the right place. Repeat this for all the stickers.

Sticker suggestions

Now you can put your designs in the sticker shapes. Here are some ideas...

Pictures A sticker can be just a picture. Design your own using Paint (see page 14) or use Clip Art or Word AutoShapes (see page 17) to make bright, bold stickers.

Words You can put words in a sticker shape, or in any other Word AutoShape, by right-clicking on it and selecting *Add Text*. Stickers also look good with WordArt (see Text Effects on page 28).

Colours Use the AutoShapes tools at the bottom of the screen to change the colours of text, background and AutoShapes. First click on your shape or highlight your text, then select one of these tools.

This tool fills in shapes with colour.

This tool changes the colour of text.

This tool colours outlines of shapes.

Clicking on these arrows shows you a range of colours to choose from.

Set both these boxes to "Page".

This is an AutoShape with text inside.

26

Leave a space, just in case

Even if you position the shapes carefully, your printer might not be able to print them in exactly the right place. Make sure you allow for this in your designs.

If you want a sticker with a white background, like this, leave some space all around your design.

White space

On the other hand, if you want to fill the sticker with colour, make your background shape bigger than the sticker really is, to make sure it's all covered. Professional designers call this a bleed.

Edge of real sticker

Bleed

Remove the guides

When you've finished, if you can still see your guide shapes, click on them and change their outline colour to "No Line", so you can't see them and they won't show on your stickers. Then, you can set up your printer (see page 44) and print out your stickers.

Badges and buttons

Badges and buttons work just like stickers. You get a sheet of shapes, usually circles. But instead of being sticky, they're made of cardboard. They come with plastic parts which you fit together to make your badge or button.

Some stickers just have a message on them.

This shark picture is from the Microsoft® Clip Gallery (see page 17).

WORKING WITH WORD

Text effects

Word will let you do all kinds of different things with text to make it look interesting. You can have coloured text, shadows, outlines and special effects, and you can even curve text around pictures.

Styles and colours

To try out some text styles, open a new Word document, write a word, and highlight it with your cursor. Then click on *Format* in the menu bar, and select *Font...*. You'll see a box with lots of options.

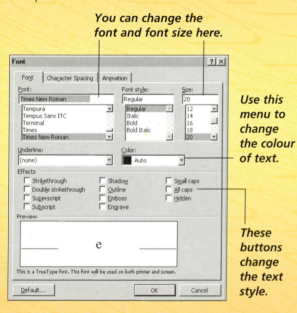

You can change the font and font size here.

Use this menu to change the colour of text.

These buttons change the text style.

This is what some of the styles look like.

WordArt

WordArt is a special facility for making text effects. It's great for exciting headings, posters and stickers.

To use WordArt, click on *Insert* in the menu bar, select *Picture*, and choose *WordArt...*. You'll see a selection of WordArt styles. When you pick one, a box will appear where you can write your text and select the font and font size. (A single word or short phrase works best.) Click on *OK* and your WordArt will appear in your document.

You can drag your WordArt around and change its size, just like a picture. To change its colour, right-click on it and choose *Format WordArt*.

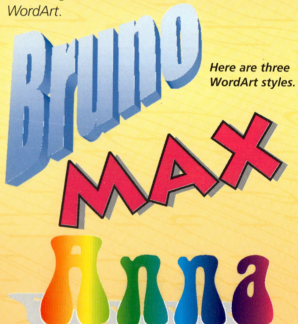

Here are three WordArt styles.

 Design tips

Remember to save amazing text effects like these for big, bold headings. If you use them for long passages of small text, you could make it hard to read.

Text wrapping

Making text fit around a picture is called wrapping. To do it, click on the picture with your right mouse button and select *Format Picture*. Under the *Position* tab, make sure the "Float over text" box is selected. Then choose the *Wrapping* tab.

You can now choose from several ways of wrapping the text. For example, *Square* leaves a square space around the picture. *Tight* wraps the text closely around the picture.

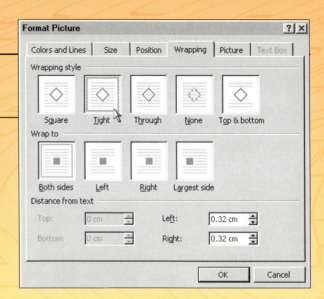

This dialog box lets you choose a wrapping style.

Text boxes

You can also put any piece of text in its own box, so you can move it around just like a picture or an AutoShape. To do this, click on *Insert* in the menu bar, select *Text Box*, and then type in your text.

Here's a one-page project on hippos, which was designed using several text effects.

— The title was made using WordArt.

— The labels are in their own text boxes.

The Autoshapes menu has an option for drawing straight lines.

The headings are in capital letters in an outline style.

The picture at the bottom has a tight text wrap. (After choosing the wrap, you may need to move the picture slightly to make the wrap look right.)

Hippos

INTRODUCTION

Hippos are among the largest land mammals in the world. They live in and around rivers in Africa and are very good swimmers. They are herbivores and eat mostly grass and a few underwater plants.

HIPPO ANATOMY

Hippos are huge. A fully grown male hippo can be up to 5m (16 ft) long and weigh up to 3,630 kilos (8,000 pounds). Even though they look fat and clumsy, Hippos are very strong and can run as fast as a human being.

Eyes
Ears
Nostrils

A hippo's eyes, ears and nostrils are on top of its head so that they stick out of the water.

A HIPPO'S DAY

Hippos spend most of the day underwater, where they can stay cool. In the evenings, they come out of the water and spend several hours eating grass at their feeding grounds.

WORKING WITH WORD

29

Make a newsletter

Word is ideal for creating newsletters, or illustrated projects. You can arrange text in columns, blocks or boxes, and put pictures wherever you like. Here's how to make a one-page newsletter for your club, school or family.

Plan your publication

First of all, collect all the items you want to include and make a list so you don't leave anything off. If you want to use any pictures, make sure they are saved in digital form (see page 14).

> Edwards family newsletter
>
> Editor's letter
> Article about American visit
> Announcement - Bob & Becky's triplets
> Photo of triplets
> Announcement - George's birthday
> Recipe

Then choose your fonts (see page 18). You'll need a serif or clear sanserif font for the main text, and an eyecatching font for the title.

Finally, set up a new Word document with a normal paper size, such as A4 or letter paper.

Make a masthead

Newspapers and newsletters have an area at the top called a masthead, which contains the title of the publication and sometimes a logo as well. It always looks the same so that the publication is easy to recognize. The masthead should be quite big and should run right across the top of the newsletter.

Columns

A typical newsletter is arranged in columns. When you've done the masthead, position the cursor just below it. Click on *Format* in the menu bar, select *Columns...*, and choose three columns.

Select the number of columns here.

"Line between" puts a rule between the columns.

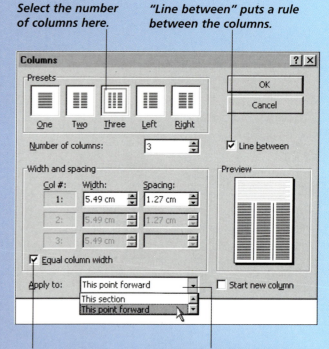

Select "Equal column width" here.

Select "This point forward" in this box, so that the columns do not affect your masthead.

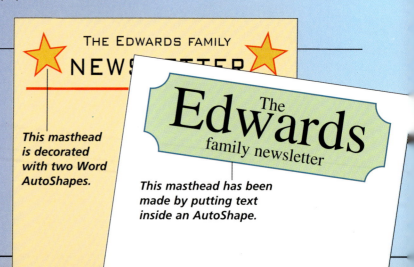

This masthead is decorated with two Word AutoShapes.

This masthead has been made by putting text inside an AutoShape.

WORKING WITH WORD

30

WORKING WITH WORD

Here's a finished newsletter full of family news.

Masthead

The main text of this newsletter is in 12-point Stone Sans font.

The picture caption uses a smaller version of the same font.

The subheadings use the same font, but in bold and slightly larger.

The box about the birthday party takes up two column widths.

The Edwards family newsletter

March 2001

Editor's letter
Welcome to the first edition of the Edwards family newsletter! There are so many members of the Edwards family that I've decided to write this newsletter to help us all keep in touch. If anyone has any announcements they'd like me to put in the newsletter, just email me at josh.edwards@coolweb.com. Or write to me at 12 Techno Terrace, Quadport QU8 1SA, England, UK.

Happy reading...

Josh

American visit
Several members of the American branch of the family visited the UK recently. Uncle Norman's daughter Maggie, her husband Elmer and their children Dexter and Paige came over on holiday from Ipswich, Massachusetts. They stayed with Magenta Edwards in London, where they visited the Tower of London, spent a day at Legoland, and had a ride on the London Eye. They also went to Scotland to see if they could spot the Loch Ness Monster, but came back with a haggis instead.

Bridget, Britney and Blodwen at 2 days old

Bob and Becky's big baby bonanza
On February 12, Bob Edwards and his wife Becky were blessed with not one, not two, but three new little girls! Everything went well and the triplets were born just after midnight. The bouncing babes have been named Bridget, Britney and Blodwen.

Roisina's recipe
Every month the newsletter will contain a recipe, top tip or handy hint from a family member. We're kicking off with my sister Roisina's recipe for roast parsnips.

Method
Cut 500g/1lb parsnips into chip-sized pieces. Spread them out on a non-stick baking tray. Drizzle them with olive oil and sprinkle with salt. Preheat the oven to its hottest setting and roast the parsnips for about 40 minutes, or until crispy and cooked through.

Next month: Uncle Bert shows how to make and decorate your own chocolate eggs for Easter.

Grandpa George turns 100!
After a century of studying sea creatures, fighting in World Wars and drinking a lot of tea, Grandpa George will celebrate his 100th birthday on Thursday 5 April.

Don't miss the party!

A birthday garden party will be held at George's house in Birmingham on Saturday 7 April. All Edwards family members are invited.
The party is being organized by Millie Edwards, George's great niece. E-mail Millie at MillieE@usborne.co.uk, or phone her on 098 765 4321, for all the details.

Design your layout

When you type in your text, Word will automatically run it into the three columns. If you add a picture, give it a text wrap (see page 29) so that the text will run around it. Try to make each text item fit into a column, not run between columns.

Boxes

For a special feature to grab the reader's attention, use a box. Click on *Insert*, select *Text Box* and draw a box using the mouse. Give it a square text wrap (see page 29) and type your text inside.

31

Four-page booklets

You can make a basic 4-page document from a single piece of paper folded in half. Booklets like this are often used for leaflets, menus and show programmes.

Plan the layout

Just like a folded card, a folded booklet has to be planned to make sure it will look right. An easy way to do this is to take a blank sheet of paper, fold it in half, make notes about what will go where, and then unfold it again. A plan for a pantomime programme is shown here.

Setting up

Start a new Word document as usual, and set it to the right paper size (probably A4 or letter paper) in a landscape layout. Then click on *Format*, select *Columns...*, and choose two columns in the box that appears.

Laying out the pages

In the first column, on the left-hand half of the paper, design the back page of your booklet. In our programme, this is made up of several text boxes (see page 29) containing advertisements. Press the *Return* key several times to move to the next column. (If any of your pictures or boxes move, move them back with the mouse.) Put the front cover in the second column. Like a poster, it should be simple with a large title and maybe a picture. At the end of the page, press the *Return* key again to move to the next page of the document, which will form the two inside pages of the booklet. As before, lay out the text for these two pages in the two columns ~ one column for each page of the booklet.

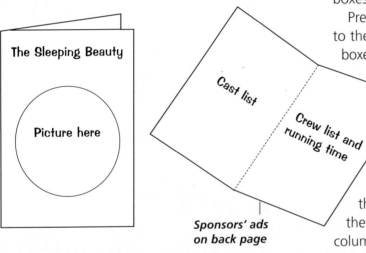

Sponsors' ads on back page

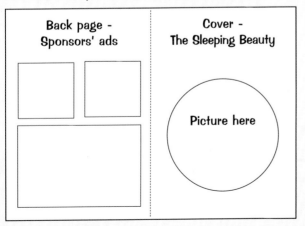

This is how the first page of the document will be laid out, to be printed on one side of the paper.

The second page of the document will be laid out like this, and printed on the other side of the paper.

Lists, tabs and bullets

Booklets often contain lists of information, such as a cast list. Tabs are very useful for lists. When you press the *Tab* key, it creates a space (called an indent) before the next word you type. The *Tab* key is at the top left of the keyboard and has two arrows on it.

Here's an example, showing how to use the *Tab* key to make a list of cast members:

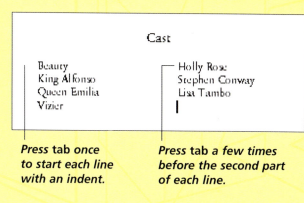

Press tab once to start each line with an indent.

Press tab a few times before the second part of each line.

You can also add bullet points to a list. Just highlight the list, click on *Format* in the menu bar, and select *Bullets and Numbering...* You can then choose from a range of different bullet point styles.

Printing booklets

To make the booklet work, you'll have to print it out on both sides of the same sheet of paper. To do this, tell your printer to print just page 1 of the document (see page 44 for printing tips). Then turn the paper over and start printing again, this time telling the printer to print just page 2. (Remember you'll need to make sure the printout is the same way up on both sides.) Finally, carefully fold the paper in half to make the finished booklet.

Design tips

When you're printing on both sides of the paper, it's best to use extra-thick or high-quality paper or thin card, so that the print doesn't show through.

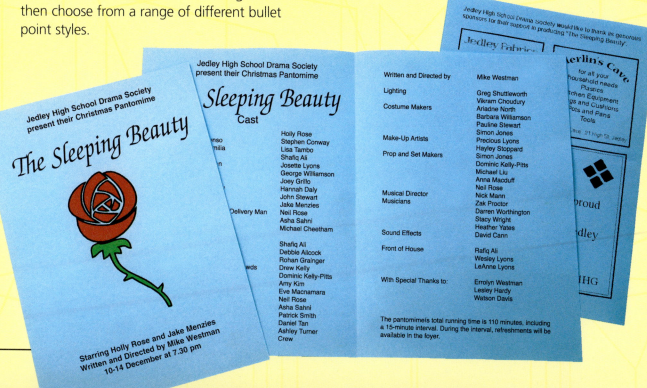

WORKING WITH WORD

Lots of pages

Once you can make a four-page booklet, it's easy to make a whole book by joining several booklets together.

Plan your book

Books are made by folding pieces of paper. This means that, as with the booklet on page 32, you have to put the pages in a particular order in your Word document, to make them appear in the right order when the paper is folded and the pages are put together.

To work out the order, make a blank book first. (Designers call this a dummy.) Take a sheet of paper and fold it in half to make the cover. Then add more folded sheets of paper inside the first one. Each extra sheet of paper will add four pages to your book.

This blank book is made up of three folded pieces of paper. One makes the cover and the other two together make eight pages.

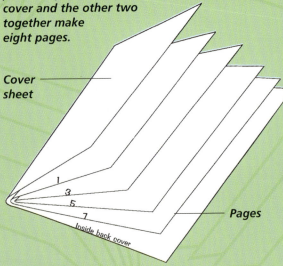

When you have as many pages as you want, hold the sheets of paper together at the fold and write in the page numbers or what you want to go on each page. Then open out the paper. You'll now be able to see how to arrange the pages in your Word document.

Setting up in Word

Start a new Word document and set the right paper size in a landscape layout. Set up two columns, as for a booklet, by selecting *Format* and *Columns...* and clicking on *Two*. Put quite a large gap between the columns, using the "Spacing" box, to make sure no text disappears into the fold, or gutter, of your book. A spacing of about 4cm works well for A4 or letter paper.

You can now write the pages of your book, using your dummy book as a guide to what order to put them in.

This is how the pages would be arranged in a Word document to make the book shown on the left. These Word pages would then be printed out on both sides of three sheets of paper.

Page 1 (front of sheet 1) — Back cover | Front cover

Page 2 (back of sheet 1) — Inside front cover | Inside back cover

Page 3 (front of sheet 2) — Page 8 | Page 1

Page 4 (back of sheet 2) — Page 2 | Page 7

Page 5 (front of sheet 3) — Page 4 | Page 5

Page 6 (back of sheet 3) — Page 6 | Page 3

Making new pages in Word

If you type past the end of a page in your document, Word will automatically add a new page. However, you can also add new pages by pressing the *Control* key and the *Return* key at the same time. This is useful for keeping bits of text separate from each other as you work.

Gutter

Toes	Contents	
My toes are like a family,	Polar Bear	2
Five little piggies snuggling up.	Snoring Patrick	3
A bunch of potatoes in a furrow,	The Hurricane	4
Or maybe like a flower's petals.	Noah's Ark	5
A row of walkers on a hill,	Robin Hood	6
One leader and four more behind.	In Winter	7
Or else like broad beans in their pod,	Toes	8
Or someone's very short, fat hand.		
And yet the lines above are wrong.		
My toes are not like anything.		
In fact they're just a row of toes,		
And all they look like is my toes.		
8		1

It's easiest to add page numbers by putting each one in its own text box (see page 29).

Remember you can use tabs, alignment and different styles when designing your text.

Book ideas

Here are some ideas for books to make:

Recipe book Put a contents list on page 1 and a different recipe on each of the other pages.

Travel guide Prepare a book about your area for someone who's coming to stay.

Book of poems Collect and type out poems you like, to make an anthology, or make a book of your own poetry.

Picture story book Write a story for a brother or sister, or a child you know. You could even write it about them.

For a smart look, use thick paper or card for the cover.

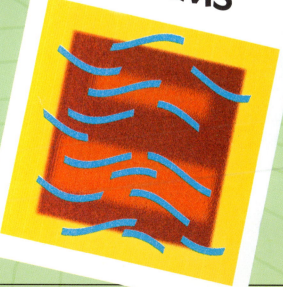

Book binding

When you've printed the book on both sides of each sheet of paper, fold and arrange them in order with the cover on the outside. Then bind the book by stapling or glueing it together at the fold, or spine. If your stapler doesn't reach, another good way is to use a needle and thread to sew the pages together along the spine.

Sew about three large stitches down the spine.

WORKING WITH WORD

Design a logo

A logo is a simple picture or symbol that stands for something. Clubs, societies and businesses often have logos, and you can have one too.

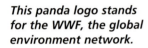

This panda logo stands for the WWF, the global environment network.

Usborne Publishing's logo is a colourful hot-air balloon.

Your own logo

You could design a logo for yourself and put it on your letterheads, envelopes, stickers or anything else you want to personalize. Or you could design one for a club, a school or college magazine, or a business.

Ideally, a logo should relate to the thing it stands for. For example, it could contain a set of initials, or it could be a simple picture that symbolizes a person, club or store.

A picture logo for a flower shop

A logo made up of initials

A music group logo

This logo for a drama club is made up of words inside a speech bubble.

Logos in Word

You could just draw your logo using Paint (see page 14) or design it on paper and scan it into your computer (see page 45). But there are lots of ways Word can help you produce a stylish logo.

AutoShapes

The *AutoShapes* menu (see page 17) has lots of shapes which make great logos. When you've drawn your shape, right-click on it and select *Format AutoShape*. Use the AutoShape tools to change the colour, outline colour and thickness.

WordArt

A word or a set of initials can make a great logo if you make them into a WordArt picture (see page 28).

Dingbat fonts

Dingbats fonts like Dingbats 1, Wingdings and

Astro are a good source of logos. Just find a picture you like and choose a font size and text colour.

Text logos

Try making a logo using a word or a set of initials in a wacky font. Remember you can also change the style (see page 28).

Put your letters in a text box (see page 29) so that you can move them around on the page.

Mix and match

You can use any combination of design techniques in your logos. Word will let you put text inside an AutoShape, or put one AutoShape on top of another. This means you can put any logo inside an outline, or build up your own image out of several different words and shapes.

Logo tips and tricks

• The most important rule of logo design is: keep it simple! Most famous logos are based around a basic shape such as a circle, triangle, square or ellipse.
• Your logo will be most effective if you use just one or two colours.
• For a complete look, use the colours from your logo in other parts of your publication ~ for example, put a rule under your letterhead in the same colour.
• There are so many logos around, it can be hard to make sure yours doesn't look like someone else's. So try to make it unique ~ most famous logos are protected by copyright, which means it's illegal to copy them.
• Want a tilted logo? Click with the right mouse button on your AutoShape or WordArt box, select *Format*, select the *Size* tab, and enter a value (such as 20) in the "Rotation" box.

A brand image

Companies who have logos make sure that everything they produce has the same logo on it. This gives them a corporate or brand "image", which means that the company logo and colours are always easily recognized.

You can give your school, your club, your band or a small business a brand image by using the same logo and colours on all its publications. Here's an example:

Compliments slip, made from A4 or letter paper cut into 3 strips.

Letterhead

You can buy blank business cards stuck to a sheet of card. You design and print them just like stickers (see page 26).

You could make brand stickers too, or even t-shirts (see page 38).

WORKING WITH WORD

Fashion design

Want to be a fashion designer? It's easy to do your own T-shirt designs and iron them onto a T-shirt using a transfer sheet. Transfer sheets come in packs of about 10 and are fairly cheap. You can also use them on bags, hats, shoes and other fashion gear.

You will need...

It's a good idea to make sure you've got everything before you start. For most T-shirt transfers, you'll need:

Transfer sheets You can use any brand of T-shirt transfer sheet, as long as it's meant for use with a computer printer. Look for them in your computer store.

Inkjet printer You must use an inkjet printer. A laser printer won't work because it will get hot inside and melt the transfer sheet.

A T-shirt Or whatever else you want to decorate, such as a bag, a hat or a pair of jeans. Whatever it is, it must be made of 100% cotton, so that it will withstand a hot iron. It should also be white, or a pale colour like pink or cream, to make the design show up properly.

An iron If it's a steam iron, make sure it has no water in it, because steam will damage the transfer.

Your design

Set up a new Word document that's the same size as the transfer sheets (usually A4 or letter size). You're now ready to create your own fashion moment! Using any of the design skills described in this book, you can design a logo or a message, or just put a picture on your T-shirt. Here are some ideas:

• Make a T-shirt for your band, club or sports team. Design a logo and then add the band, club or team name.
• Make decorative symbols or patterns using dingbats fonts (see page 18) or Word AutoShapes (see page 17).
• Write a funny or fashionable slogan such as Chill Out, Jet Set, or Hippy Chick. Or use your T-shirt to send out a message, such as Girl Power or Go Veggie! You can add a picture as well, to go with the message.
• You can put a photo of yourself, a pet, your home or anything you like on a T-shirt. You'll have to scan the photo into your computer first (see page 45).

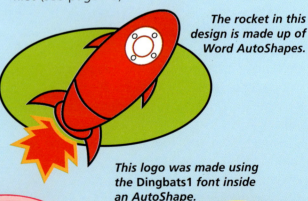

The rocket in this design is made up of Word AutoShapes.

This logo was made using the Dingbats1 font inside an AutoShape.

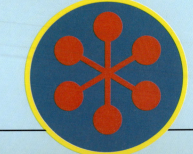

This Girl Power logo is made up of several Word AutoShapes. The main one has text inside.

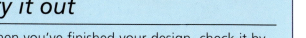

Try it out

When you've finished your design, check it by printing it out on a normal piece of paper and holding it up against your blank T-shirt to see how it will look. To avoid waste, don't print it onto a transfer sheet until you're completely happy with it.

Design tips

Remember you'll have quite a lot of space for your design ~ up to the size of the transfer sheet. A small logo or message looks sophisticated, but a big one has lots of impact. Experiment with different effects ~ try putting the design in the middle, at a top corner, or even on the back of the T-shirt.

Mirror image T-shirt designs printed onto transfer sheets.

Printing and ironing

Follow the transfer instructions carefully on how to print out and iron your transfer. In most cases, you'll have to set your printer to "special paper" or "T-shirt transfer", and print a mirror image of your design onto the transfer sheet so that it ends up the right way round. Most printers have an option for doing this. Look in the printer settings for an option called "Flip Horizontal" or "Mirror Image", and select it.

Print your design on a transfer sheet and iron it onto the T-shirt, pressing the iron very hard. Let it cool, then carefully peel it off. If your printer doesn't have this option, print onto good quality paper instead and take it, with a T-shirt, to a printing shop. For a small fee, they'll transfer it for you.

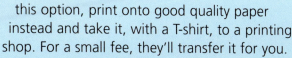

Magazines

If a booklet or newsletter isn't big enough for everything you've got to say, why not design and publish your own full-length magazine?

Plan your magazine

As with a book (see page 34), it's best to make a dummy magazine first, to work out how many pages you need and what will go on each page.

Magazines are usually designed in double-page spreads made up of two facing pages. Usually, one spread will hold one article or story. Or it can be made up of several items in boxes, or lots of small items in columns, such as classified advertisements.

Before using the computer, make a "rough" of each spread by sketching it on paper.

This is a rough for a school magazine spread, containing an interview with a famous writer who came to visit.

Here's a rough for a gossip spread, with photos of people on a day out.

Design decisions

There are several ways of designing and constructing a magazine. Think about the options before you start working in Word.

Small format
You can make a small magazine in just the same way as the book on page 34.

Full-size format
For a bigger magazine you'll need paper twice the normal size, such as A3. If, like many printers, yours won't take paper this big, the easiest thing to do is to design your magazine on smaller paper, as above, making everything smaller than you want it to be. Then enlarge it to twice the size on a photocopier.

Black and white or colour?
If you want to make lots of copies of your magazine, you'll have to photocopy it or send it to a printing shop. Black and white copies are much cheaper than colour, so if you want to save cash, think about making your magazine black and white only. It will still look great if you use interesting fonts and a good layout.

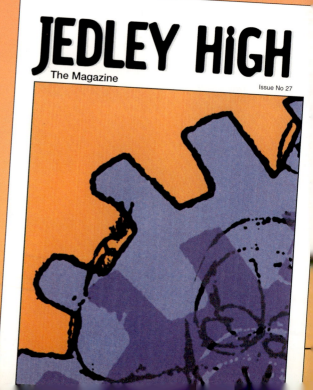

WORKING WITH WORD

Set up your document

Start a new Word document and set the paper size you're going to print on. Select "Landscape" so that you can put two pages side by side on each sheet. Then hold down the *Control* key and press *Return* to create the number of pages you need.

Remember, you have to put the pages in a particular order in your document, to make them appear in the right order when you print them out and staple or sew the magazine together. (Look at page 34 for a reminder of how to work out the order.) This means you'll be designing half of one spread opposite half of another. For example, in a 16-page magazine, you might be designing pages 7 and 11 opposite each other.

As with a book, print out the finished pages on both sides of the paper, and then assemble them into the right order.

 Magazine tips

- **Don't forget the gutter!** Leave a gap in the middle of each page of the Word document, where the stapling will go. Don't put pictures or text in the gutter.
- **Titles and straplines** Use a big, bold font for titles. Then use a smaller font to give a taster of what the article is about. This is called the strapline.
- **Use AutoShapes** Word AutoShapes with text inside are great for funky titles and captions. Ovals and round-cornered boxes look modern. Try a star or thought bubble for a special effect.
- **Columns and breakers** Long pieces of text look best arranged in three columns per page. Jazz them up with breakers ~ mini-headings halfway down the columns.

Gutter

GOING FURTHER

What is DTP?

Desktop Publishing software, or DTP, is what most professional graphic designers use to arrange words and pictures together on a computer screen. These two pages explain how it works.

DTP programs

The main DTP programs are Quark XPress™, Adobe® Indesign™, Adobe® PageMaker® and Microsoft® Publisher. They are used to design magazines, posters and books (like this one, which was designed using QuarkXPress). DTP software can be expensive. If you want to try it, Microsoft® Publisher is the cheapest and easiest package to begin with.

How DTP works

In DTP, all the text is in boxes (they do not show on the printout). The boxes can be linked together so that text runs from one to another. Pictures and photos are also put in boxes. You can create more complicated shapes and special effects than you can in Word.

A professional book designer at work using QuarkXPress

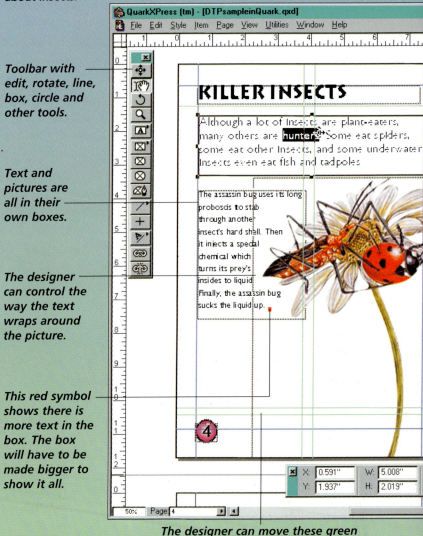

This screenshot shows a DTP program being used to design a double-page spread of a book about insects.

Toolbar with edit, rotate, line, box, circle and other tools.

Text and pictures are all in their own boxes.

The designer can control the way the text wraps around the picture.

This red symbol shows there is more text in the box. The box will have to be made bigger to show it all.

The designer can move these green guide rules to any part of the spread.

A picture in an ellipse

A circle with a colour blend

Curved text...

Stretched text...

42

Image manipulation

As well as DTP software, many graphic designers use programs such as PhotoShop, which allow you to make changes to pictures. For example, using PhotoShop, a designer could make a picture look semi-transparent, create swirls of colour to use as a background, or combine two photos so that one person's head was joined onto another person's body.

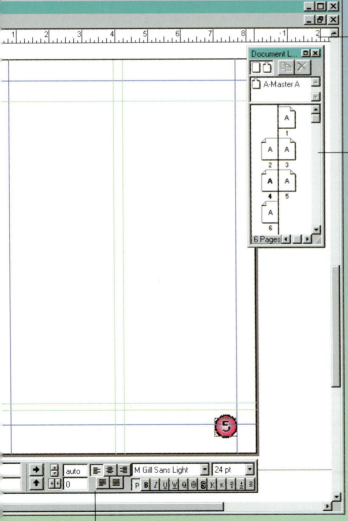

This photo of a girl has been altered in PhotoShop.

The designer has made copies of her arms and attached them to her body, so that she now has four arms.

Rulers along the edges of the screen help with positioning.

This box shows all the pages in the document. The designer clicks here to go to another page.

This box contains information about the highlighted text.

Becoming a designer

Want to be a real graphic designer? You're in luck! Media industries such as magazine publishing, book publishing, advertising and Web site design are expanding at an amazing rate. So, in the 21st century, good designers are more in demand than ever.

If you want to become a graphic designer, it helps to pick art, design and computer-related subjects to study at school. Most designers then study art and design at college or university.

New design programs are always being invented, so working designers sometimes go on courses to help them keep up with the latest technology.

GOING FURTHER

Saving, printing and scanning

These two pages contain some more useful information about saving files in Word, printing your designs, and using scanners.

Saving and naming your file

Each Word document you work on has to be saved, so that you can store it, find it and open it again whenever you want. The first time you save a file, click on *Save* in the *File* menu. A dialog box will appear.

Type the name of your document in this box.

Word will give your document a name such as Doc1.doc, but you can change this to something else, such as Letter.doc or Xmasparty.doc, to make it easier to find again later. Make sure the file name includes the ending .doc, so that your computer will identify it and open it again as a Word document.

Word will also ask you where you want to put your file. You can select a folder on your computer to store it in, or create a new folder for your designs. Finally, click on *Save* to save the file.

When you save the same file again, use the *Save As* command instead, and click on *Yes* to save the new version.

Closing Word

To close Word down, click on *Exit* in the *File* menu, or click on the X symbol in the top right-hand corner of the screen. Make sure you save your file before closing Word.

Printers

There are several types of printers. The cheapest and most common are inkjet printers, which are easy to find in computer stores and often come free with computers. This is the best type of printer for the projects in this book. Laser printers are not recommended, because they get very hot inside, which can damage some types of special paper.

This picture shows a typical inkjet printer and its main parts.

The output tray collects your printouts.

The power cable plugs into a wall socket.

Most printers take refill cartridges that look like this.

The feed tray holds blank paper and feeds it into the printer.

This cable plugs into the back of your computer.

GOING FURTHER

44

Printer settings

When you buy a new printer, follow the instructions on how to set it up and install the printer software that comes with it.

To print something, click on *File* in the menu bar, and select *Print...* A dialog box for your printer will appear. This lets you set the printer to the right paper size, paper type, number of copies, colour settings and print quality (known as the "resolution"). A high resolution printout will take longer to print. You may need to click on *Properties* to see some of these options.

When you've selected the settings, click on *OK* or *Print* to start printing. With most printers, another dialog box appears during printing. It will have a *Stop* or *Cancel* option so that you can stop printing if you change your mind.

Printer paper

Computer stores sell all kinds of paper and special media for inkjet printers, including letter paper, coloured paper, thin card, photo quality paper, blank business cards, postcards, T-shirt transfers and stickers. Remember that when you print on these, you have to set the printer settings to the right size and paper type, and make sure the feed guides on your printer are set to the right width.

Scanners

A scanner is useful if you want to copy photographs, or your own artwork, into the computer to use in your designs.

This section explains briefly how it works, but remember that all scanners are different. Like printers, they come with their own software and instructions, which you should read carefully.

Scanning an image

The most common type of scanner is a flatbed scanner. This is how it works.

First, you open the lid and place the thing you want to scan face down on the scanner window.

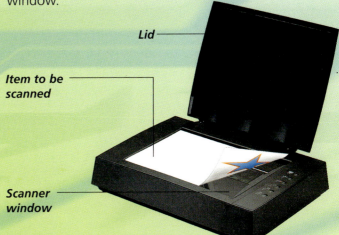

Lid

Item to be scanned

Scanner window

As with a printer, you use the on-screen settings to select the quality, or resolution, of your scan, and to choose colour or black and white. Most scanners do a rough scan first, and show you a preview so that you can move your picture if necessary, or select just one part of it to scan. Once you're sure, you click on *Scan* or *OK* to do the final scan.

You then name and save the image as a picture file. Almost all scanners will let you save it as a .bmp (bitmap) file, which is what you need if you want to import the picture into Word.

45

Glossary

This page explains some of the unusual design words and computer jargon used in this book.

Alignment The way rows of text line up with each other.

Bitmap (.bmp) A type of computerized picture file which can be used with Word.

Breaker A small heading used to break up a column of text.

CD-ROM A CD containing software or information for use on a computer.

Clicking and dragging Holding down your mouse button while you move the mouse. This method is often used to "drag" objects around on your computer screen.

Clip Art Computerized pictures which can be used in Word documents.

Crash When a computer crashes, it stops working and the screen freezes up or goes blank. To fix it, you need to switch off your computer and restart it.

Desktop PC A large computer that sits on top of a desk.

Dialog box A box which appears on your computer screen to allow you to choose various options or settings.

Digital To do with the way a computer stores information. A digital picture is a picture stored on a computer.

Dingbats Fonts that are made up of little pictures instead of letters and numbers.

Dummy A pretend version of a book, made to help with the design process.

Font A style of lettering. Also known as a **typeface** or **type**.

Graphic design Designing pictures and text for paper or computer publications, such as books, magazines or Web sites.

Icon A small, easily recognized picture used on a computer screen to stand for something.

Internet Service Provider (ISP) A company that handles e-mail and access to the Web. You need an account with an ISP if you want to use the Internet.

Landscape Used to describe any picture which is wider than it is tall.

Laptop A small, portable computer.

Masthead The area of a newsletter or newspaper that contains the title.

Menu A list of options on your computer screen. Sometimes, when you click on one option, a new menu appears.

Modem A device which converts computer information into signals which can be sent down a telephone line.

Notebook Another name for a laptop.

Point size A way of measuring type. One point is 0.35 mm or 1/72 of an inch. This sentence is in 11-point type.

Portrait Used to describe any picture which is taller than it is wide.

Resolution The sharpness of a computer picture, scan or printout.

Rough A rough design sketch.

Sanserif A font without serifs (see below).

Score To cut or press a line into a piece of paper or card to make it fold easily, without cutting all the way through it.

Serif A small, sticking-out tab on a letter of the alphabet. A serif font is a font with letters that have serifs.

Strapline A short sentence which comes after a title to explain briefly what the text is about.

Tab A computer function that inserts a space before the next word you type. Also the name for the parts of a dialog box that you click on.

Thumbnail A small design sketch.

Typeface or **type** Alternative names for a font.

Wrap To make text flow closely around a picture.

Web sites

This page lists Web sites where you can find free fonts and Clip Art pictures. Remember that the Web can change quickly, so don't worry if you can't find all these sites. You can find others by doing a search in any search engine. Use keywords such as "fonts" "Clip Art" and "download" to make sure you find the right kind of site.

Fonts

FreebieSource.com
www.freebiesource.com/fonts.html
Fonts for Kids
home.att.net/~mickeymousemania/fonts.htm
Free Windows Fonts for Kids
www.billybear4kids.com/fonts/fonts.htm

Downloading fonts

Most font sites will explain how to download, or copy, fonts from the Web onto your computer. You usually have to click on the font you want with your mouse. Select *Save this file to disk* in the dialog box that appears. You can then choose a folder on your computer to put the font file in. It's best to put all your fonts in a folder called *Fonts* which you should find under the *Windows* folder.

When you download your font file, it may be compressed, or "zipped", so that it takes up less space. To use it, you need to "unzip" it using a program called Winzip. You can download this from the Web at **www.winzip.com.** This site also explains how to use Winzip to unzip files.

Once a font is unzipped and in your font folder, you will be able to select it from your font list when you're using Word.

Clip Art

Original Free Clip Art
www.free-clip-art.net/index4.shtml
Barry's Clip Art Server
www.barrysclipart.com/ClipArt
Free Clip Art for Kids
www.thekidzpage.com/freekidsclipart/index.htm
Judy's Free Clip Art
members.nbci.com/galaxy777
Three Birds Studio Clip Art
www.countryfriends.org/KWClipArt.html
Clips Ahoy!
www.clipsahoy.com
Clip Art Connection
www.clipartconnection.com/clipart.html

Clip Art on the Web

The sites listed here are just a few of the hundreds and hundreds of Clip Art sites on the Web. When you get to a Clip Art site, you'll probably see a list of different types of pictures, such as Animals, Cartoons, Flowers, Food, People and so on. Click on the one you want, to view the pictures. If there are too many to fit on one screen, there will be a "Next" button which you can click on to see the next screen. When you find a picture you want, click on it and save it on your computer, as described on page 17.

Most Clip Art sites also have lots of links to similar sites. If you can't find the picture you want, just try a different site.

Remember that Clip Art and fonts on the Web belong to the people who designed them and put them there. They are usually happy for you to use them for your own personal designs. But if a site says you can't copy its pictures, then it is illegal to use them and you should look somewhere else.

Index

alignment 13, 35, 46
AutoCorrect 10
AutoShapes 17, 19, 20, 21, 24, 26, 29, 36, 37, 38, 41

badges 27
bitmaps (.bmps) 15, 16, 17, 46
black and white publications 40
bleeds 27
booklets 32-33
books 34-35
brand image 37
breakers 41, 46
bullet points 33
buttons 27

cards 24-25
CD-ROMS 5, 17, 18, 46
Clip Art 17, 18, 19, 26, 27, 46, 47
colours 6, 7, 20-21, 26, 37
columns 24, 25, 30, 32, 34, 41
compressed files 47
copyright 37
crashing 10, 46
cursor 9, 10

design elements 6, 7
design process 7
desktop computers 4, 46
Desktop Publishing (DTP) 2, 3, 42-43
downloading files 47
dummies 34, 46

fonts 5, 6, 7, 12, 13, 18-19, 30,

36, 46, 47
groups 18
sizes 13, 18

gutter 34, 35, 41

highlighting 12
homework projects 29

Internet, the 5
Internet Service Providers (ISPs) 5, 46
invitations 23

layout 6, 7, 13, 24, 32
leaflets 24-25, 32
letterheads 12-13, 16, 36, 37
lettering see fonts
lists 33
logos 7, 20, 36-37, 38

magazines 40-41
margins 9, 22, 24
mastheads 30, 46
Microsoft® Clip Gallery 17, 27
modems 5, 46

newsletters 30-31

Paint 5, 14-15, 16, 20, 22, 26,
changing colours in 21
paper size 9
PhotoShop 43
picture files 15

pictures
adding to Word 16
creating with Paint 14-15
digital 14
postcards 22
posters 18-19, 28
printing 4, 5, 13, 22, 25, 38, 39, 44-45

resolution 46
rotation 37
rules 13

saving files 44
scanners 5, 45
special media 5, 22
stickers 26-27, 28, 36
straplines 41, 46

tables 23
tabs 33, 46
text boxes 22, 24, 29, 31
text styles 12-13, 28
text wrapping 28, 29, 46
thumbnails 7, 46
T-shirts 38-39
typeface see font

Windows® 4, 14
WordArt 28, 29, 36, 37
World Wide Web, the 5, 17, 18, 47
wrapping see text wrapping
wrapping paper 20-21

zipped files 47

Acknowledgements

Microsoft® Word 97, Microsoft® Paint, Microsoft® WordPad and Microsoft® Windows 95 and 98 are either registered Trade Marks or Trade Marks of Microsoft corporation in the United States and/or other countries. Product images, icon images and screen shots of Microsoft products are reprinted by permission from Microsoft Corporation.
Every effort has been made to trace the copyright holders of the material in this book. If any rights have been omitted, the publishers offer their sincere apologies and will rectify this in any future editions following notification.

Usborne Publishing are not responsible and do not accept liability for the availability or content of any Web site other than our own, or for any exposure to harmful, offensive, or inaccurate material which may appear on the Web. Usborne Publishing will have no liability for any damage or loss caused by viruses that may be downloaded as a result of browsing the sites we recommend.

First published in 2001 by Usborne Publishing Ltd., Usborne House, 83-85 Saffron Hill, London EC1N 8RT, England. www.usborne.com. Copyright ©2001 Usborne Publishing Ltd. The name Usborne and the devices ⚉⚉ are Trade Marks of Usborne Publishing Ltd. All rights reserved. No part of this publication may be reproduced, stored in a retrieval system, or transmitted in any form or by any means, electronic, mechanical, photocopying, recording or otherwise without the prior permission of the publisher. Printed in Spain.

Computer monitor on front cover reproduced with permission of Hewlett-Packard/Beattie Media. "10,000 Clipart" CD cover on page 17 reproduced by permission of greenstreet ©Copyright 2000. Panda logo on page 36 reproduced by permission of WWF-UK. Photos on page 40-41 ©Digital Vision